Home Ownership in America

A wide-ranging cultural history centered around the concepts of real estate, the family home, and the American dream, and how they evolved over the years, *Home Ownership in America: A Socio-Cultural History of Housing in the United States* traces narratives around home ownership from the 1920s to today.

As a product of the emergence of a large middle class during the Roaring Twenties, the modern concept of home ownership continued through the shaky Great Depression years, holding pattern of World War II, and glory days of the postwar era, when home ownership became a reality for much of the White middle class. While the late 1960s and 1970s were difficult years for home ownership as the postwar economic engine ran out of steam, a renaissance took place in the 1980s and 1990s due to tens of millions of baby boomers wanting to nest. Although there have been a few bumps in the road over the last couple of decades, home ownership, or at least the pursuit of it, is once again booming, making the subject as relevant as ever.

With the single-family home central to the American idea and experience, this book touches on a host of issues related to our social divisions of race, gender, and class. *Home Ownership in America* is a truly interdisciplinary study, crossing over into a wide variety of subjects including sociology, family, urban history/planning, suburban studies, the built environment, public policy, business, finance, economics, politics, architecture, design, technology, and popular and consumer culture.

Lawrence R. Samuel is a Miami-based author and independent scholar. He holds a PhD in American Studies from the University of Minnesota and is the author of many books including *Diversity in the United States: A Cultural History of the Past Century* (Routledge, 2023), *Age Friendly: Ending Ageism in America* (Routledge, 2022), and *The American Middle Class: A Cultural History* (Routledge, 2014).

"A fascinating text that covers 100 years of housing ownership in the United States through wars, depressions, recessions, and times of prosperity. Home ownership as an integral part of the American dream is explained and explored from different angles that most of us often overlook. An interesting read for all."

Eli Beracha, *Director of the Tibor and Sheila Hollo School of Real Estate at Florida International University*

"*Home Ownership in America* takes a deep dive into one of the most compelling aspects of the American Dream: the ownership of one's own home. Larry Samuel provides a lively, insightful and innovative interdisciplinary examination of the hopes, experiences, and limitations of American home ownership over the last century."

Elaine Tyler May, *Regents Professor of American Studies and History at the University of Minnesota*

Home Ownership in America

A Socio-Cultural History of Housing in the United States

Lawrence R. Samuel

Routledge
Taylor & Francis Group
NEW YORK AND LONDON

Designed cover image: Anne Richard, Shutterstock #2339204451

First published 2025
by Routledge
605 Third Avenue, New York, NY 10158

and by Routledge
4 Park Square, Milton Park, Abingdon, Oxon, OX14 4RN

Routledge is an imprint of the Taylor & Francis Group, an informa business

ISBN: 978-1-032-77143-4 (hbk)
ISBN: 978-1-032-75803-9 (pbk)
ISBN: 978-1-003-48148-5 (ebk)

DOI: 10.4324/9781003481485

Typeset in Sabon
by Deanta Global Publishing Services, Chennai, India

Contents

Introduction

Let the American people live in their own homes and you'll see the greatest nation in the world.

Abraham Lincoln

Home Ownership in America: A Socio-Cultural History of Housing in the United States is, as the title suggests, a history of home ownership in this country with special attention paid to its intersection with the nation's major social divisions. In short, the work is a wide-ranging cultural history centered around the concepts of real estate, the family home, and the American dream and how they evolved over the years.

Told chronologically and divided into ten decades, *Home Ownership in America* traces the narrative of the subject from the 1920s right up to today. It was in the 1920s when our modern concept of home ownership emerged, I argue, a function of a much-expanded managerial class, the aggressive development of suburbia in many cities, and the professionalization of the real estate industry armed with "scientific" marketing methods. Naturally, history doesn't operate neatly in ten-year chunks, but I find defined chronology to be a convenient framework to organize large amounts of material. And, as an American cultural historian, I believe that the overarching societal, economical, and political happenings of each decade clearly played a role in shaping home ownership (and the attitudes toward it) over the course of the past century.

Sources for this work are primarily period articles published in a wide array of national and local newspapers, magazines, and trade publications. Newspapers are prioritized as reporters covering the real estate beat provide a fluid, in-real-time narrative, supporting my view that journalism really is the first draft of history. In addition to these mainstream publications, African American newspapers (the *Atlanta Daily World*, *Baltimore Afro-American*, *Chicago Defender*, *Cleveland Call and Post*, *Los Angeles Sentinel*, *Michigan Chronicle*, *New York Amsterdam News*, *Norfolk Journal and Guide*, *Philadelphia Tribune*, and *Pittsburgh Courier*) are also heavily drawn upon. Scholarly articles are sourced from JSTOR, and other books

DOI: 10.4324/9781003481485-1

about home ownership that have been published over the years help frame the story.

The home has featured prominently in both American popular and consumer culture, of course, not a surprising thing given how much time we actually spend in houses or apartments (and how much money we spend on them). Home ownership has been used as a convenient plot device in movies over the years, as both a sacred thing (*The Wizard of Oz*; *It's a Wonderful Life*) and something that one might better avoid (*Mr. Blanding Builds His Dream House*; *The Money Pit*). Also, the image of the white picket fence is firmly etched in our minds, as pleasing a symbol of private property as one can imagine.

Consistent with the work's methodology/conceptual framework and its structure and coverage, the story is told primarily through the voices of journalists and scholars who have weighed in on the many different dimensions of home ownership over the past century. I draw heavily on sources originating from New York, Chicago, and Los Angeles both because they are the biggest real estate markets in the country and to get a broad geographic perspective. Still, I examine home ownership in many other smaller cities and towns in an attempt to get a balanced view of the nation's general housing scene.

I begin *Home Ownership in America* after World War I, when both the buying and selling of real estate (and much of everyday life) entered a new and different kind of era grounded in "modernism." The story continues through the shaky Great Depression years, holding pattern of World War II, and "glory days" of the postwar era, when home ownership became a reality for much of the White middle class. While the late 1960s and 1970s were rough ones for home ownership as the postwar economic engine ran out of steam, a renaissance took place in the 1980s and 1990s due much in part to tens of millions of baby boomers wanting to nest. Although there have been a few bumps in the road over the last couple of decades, home ownership, or at least the pursuit of it, is once again booming, making the subject as relevant as ever.

The story of home ownership in America is a truly remarkable one, offering new insights into who we are as a people. Property has been central to the American idea and experience, we know, a legacy of the Founding Fathers' vision to allow private ownership of land. ("Small landholders are the most precious part of a state," Thomas Jefferson once remarked, although it was he who changed John Locke's "life, liberty, and the pursuit of property" to "life, liberty, and the pursuit of happiness" in the Declaration of Independence.) Much of the American dream is steeped in home ownership, of course, as it has been the latter that has arguably most symbolized our core values of freedom and independence. It should be noted, however, that James Truslow Adams, who is credited for originating the phrase "American dream" (he undoubtedly popularized it), did not equate the concept with home ownership. "The dream is a vision of a better, deeper, richer life for every individual, regardless of the position in society which he or she may occupy by the accident of birth," he explained in 1933, not realizing the degree to which the home would come to define the American dream.[1]

Home ownership, or again at least the pursuit of it, has been and continues to serve as the principal driver of our economic engine, making it no wonder that it touches upon so many areas of everyday life. Fittingly, *Home Ownership in America* is truly interdisciplinary, crossing over into a wide variety of subjects including sociology, family, urban history/planning, suburban studies, the built environment, geography, public policy, business, finance, economics, politics, architecture, design, technology, and, last but hardly least, popular and consumer culture. With its ambitious scope, the work aims to be recognized as a seminal guide to the history of home ownership in the United States.

To be clear, rather than a research study itself, *Home Ownership in America* draws on what I consider to be the most important literature related to home ownership that has been completed over the years. The work is a big, sweeping picture of the history of American home ownership designed to complement more academic books that take a more in-depth analysis of particular topics with original research. I am more interested in the threads that have connected issues such as race and economic status over time than focusing on a single topic. In short, I felt there was a need for a synthetic, narrative-driven study that brought together in one place what I believed to represent the essential research and writings in the field. And like any good cultural history, the book shows how mining the stuff of everyday life serves as the richest way to learn more about a group of people at a particular time and in a particular place.

Also, readers might be advised (or warned) that there is much discussion of real estate agents and brokers in this work. I find agents to be a source of fascination, perhaps in part because I know many personally; where I live (Miami), it sometimes seems that the majority of working adults are somehow involved in real estate, either part- or full-time. Regardless, it is hard to overestimate agents' influence in facilitating (and sometimes preventing) residential home ownership throughout the years. In certain ways, not much has changed since 1968 when Charles M. Barresi assessed the multifaceted functions of the real estate agent in an article for *Sociological Focus*. In each transaction, the agent brings the buyer and seller together, appraises the market value of the property, and facilitates the process of lending and borrowing money. It's thus clear that the agent wields much control in this quite complicated process where there are many moving parts, a function of her or his expertise (in contrast to that of the client).[2]

But there is even more to the real estate agent than may meet the eye, "Part of his power flows from his interpretation of social values in the community," Barresi noted, "and his subsequent actions consistent with these values." As a principal gatekeeper to home ownership, the agent selects certain clients and certain properties, sets prices, and decides what kind of loans the buyer should assume. With that kind of control, the agent can and has strongly shaped the social dynamics of an area, including those related to race, class, and even gender. Over the years and to this very day, such influence has been made most apparent in a long list of unethical, discriminatory practices directed at people of color, including but hardly limited to town or neighborhood redlining, discouraging purchases based on property "flaws," and steering clients to designated areas.[3]

Perhaps more than anyone else, however, real estate agents have recognized the profound symbolic value of home ownership, as it is that which will heavily determine how successful they are. Most of the rationale assigned to buying a home has been based on money, specifically the financial benefits to be had through the deduction of property taxes and mortgage interest and the building of wealth through equity. It is the psychological or emotional value that has perhaps accounted for a larger share of home buying (and selling), however, something Diana Loercher observed in the *Christian Science Monitor* in 1978 after she and her husband searched for a house in the suburbs. "I began to realize the degree to which a house is a symbol," Loercher wrote, seeing whatever dwelling one happened to choose as:

> a symbol of independence because it is one's own (even if one is still paying off the mortgage) and not one's landlord's. It is a symbol of security because it represents a relative degree of performance ... Land promises freedom of movement, however small the area, the opportunity to plant, and a margin of privacy ... There are aspects of owning land that seem to satisfy one of man's most basic needs. One thinks of pre-historic man searching for a stable shelter and finding it for the first time in a cave.[4]

Home Ownership in America joins an impressive list of scholarship in the area, particularly those works falling within the rather new arena of the sociology of housing. In my view, the classic books in the field are (my ex-advisor) Elaine Tyler May's *Homeward Bound* and Kenneth T. Jackson's *Crabgrass Frontier*, each a work to which this one owes a debt. Other important works related to home ownership and real estate include Jeffrey M. Hornstein's *A Nation of Realtors®: A Cultural History of the Twentieth-Century American Middle Class*, which traced the development of the real estate business and how it helped to make the owner-occupied, single-family home a key feature of American life in the 20th century.[5] In her *City of American Dreams: A History of Home Ownership and Housing Reform in Chicago, 1871–1919*, Margaret Garb showed how the owner-occupied, single-family house "came to embody the American ideal of the family home," focusing on Chicago in the latter decades of the late 19th century and early decades of the 20th century. "Struggles over property rights in housing fundamentally transformed living conditions and social relations in American cities," Garb wrote, delving into major issues related to working-class culture during these pivotal years.[6]

Lee Anne Fennell's *The Unbounded Home: Property Values beyond Property Lines*, meanwhile, nicely illustrated how today's private dwellings are actually less private than we may like to believe. All kinds of variables—one's neighbors, city services, and the local airport's flight pattern, to name just a few—have a major effect on both quality of life and property values, something to which many homeowners can testify.[7] In their *Well Worth Saving: How the New Deal Safeguarded Home Ownership*, Price Fishback, Jonathan Rose, and Kenneth Snowden examined the economic effects of the Home Owner's Loan Corporation and drew parallels to the 2008 subprime mortgage crisis.[8] Brian J. McCabe's *No Place Like Home: Wealth, Community and the Politics of Home Ownership* parsed the politics of home ownership, especially the popular idea that home ownership made residents into "better neighbors, citizens, and Americans." (McCabe found scarce hard evidence to support the claim.)[9]

Race has deservedly been the focus of recent histories of home ownership in the United States. Richard Rothstein's *The Color of Law: A Forgotten History of How Our Government Segregated America* revealed how and why government at all levels legalized racial segregation in metropolitan areas across the country, while Keenanga-Yamahtta Taylor's *Race for Profit: How Banks and the Real Estate Industry Undermined Black Home Ownership* demonstrated how inequitable real estate practices persisted long after discrimination in housing was made illegal.[10] *The Sociology of Housing: How Homes Shape Our Lives*, a collection of essays edited by Brian J. McCabe and Eve Rosen, made a firm case that housing represents a legitimate area of inquiry within sociology, particularly as related to the many inequalities based on race, ethnicity, and class.[11] *Home Ownership in America* is different from all these fine books via its broad sweep, focus on the United States over the past century, weaving of race, class, and gender in the general narrative of home ownership, and reliance on a diverse array of period sources, both popular and scholarly.

While more researchers are exploring contemporary problems in home ownership in America, there has also been an effort to mine relevant stories from the past that add to our understanding of the residential development of the nation. For centuries, we well know, immigrants have looked to America as a place to realize greater economic independence, with owning property a central part of that. Land was cheap through the 18th century and much of the 19th century, drawing both immigrants and the native-born to the countryside to exploit the local natural resources. Also, a homestead on the prairie, log cabin in the woods, or fisherman's shack was often romanticized in literature, reflecting the core American values of autonomy and self-sustenance. In his tour of the country in the 1830s, Alexis de Tocqueville took note of Americans' independent spirit and desire to have their own home, seeing it as a rejection of the European feudal system in which only the wealthy or politically powerful owned property.

The Homestead Act of 1862 and subsequent laws made available millions of acres of government-owned land for virtually any White person to settle at no cost, and some 1.6 million people took the federal government up on its offer. (Women and immigrants who had applied for citizenship were eligible.) The steady influx of the "huddled masses" further glorified the one-family settlement surrounded by nature despite what were often harsh conditions. "Nineteenth century reformers, as well as journalists, documented the development of America's land through colorful accounts of burgeoning urban centers and immigrant living conditions laced with social deterioration, disease, and despair," Suzanne M. Zukowski wrote in her account of home ownership among Polish Americans in Milwaukee.[12]

Studies of the development of certain cities or particular neighborhoods have challenged prevailing beliefs and assumptions regarding home ownership in this country. In his *The First Suburbs: Residential Communities on the Boston Periphery, 1815–1860*, for example, Henry C. Binford argued that neither "ethnic flight" (from the Irish) nor advances in transportation were primarily responsible for the development of the suburbs in that city. (It was rather the emergence of "fringe" businesses, i.e., the manufacturing of soap, bricks, glass, rope, and other products not particularly welcome in an urban setting, that led to the growth of suburbs such as Cambridge and Somerville, he proposed.)[13]

New theories too have emerged within the ascendant field of the sociology of housing. Richard Harris and Chris Hamnett, for example, have suggested that it was robber barons' greed that indirectly led to a vast increase in American home ownership, initially in rural areas and later in cities. "By the turn of the twentieth century, the concentration of industry, banking, and commerce was leaving fewer and fewer opportunities for small-scale urban enterprise," they wrote in 1997 in *Annals of the Association of American Geographers*, positing that "the desire to acquire wealth found expression in the home." While it was highly unlikely that skilled labor would ever get rich, in other words, their wages were relatively high, allowing workers to feel like they were kings or queens of their own castle.[14]

The most significant shift in the history of home ownership in the United States was the transformation from the nation being primarily rural to one primarily urban, most scholars agree. In 1880, three-quarters of the population was rural, while by 1939 three-quarters of the American people lived in or near cities, reflecting the recasting of the country's economy from agriculture-based to industry-based. Not coincidentally, the modern real estate industry took shape over this stretch of time, as there was much money to be made for helping new urbanites find homes in metropolitan areas and the suburbs that ringed them. (Commercial real estate too was of course a thriving business.) Creating many homes where there had previously been one large estate was a big part of this transformation, a conversion in the use of land that would be perfected in the mass production and selling of houses in the post-World War II years.[15]

The formation of local real estate boards across the country certainly fueled the expansion of home ownership in the late 19th century and early 20th century. In 1908, the National Association of Real Estate Boards (NAREB) was founded in Chicago; the organization was composed of nineteen real estate boards with 1,435 members. (A similar organization had been formed in 1891 but was dissolved in 1894.) Through much of the 20th century, the NAREB would play a key role in all things real estate by establishing industry standards, collecting and exchanging information, and promoting home ownership.[16] As Donald H. Bouma showed in a 1962 article published in the *American Journal of Economics and Sociology*, local real estate boards held enormous social power in their respective communities, so much so that city commissions and boards of education commonly sought their blessing before making land-related decisions.[17]

Alongside real estate agents, the business community, especially bankers and other financiers, was instrumental in forging an ethos of home ownership in America. Long-term economic growth could be achieved by many Americans owning their homes, it was believed, particularly as the consumer society of the early 20th century emerged. Cleverly, lenders based the mortgage system on the increasingly popular "installment plan," in which consumers could pay off the cost of an expensive item in small amounts over time. "If people could purchase a house with a small initial outlay and modest monthly payments, then the economic barriers to home ownership would disappear for the majority of moderate-income families," Marc A. Weiss noted in *Business and Economic History* in 1989.[18]

That financial plan, which was also similar to renting but with the bonus of creating equity, would soon be complemented by an intensive marketing effort, the "Own Your Own Home" campaign (discussed in Chapter 1). For industry, the campaign was intended to "stimulate new investment, construction, and sales in the private residential property market," Weiss wrote, while for the government, the objective was to "defeat radical protest and restore political stability by encouraging urban workers to become homeowners."[19] As McCabe's *No Place Like Home* made clear, it was commonly believed that having "a stake in the system" would encourage homeowners to subscribe to status quo thinking and be more community-minded, but other studies have shown this to be not so.[20] With the 1932 passage of the Federal Home Loan Bank Act, however, home ownership became official United States policy, perceived by the FDR administration as a means to bring economic and social stability during the worst days of the Great Depression.[21]

Despite there being a "code of ethics" that supposedly guided real estate transactions, more influential was the "gentlemen's agreement" that for decades existed between the private and public sectors (and at some level can still be found in certain areas of the country). The aim of this unofficial pact was to prevent people of color from owning property, particularly in or near where White people lived. (Hence the existence of a different NAREB—the National Association of Real Estate Brokers—a trade organization and network of Black real estate professionals. That organization, which was formed in 1947, is charged with "promoting democracy in housing and advocating for public policies that protect and expand sustainable home ownership," a much-needed thing given the rather ugly history of real estate in this country.)[22]

More scholarship has recently been devoted to that history, with the turn of the 20th century recognized as a key juncture in African American home ownership. Steven Mintz wrote for *Phylon* in 1983:

> Historians have come to see that the period from 1890 to the race riots coinciding with the First World War witnessed the origins of the social structure, institutional developments, and racial outlooks that would characterize black urban communities throughout much of the twentieth century.

Discrimination in various forms, notably segregation and limited job opportunities, collided with a rising Black professional class between the world wars, ultimately coming to a head in the post-World War II civil rights movement.[23]

More attention is being given to the development of what has been referred to as "Black suburbanization." "Early black suburbanites formed an important component of the Great Migration," noted Andrew Wiese, adding that this group of people was "much more likely to own their own homes than central city blacks," despite being poorer. How could such a thing be? Land was less expensive in the suburbs, for one thing, and it was not uncommon for African Americans to build their houses themselves. Getting a mortgage was essentially impossible—credit would not be extended to people of color—the saving grace being that Black suburbanites would have a house free and clear, something unlikely for White homeowners.[24]

In their 2011 essay for the *American Economic Review*, William J. Collins and Robert A. Margo did yeoman's work by estimating levels of home ownership among both African American and White households between the years 1870 and 2007. Over this long stretch of time, Black households increased their rate by 46% versus 20% for White households. While the spread was thus narrowed by 26%, almost all of it (25%) took place between 1870 and 1910, a remarkable and important finding. "After four decades of increase, black owner-occupancy stagnated after 1910," they wrote, citing the "Great Migration" to urban areas, redlining, and segregation in suburbia as key factors in the failure to make further gains. As other scholars have noted, the Fair Housing Act of 1968 did little to slow racial discrimination in housing, a fact confirmed by Collins's and Margo's data.[25]

Finally, any study of home ownership would be incomplete without acknowledging the major role of the Federal Housing Administration (FHA). David's Reiss's 2017 essay in the *Journal of Affordable Housing & Community Development Law* is a concise but thorough analysis of how the FHA both enabled and limited home ownership among African Americans (and Whites, it could be safely said). Created during the Great Depression, the FHA achieved great success and equally great failures, especially with regard to facilitating sustainable home ownership among African Americans. While being part of the redlining machine early in its history and decades later heavily responsible for defaults and foreclosures among African Americans, the FHA was also instrumental in making the American dream real for people of all colors, making its story a complex one.[26] Home ownership in America as a whole can be legitimately said to be complex, however, a story that now begins.

Notes

1 James Truslow Adams, "America Faces 1933's Realities," *New York Times*, January 1, 1933, SM1; James Truslow Adams, *The Epic of America* (New York: Little, Brown, and Company, 1931).
2 Charles M. Barresi, "The Role of the Real Estate Agent in Residential Location," *Sociological Focus*, Summer 1968, 59–71.
3 Barresi, "The Role of the Real Estate Agent in Residential Location."
4 Diana Loercher, "And Know the Place for the First Time,'" *Christian Science Monitor*, June 21, 1978, 20.
5 Jeffrey M. Hornstein, *A Nation of Realtors: A Cultural History of the Twentieth-Century American Middle Class* (Durham, NC: Duke University Press, 2005).
6 Margaret Garb, *City of American Dreams: A History of Home Ownership and Housing Reform in Chicago, 1871–1919* (Chicago: University of Chicago Press, 2005), 2; For more on Chicago, see also Joseph C. Bigott, *From Cottage to Bungalow: Houses and the Working Class in Chicago, 1869–1929* (Chicago: University of Chicago Press, 2001); Amanda Seligman, *Block By Block: Neighborhoods and Public Policy on Chicago's West Side* (Chicago: University of Chicago Press, 2005).
7 Lee Anne Fennell, *The Unbounded Home: Property Values beyond Property Lines* (New Haven, CT: Yale University Press, 2009).
8 Price Fishback, Jonathan Rose, and Kenneth Snowden, *Well Worth Saving: How the New Deal Safeguarded Home Ownership* (Chicago: University of Chicago Press, 2013).
9 Brian J. McCabe, *No Place Like Home: Wealth, Community and the Politics of Home Ownership* (New York: Oxford University Press, 2016), 15.
10 Richard Rothstein, *The Color of Law: A Forgotten History of How Our Government Segregated America* (New York: Norton, 2018); Keenanga-Yamahtta Taylor, *Race for Profit: How Banks and the Real Estate Industry Undermined Black Home Ownership* (Chapel Hill: University of North Carolina Press, 2019).
11 Brian J. McCabe and Eve Rosen (eds.), *The Sociology of Housing: How Homes Shape Our Lives* (Chicago: University of Chicago Press, 2023).
12 Suzanne M. Zukowski, "From Peasant to Proletarian: Home Ownership in Milwaukee's Polonia," *Polish American Studies*, Autumn 2009, 5.
13 Henry C. Binford, *The First Suburbs: Residential Communities on the Boston Periphery, 1815–1860* (Chicago: University of Chicago Press, 1985).
14 Richard Harris and Chris Hamnett, "The Myth of the Promised Land: The Social Diffusion of Home Ownership in Britain and North America," *Annals of the Association of American Geographers*, June 1987, 173.
15 "Many Factors, Mainly Needs, in Real Estate," *Washington Post*, May 19, 1940, R7; W. Clifford Harvey, "Real Estate or Housing: Difference?," *Christian Science Monitor*, March 27, 1953, 15; See Henry McCulley Muller, *Urban*

Home Ownership: A Socio-Economic Analysis with Emphasis on Philadelphia (Philadelphia: The Author, 1947); Albert Chevan, "The Growth of Home Ownership, 1940–1980," *Demography*, May 1989, 249–266.

16 "Chicago—America's Real Estate Capital," *Chicago Daily Tribune*, May 15, 1958, F8; For more on the history of the NAREB, see Pearl Janet Davies, *Real Estate in American History* (Washington, DC: Public Affairs Press, 1958).

17 Donald H. Bouma, "The Legitimization of the Social Power Position of a Real Estate Board," *American Journal of Economics and Sociology*, October 1962, 383–392; See also Donald H. Bouma's, "Analysis of the Social Power Position of a Real Estate Board," *Social Problems*, Autumn 1962, 121–132.

18 Marc A. Weiss, "Marketing and Financing Home Ownership: Mortgage Lending and Public Policy in the United States, 1918–1989," *Business and Economic History*, 1989, 109.diff

19 Weiss, "Marketing and Financing Home Ownership."

20 See, for example, Paul W. Kingston and John C. Fries, "Having a Stake in the System: The Sociopolitical Ramifications of Business and Home Ownership," *Social Science Quarterly*, September 1994, 679–686.

21 Isaac F. Megbolugbe and Peter D. Linneman, "Home Ownership," *Urban Studies*, May 1993, 659–682.

22 nareb.com.

23 Steven Mintz, "Sources of Variability in Black Home Ownership in 1900," *Phylon*, 4 Qtr., 1983, 312–331.

24 Andrew Wiese, "Black Housing, White Finance: African American Housing and Home Ownership in Evanston, Illinois, before 1940," *Journal of Social History*, Winter 1999, 429–460.

25 William J. Collins and Robert A. Margo, "Race and Home Ownership from the End of the Civil War to the Present," *American Economic Review*, May 2011, 355–359; See also Trevon D. Logan and John M. Parman, "Segregation and Home Ownership in the Early Twentieth Century," *American Economic Review*, May 2017, 410–414; Wilhelmina A. Leigh, "Civil Rights Legislation and the Housing Status of Black Americans: An Overview," in Wilhelmina A. Leigh and James B. Stewart, eds., *The Housing Status of Black Americans* (New Brunswick, NJ: Transaction, 1992), 5–28. Leigh's research found that the rate of Black homeownership in the 1980s matched those of Whites in the 1940s.

26 David Reiss, "The Federal Housing Administration and African-American Home Ownership," *Journal of Affordable Housing & Community Development Law*, 2017, 123–150.

1 Own Your Own Home

I wish I had a pretty house, the littlest ever seen...

Wendy to Peter Pan

In Los Angeles in 1925, a married couple appeared in court before a judge after the wife filed for divorce. The wife, Myrna Lawson, had started a career in real estate, something many Americans, including women, were doing at the time. "I did it because I wanted to increase the family income," she told the judge, but "he made so much fuss about it that I finally had to put him out." Perry Lawson, the woman's husband, then told his side of the story to the judge. "She took my salary and sold me lots for it," he explained, meaning his wife used the family's money to buy real estate which she would later sell, presumably at a profit. "She was never home," the man continued, adding that "I finally offered to pay her a salary to stay at home, but she wouldn't even do that." After deliberating, the judge decided there was "altogether too much work in this family," and advised the couple to come to some agreement before granting a divorce.[1]

The true story offered interesting insights into not only gender dynamics and the legal system circa 1925 but the pronounced role of real estate in everyday life in the United States. It was the 1920s when the modern era of real estate began in this country, as social and economic forces came together to forge an ideal climate for the buying and selling of property to take place. Much of this had to do with the Own Your Own Home movement, a national campaign launched by the U.S. Department of Labor and championed by the real estate industry that was designed to persuade Americans to invest in property rather than continue to rent. Home ownership became a symbol of a citizen's commitment and loyalty to the United States, an expression of patriotism during what were anxious times.[2] Over the next decade, many Americans would indeed invest in property not just for political reasons but for financial and personal ones, finding that making the decision to own a home was one of the best things they ever did.

DOI: 10.4324/9781003481485-2

A Manifest Desire

African Americans, however, were routinely denied the chance to build their white picket fence a century ago, particularly in neighborhoods that were exclusively white. In fact, local real estate organizations in many cities across the United States actively took steps to prevent Blacks from owning property in designated areas. The Great Migration—the movement of millions of African Americans from the South to points north and west—was in full swing, making whites concerned about property values and who might be living next door. In St. Louis in 1920, for example, that city's Real Estate Exchange adopted a resolution stating that any member of that group who sold, bought, or otherwise transferred property from a white person to an African American in a specified district would be expelled. The St. Louis Negro Businessmen's League condemned the exchange for its discriminatory policy, declaring it a "blow to the rise and progress of a whole group of people."[3]

The same action was taken the following year in Chicago by that city's Real Estate Board, a reminder that Jim Crow segregation was hardly limited to the South, and the Baltimore Real Estate Board was considering a similar policy (while allowing whites to reside in Black areas if so desired).[4] In Harlem, meanwhile, it was more egregiously high rents that were the main problem, as white landlords took advantage of the inability for African Americans to move into white-dominated neighborhoods and buildings.[5]

Housing for all remained tight in many cities, and none more so than in Washington, DC. A good number of war workers had left the nation's capital by the early 1920s but finding an apartment to rent was still quite a challenge. Purchasing an apartment, however, was no problem at all. One generally thinks of the mass conversion of apartments into cooperatives and condominiums as a 1970s or 1980s phenomenon, but the practice was actually common more than a half century earlier. "There is a manifest desire to sell, especially apartments," a journalist for the *Christian Science Monitor* reported in 1920, noting that "hardly a day passes without several apartment houses are put on the market for so called 'co-operative selling.'" As would happen decades later in such situations, tenants were notified that they would have to vacate their apartment when their lease expired or buy it, with the same holding true for house rentals. Many believed a postwar recession was coming, encouraging property owners to try to sell before values fell.[6]

The "co-operative plan," as it was sometimes called, was gaining popularity in Chicago and New York City as well. Less than 3% of dwellings in the latter were occupied by their owner, but that was slowly changing as rents rose after the war. Then, as now, cooperative apartments were different from the single-family home in many respects, making it vital for potential buyers to know what they were getting into. The benefits—no lease, not being subject to whims or demands of a landlord, building equity, and possible appreciation—were the same, however, good reason why more urbanites with some cash were exploring the opportunity. Cooperative apartments were much more popular in Europe, but Americans were gradually embracing the idea.[7]

Real estate speculators had by no means ceased to buy land and divvy it up into lots for development, however, especially as more suburbs sprang up around the country. In fact, local real estate groups supported the "Own Your Own Home" campaign by flaunting the benefits of being the king or queen of one's castle. Folks who would today be called locavores were critical of the approach developers were taking, however, believing that the goal to maximize profits was not serving the best interests of the homeowner or community. The tendency for many builders at the time to squeeze as many houses into a parcel of land didn't allow room for gardens in which to grow fruit or vegetables, an unfortunate thing given the lost opportunity to enjoy or sell produce. "There is altogether too much home plotting from the viewpoint of the engineer and the academic and too little from that of the homemaker," bemoaned Philip Foster, a Cambridge, Massachusetts-based town and city planner.[8]

Also subscribing to the anti-cookie-cutter school of houses was Henry Ely, a Cedar Rapids, Iowa, builder. Ely was a big believer in the "Own Your Own Home" campaign, and decided to build a house that would make people want something, well, homey. True to form, the gray house in downtown Cedar Rapids was not grand or fancy but had a distinct charm about it, just as the man intended. Ely held a three-week open house during the Christmas holiday season of 1920, when shoppers filled the streets, and more than ten thousand people took the builder up on his offer to see the inside. Requests poured in for copies of the plans, with the innovative promotion becoming something of a national phenomenon. Ely was confident that each new homeowner would use the plan just as a starting point, however, and customize theirs to their own liking.[9]

Such selling techniques were just what the real estate industry believed were necessary to get more Americans to own their own homes. More than 2,000 brokers and agents gathered at the annual gathering of the National Association of Real Estate Boards (NAREB) in 1922 in San Francisco, agreeing that Americans had to be taught that real estate was the best security to own. Even small investments in real estate were preferable to the purchase of stocks due to the former's relative stability, the group advised the attendees to tell potential homeowners, preferably via advertising to reach as many people as possible. Some companies were promising that their respective stock would soon deliver tremendous profits, something real estate was admittedly unlikely to do. Also, the NAREB's leaders recommended that attendees spread the word that real estate investors were more stable citizens of a community than those who played the volatile stock market because homeowners possessed a literal stake in it.[10]

Good ammunition, no doubt, but convincing renters to invest in a house was at the time not an easy thing to do. Apartment dwellers (especially those with a baby or one on the way) considering such a move were typically motivated by seeing how their $50 or so per month rent payment would be roughly equivalent for a monthly mortgage payment. Next came the house tour, which usually ended in disappointment. For that kind of money, homes were usually located in less desirable parts of town (possibly near the railroad tracks), and they had had previous owners with questionable aesthetics. Considerable beautifying and yardwork were often needed, making the renters think apartment life wasn't so bad after all.[11]

Other renters thinking about becoming homeowners were discouraged after tumbling the numbers. The $50 payment per month might be the same, but a surprising amount turned out to be interest rather than principal. Then there were property taxes, improvement costs, the occasional assessment levied by the town or city (such as paving streets, a common thing in the burgeoning suburbs), and income tax if the property was sold at a profit (an issue of much contention). Again, renting an apartment, despite all the nuisances—like getting the heat turned on or having the super fix the annoying leak—seemed like the better way to go.[12]

A third barrier to renters making the leap to ownership was the fear of taking on such an expensive possession—almost always far more than anything else that could be bought. For the majority of Americans, $5,000 was an enormous amount of money in 1922 ($90,000 in today's dollars), making the more cautious balk at signing on the line. "You must have faith if you're going to buy on a small income, and then bend every energy to justify that faith," Zelia M. Walters, a successful real estate broker, recommended to those in the same profession.[13]

Despite all those valid reasons to think twice about home ownership, many Americans were taking that leap of faith. Los Angeles was certainly booming, with the number of real estate transfers between 1921 and 1923 equal to those completed between 1910 and 1920. That decade had been a terrible one for the real estate business in most cities, as the nation's involvement in the Great War triggered a major slump in building activity. Public service utilities were struggling to keep up with the rapid development of Los Angeles and demand for gas, water, and electricity, with considerable further growth anticipated due in part to the movie industry relocating from New York to the West Coast.[14]

The Best Type of Citizenship

Los Angelenos' greater interest in buying property in the early 1920s was a good indicator of what was taking place across the country. "The nation has turned to real estate," declared a headline in the *New York Tribune* in 1923, with records of transfers consistently rising. "Builders are active, money is plentiful, and real estate is far more popular with investors than ever before," the article continued. As the National Association of Real Estate Boards had pointed out, the stock market was fluctuating widely, an incentive for those with some extra cash to look to property as a better place to store it. Rents were rising and the postwar housing shortage persisted in larger cities, making being a landlord a profitable venture if one was up to it. Also, with Henry Ford's inexpensive Model-T, traffic congestion had become a major problem in downtown areas, an additional reason to invest in suburban property.[15] Small single-family homes accounted for the greatest demand, a reflection of those with average incomes to now be able to afford a place of one's own as the economy improved.[16]

"Film folk," as they were sometimes called, were a very active part of the real estate scene in Los Angeles. Silent movie star Buster Keaton bought a home on South Ardmore for $55,000 in 1923, quite a large sum in those days (about $1 million today), with Ruth Roland, Dorothy Talmadge, and others scooping up property around Wilshire Boulevard and Western Avenue.[17] Roland, who appeared in more than 200 films between 1909 and 1927, was herself a big-time real estate entrepreneur when not appearing on the silver screen. In 1923, she was busy developing a subdivision in the Wilshire district aptly named Roland Square, thinking Los Angeles would one day be recognized for what the *Los Angeles Times* described as "a paradise for home seekers."[18]

Roland had excellent business sense (she also formed her own production company), taking advantage of the fact that Los Angeles was leading the nation in home buying. In addition to that, California was reportedly the world leader in real estate, at least judging by the number of broker and agent licenses being taken in the state. More than 30,000 people were legally permitted to sell real estate in California in 1923 as a bona fide land rush took shape.[19] (Many more were practicing the trade without a license, some of them making sketchy if not downright fraudulent deals.) Lots were selling both day and night, including those in Alhambra Hills, a new subdivision, whose roads had just been paved.[20] Courses in real estate were being given in Los Angeles and many other cities in the United States as many—including a good number of women—recognized the opportunities to be had in this rapidly expanding profession. (Some society women were entering the field to pick up some extra pin money.)[21] Like today, selling real estate could be a part-time gig rather than a full-time job. Zeb Terry, the second baseman for the Chicago Cubs, for example, was peddling real estate in the off-season, finding it an excellent way to supplement his income.[22]

With so many Americans new to the real estate game, experts stepped forward to advise novices on what to look (and look out) for when considering a particular property. There were many factors involved, needless to say, the number one being, not surprisingly, location. Was the house relatively near a retail area, preferably within walking distance (eight blocks, according to some)? Was the ground relatively level? Was the city making infrastructural improvements to the area so that more people could move in (raising values)? Importantly, what were the values (and, if recently sold, prices) of adjacent properties? Running the "comps," as we would say now, was seen a century ago as a prime means of determining whether the ask was too much, too little, or just right.[23]

Although some bargains could still be had in town, investors in property were more likely to look for cheaper land outside of cities. Considerable numbers of farmers were selling their land, realizing more money could be made by doing so than by growing crops. A combination of factors—high taxes relative to income, tight margins, a labor shortage, and a decreasing population in rural areas—was making farmers take developers' offers seriously when the latter or real estate agents knocked on the doors of the former.[24]

While developers' and agents' primary goal was naturally to make money, authority figures positioned home ownership as a morally responsible act. Renting an apartment, especially an expensive one, was portrayed by some officials as an extravagant and wasteful thing to do. Within such a view, rent was presented as spending money while paying off a mortgage was framed as saving money; the former was consuming, the latter producing. Renting was "not a healthy, progressive and constructive situation," argued W. Franklin Burnham, former president of the Massachusetts Real Estate Exchange, in 1925, nor was it "conducive to the best type of citizenship." Rather than being an indulgence, then, owning was a symbol of thrift, an interesting take on the pursuit of private property. Taking on debt via a mortgage was seen as a good thing, somewhat paradoxically, as it reinforced a work ethic. A subtext of all this certainly was that by owning property, one presumably was less likely to engage in subversive activity, a major concern vis-à-vis the First Red Scare of the early 1920s.[25]

Major William Kennelly, one of the top real estate people of the day, addressed this idea head-on in a 1925 piece in the *New York Herald Tribune*. For Kennelly, it wasn't the big investors who symbolized the ideological importance of real estate but rather the small ones. It was the buyer with modest means who ventured into home ownership for the first time, as it was he or she who "augured a bright future for the perpetuation of real American institutions."[26] Kennelly continued:

> It does more than reflect the time honored and traditional dream of every man to own in his own right a bit of God's green earth. It means the creation of a nation of land owners and home owners, the greatest bulwark against propagandists of unrest and the greatest possible guarantee that our country will successfully withstand the vicious political and economic onslaughts which for a time seemed to menace our traditions.[27]

In short, distributing real estate holdings among the many rather than a rich and powerful few served as a tool of democracy, and as one important way that we were different than foreign nations.[28]

A notable exception to the Own Your Own Home movement in the mid-1920s was, in a word, Florida. Many investors from across the country had been taken in by unscrupulous brokers (or, more accurately, swindlers) in that state who boasted of fortunes to be made overnight by buying property. Inspection of such property often revealed that, if it existed at all, it was as likely as not to be under water or in an area better suited for occupancy by alligators and crocodiles rather than humans.[29]

Modern means of transportation—specifically the "flivver" (a cheap automobile) and improved mass transit systems—were instrumental in Americans' interest in owning property in the suburbs. (Automobile sales drove sales of suburban real estate and vice versa.) The need to pave roads for cars played a large role in the development of towns outside major cities. Being as little as twenty miles from a city's downtown area not long ago meant a rather remote existence but that had all changed with speedier ways of moving to-and-fro. Now, being as much as a hundred miles from a metropolitan area didn't mean being cut off from civilization, a huge stride in terms of cultural geography. "While the modern apartment is popular with some, there are many others who have always wanted country life, with its trees, flowers, and bit of green grass," a journalist for the *Christian Science Monitor* noted in 1925, that pretty scene now being made real by effectively shortening the distance to the city. Commuting to work was becoming an increasingly desirable thing to do among salary men with families, with some keeping a *pied a terre* in town during the week. The suburban exodus was a good thing for cities too, it could be argued, as it relieved some of the congestion that was making urban life an ordeal.[30]

A New Phase

The year 1925 appeared to be a turning point in home ownership in America as the Roaring Twenties swept the nation. Traffic coming into cities in the morning and out at the end of the business was already heavy, and commuting trains had become crowded, a clear sign of the increasing popularity of suburban life. It was "the newer residential sections where 'the man on the street' has a home of his own and has learned to appreciate the value of fresh air, sunshine, and living rooms that are wholesome, clean, and safe," Joseph P. Day wrote for the *New York Herald Tribune* in 1925. Near New York City, great estates were being broken up, with developers dividing them neatly into lots for sale. With the stock market reaching record highs, companies were sending hefty dividend checks to shareholders, many of whom were using the funds as down payments on a home. "Every man in every walk of life has become a 'realtor' and real estate is king!," Day, a notable real estate broker and auctioneer, exclaimed, with who was buying what the talk of the town in Manhattan. While Day was overstating—a habit of the trade—his claim that real estate had entered "a new phase" was entirely true, as it was members of the ballooning middle class who were leading the grabbing of property.[31]

Knowing that it had a good story to tell, the NAREB commissioned a researcher to learn how much money was currently lent by banks and financial institutions for real estate mortgages in the country in 1925. Using a variety of sources, the researcher came up with the figure of $25 billion ($437 billion today), which happened to be more than all the money in circulation at the time plus the value of all the gold and silver reserves in the United States Treasury. (The country began phasing out the backing of currency in gold and silver in 1933 and it ended in 1973.) "The availability of mortgage credit has been a mighty factor in the development of the United States," the NAREB boasted in a press release, making possible millions of homes, farms, and businesses that otherwise wouldn't exist. In short, real estate was essential to the American way of life, the organization suggested, taking full advantage of the current rush to buy (and sell) property.[32]

While real estate was clearly a profession that was in the right place at the right time, the job was hardly an easy one. Brokers and agents had to deal with many different kinds of situations and many different kinds of people, making flexibility and patience key attributes to possess if one hoped to succeed. Those who had recently come into a large sum of money, perhaps from oil, were one type, a welcome sight for realtors given the commission they would likely reap from a luxury rental or pricy house. Subletters were another category; they typically arrived in a real estate office in the spring, hoping to rent their place in order to generate enough cash to go to Europe for the summer. Elderly tenants were known to come in to complain about noisy neighbors, and then there were those who (shades of *Glengarry Glen Ross*) simply liked to talk with real estate people but not actually complete any transaction. Finally, there was the type with high expectations but small pocketbooks, thinking a modest sum would and should reap huge square footage, a gorgeous space, or a prime location.[33]

Despite such challenges for realtors, business was very good particularly given the fact that new construction was booming. Virtually any builder could get financing to put up a structure to sell or rent out, a function of the easy credit that the NAREB was so proud of. Going against the mid-1920s development-at-any-cost grain was J. H. Tregoe, executive manager of the National Association of Credit Men. He felt that credit had become too easy, a potentially dangerous thing given past boom periods. Tregoe knew his history and pointed out that previous economic panics were (with the exception of the one that occurred in 1907) all a result of overspeculation in real estate. Way back in 1819, it was loose "paper" credit for building in the American Southwest that caused the bubble to burst, and Tregoe saw parallels with the situation a century and change later. "It is not good sense to applaud the speed of any movement if there is some danger of a wheel coming off and the drivers and passengers having a bad spill," he stated, recommending "a closer cooperation between lender and builder" lest the public suffer.[34]

There were others who believed that there was too much speculation in the real estate market. (A giant bubble in Miami was in fact currently bursting.) The big money being made was newsworthy, but there was little attention being paid to losses, which were more common than one might have thought. Purchasing a property for occupancy was one thing, buying one to rent out or flip was quite another. Investing a lot in a subdivision with the belief or promise that people would soon flock to the area could be a costly mistake, something many were learning after coming under the spell of real estate mania.[35]

There was risk enough in legitimate projects, but there were plenty of fraudulent ones that almost certainly spelled financial doom for the less cautious. A scheme in Muscle Shoals, Alabama, had become legendary due to the number of people who fell for the venture (that Henry Ford was going to build a car plant was used as bait). Another con making the rounds in Chicago was the giving out of tickets in movie theaters with the good news that the bearer has won a free lot. To collect, all one had to do was pay a nominal sum for transfer and recording of title, the bad news being that the cost of that exceeded the value of the lot.[36] An alternate version was to advertise a puzzle that a six-year-old could solve, with "winners" again receiving a "free" lot. Said lot was worth a few dollars at best, and considerable pressure was applied for the smart puzzle solvers to buy the adjacent, exorbitantly priced lot.[37] To its credit, the industry was trying to weed out these "wildcatters" and raise professional standards, knowing the crooks hurt its image (and business).

Indeed, with prudence, a home could be a very good investment, even compared to the bullish stock market (whose profits were for many largely funding the purchasing of property). Real estate could be improved and made more valuable, for one thing, something that couldn't be said for securities, and it could be used by the owner for personal or professional purposes. There was also the matter of control; one could determine how a property was used while finance professionals managed stocks and bonds, the latter making some uneasy. Finally, and perhaps most important, real estate was tangible, an asset that could be seen and was impossible (or at least difficult) to be stolen. Financial assets were simply paper certificates, with a sense (sometimes justified) that they could vanish into thin air. Real estate people pointed out these advantages to those considering where to put their money, with genuinely ethical ones advising to never buy a property sight unseen. (For oceanfront property, they recommended seeing it twice—once at low tide, once at high tide.)[38]

Encouragingly, African Americans were taking part in the home ownership frenzy of the mid-1920s in what were considered suburbs of New York City. In the summer of 1925, Blacks were actively buying property in both Jamaica, Queens, and in Brooklyn, more often than not via real estate operators of color. There was an "army of home seekers," according to the *New York Amsterdam News*, some of them newlyweds who wanted to be their own landlords after paying race-based rent. Such African Americans sought out Black brokers such as William Weir in Jamaica as it was well known that many white brokers would add hundreds of dollars to the list price of property, in part to discourage them as buyers. In just a few years, the Carrington Brothers, an African American-owned firm based on Fulton Street in Brooklyn, had sold almost a hundred homes to people of color, blazing a trail that would accelerate in the years ahead.[39]

As more Americans headed to the suburbs, home ownership became a more complex affair. In addition to working with the broker and builder, new homeowners may have hired landscape gardeners and interior decorators in the pursuit to make the dwelling as beautiful as possible and magnify the "curb appeal." In many communities, homeowners had to follow prescribed standards in building design and landscape treatment. Interior decorating was evolving into a sizable profession all its own, in part due to the emergence of a modern aesthetic—specifically art deco—that challenged more traditional design and furnishings.[40]

Home expositions—trade shows where the public could receive inspiration in how to build or decorate their domicile—were also getting more popular. The 1926 Own Your Own Home Exposition in Chicago sponsored by that city's Real Estate Board was the sixth annual event of its kind. Architects and other professionals connected to real estate showed off their products and services at the expo as a way to attract clients. To promote the show, organizers held a slogan contest which received no less than 20,000 submissions. $50 would go to the slogan that best described the reason that one should own one's own home. First prize went to Mrs. G.F. Finer of Waukegan, Illinois, whose entry went as follows: "A home is the birthplace of independence, a workshop for character building, and a foundation for social and financial standing." A bit wordy, perhaps, but Mrs. Finer was no doubt happy to see her submission painted in large letters in gold over the entrance to the exposition.[41]

A Golden Glow

While it may have been a stretch that owning a home was all the things Mrs. Finer claimed, the real estate industry could look back with pride at the strides made so far in the 1920s. Immediately after the end of World War I, many Americans were hesitant to buy property because they feared they would have trouble selling it if they chose to do so later. There were now thousands of brokers and agents who made that process much easier, and millions more people interested in investing in property. Beyond that, the population of the country had grown, and there was a sense that cities couldn't expand much beyond their current size because of limited land. Finally, the financing of a home had become more buyer-friendly through the introduction of the installment plan. The 1920s were the golden days of this arrangement in which small payments could be paid monthly for big-ticket items, allowing consumers to own cars, appliances, and even houses before having all the money needed.[42]

Some, however, traced the home ownership surge to 1914 when the war caused a housing shortage in larger cities and thus a greater demand for property. The rise in building construction after the war was thus a catching up of sorts, making the expansion into the suburbs essentially inevitable.[43] Money was tight and interest was high between 1918 and 1920, however, with credit and rates becoming far more favorable to investors beginning in 1921.[44] Also, in the early 1920s, Wall Street figured out a way to finance new construction by issuing bonds that ordinary investors could buy, a major step in the real estate business that would eventually lead to the offering of REITs (real estate investment trusts).

If there was any doubt that real estate had in the 1920s taken on the characteristics of a consumer product, albeit a high-priced one, all one had to do was go to the Fair Department Store in Chicago. In 1926, the store began selling lots and houses over the counter, reportedly the first retailer in the country to transfer real estate as if it were cosmetics or socks.[45] That year more than half (54%) of the nation's total wealth ($330 billion) was in real estate, according to a prominent engineering and construction company. This $180 billion in real estate exceeded the worth of all other industries, with railroads coming in a distant second.[46]

Home ownership had become such a part of the national conversation that the kind of language used by agents and brokers had become cliché. There were a number of lines commonly employed when convincing renters to buy or when trying to sell a particular piece of property. These included:

> This is the greatest opportunity of the age.
> Why help make your landlord rich?
> Warm in winter and cold in summer.
> On the crest of a hill.
> In a sheltered valley.
> If you don't buy it, you'll regret it all the rest of your life.
> All the great fortunes have been made in real estate.
> Grow your own vegetables.
> Near schools and churches.
> Where only the best people live.
> Almost around the corner from the railroad station.
> We're not trying to sell you; we're doing you a favor.[47]

There seemed to be no limit to the array of phrases that agents had at their disposal to motivate clients to action. Some other classics were "Opportunity knocks but once," "Easy terms," "Lots of trees," "Better act now as these lots won't last long at these prices," "The sidewalks are coming soon," and the ultimate, "Better bring your checkbook." Also, a new subdivision might very well consist of an open field with muddy ground, but future streets were likely to already carry lovely names like "Tulip Avenue," "Raspberry Road," or "Carnation Lane."[48]

Another old saying that had a good bit of truth was that there were only two kinds of people who should rent—the very wealthy, who needn't worry about money, and the poor, who couldn't afford to buy a property. For everyone else, however, owning made more sense than renting, agents were quick to point out, and was the best part toward realizing financial independence. Over the long term, they were also apt to mention, monthly rent added up to a very large sum, more reason to use those funds as "capital" if at all possible. Nothing less than success in life was contingent upon building wealth through real estate, more ambitious agents might say, playing upon the fear that one was being left behind in the race to riches that heavily informed the Roaring Twenties.[49]

Agents had also earned a reputation as go-getters if not hustlers as more men and women entered the field and competed for listings and sales. After hopping into a car with the agent at the wheel, clients were sometimes surprised that the eager beaver had not actually seen the property himself or herself. Getting lost was also not unusual, and the property often turned out to be much further from town than described. Upon arrival, clients could be quite disappointed by the appearance of the house, but the agent was prepared for such a thing. "Well, we're here so you might as well take a look inside," he or she would say, adding that one could always paint the outside or repair those broken shingles. The agents would then point out all the positive aspects of the house—especially a fireplace, if there was one—while ignoring all the negatives or dismissing them with a flippant "That's easily fixed."[50]

Agents also had as ammunition entirely true stories of how real estate had made many Americans rich. For example, the Seeger family of New Orleans owned a property valued at $500,000 in 1924 and, although tempted to sell two years later at $1.7 million, hung on another two years to reap $2.2 million. The owner of two lots in Wichita, Kansas, worth $10,000 in 1912 sold them for $40,000 in 1925, while a strip of land in Houston costing $2,600 a front foot in 1913 was worth four times that in 1926. A piece of property in Birmingham, Alabama, bought for $57,000 in 1920 was sold for $112,000 just three years later, and another in Minneapolis bought for $125,000 in early 1921 went for twice that just six months later. Not surprisingly, the biggest profits were made by those who decided to hold onto a property in what would become a prime location. In 1889, a corner lot in downtown Los Angeles that was advertised for sale for $12,000 was valued at $2.5 million forty years later, illustrating the possibilities for those with vision (and patience).[51]

Given the good times, it was understandable how most saw no end to the nation's flourishing real estate market. "National Prosperity Will Operate in Favor of Real Property," proclaimed a headline in the *New York Herald Tribune* in early 1929, with little reason to believe conditions would dramatically change. "Too many signs clearly point the way to one of the best, and perhaps the very best, years that our country has ever had," Fisher P. Weaver stated in the article. Wages were up, the auto industry had just had a record year, and, most excitingly, the stock market was climbing to unprecedented heights. Somewhere between fifteen million and twenty million Americans owned stocks or bonds—thirty to forty times the number not that many years before, with much of the gains being made invested in property. About 10% of American households owned stocks by 1929, while the home ownership rate was 47.8% the following year. "This country is a golden glow upon the face of the earth," Weaver poetically wrote, joining the chorus of voices saying that nothing could stop the momentum.[52] Something much different lay in store for home ownership and the nation as a whole, however, as the golden glow of the 1920s became significantly tarnished.

Notes

1 "Home Woes are Blamed on Business," *Los Angeles Times*, June 10, 1925, A13.
2 LeeAnn Lands, "Be a Patriot, Buy a Home: Re-Imagining Home Owners and Home Ownership in Early 20th Century Atlanta," *Journal of Social History*, Summer 2008, 943.
3 "Negroes Opposed to Real Estate Policy," *Christian Science Monitor*, March 25, 1920, 2. Slightly more than a quarter of African Americans lived in urban areas in 1910, rising to a third by 1920 largely due to the Great Migration. By 1930, more than two-fifths of African Americans lived in cities. Theodore Kornweibel, Jr., "An Economic Profile of Black Life in the Twenties," *Journal of Black Studies*, June 1976, 307.
4 "Segregation Idea Starts in Chicago," *Norfolk New Journal and Guide*, May 21, 1921, 6; "Real Estate Board Asks Segregation Measure," *Baltimore Afro-American*, September 7, 1923, 3.
5 "Color Line Bobs Up in Harlem Over Real Estate," *Chicago Defender*, August 6, 1921, 9.
6 "Housing Situation Acute at Capital," *Christian Science Monitor*, September 8, 1920, 5.
7 "Need Investigation Before Buying on Co-operative Plan," *New York Tribune*, August 29, 1920, A4; Al Chase, "Co-op Flat Idea, After a Year of Trial, a Success," *Chicago Daily Tribune*, October 16, 1921, H22. Of all cities with a population over 100,000, the lowest percentage of home ownership in 1920 was in New York City, according to figures from the Bureau of Census, the Bureau of Standards, and the Department of Commerce. A whopping 51% of residents of Des Moines, Iowa, owned their homes, this data showed. "Percentage of Home Ownership in Cities of the United States," *Scientific American*, May 1922, 318.
8 "More Land as Need for Homes," *Christian Science Monitor*, October 11, 1920, 9.
9 Beth Stewart, "Selling 'Own Your Own Home' Idea," *American Builder*, April 1, 1921, 94.
10 "National Real Estate Boards Favor Zoning," *Christian Science Monitor*, June 10, 1922, 15.
11 Zelia M. Walters, "Selling the Home Seeker," *American Builder*, December 1, 1922, 100.
12 Walters, "Selling the Home Seeker."
13 Walters, "Selling the Home Seeker."
14 Mason Case, "Los Angeles Claims Million With Real Estate Booming," *Los Angeles Times*, December 20, 1923, 19. The iconic "Hollywoodland" sign was erected in 1923.
15 "Nation Has Turned to Real Estate," *New York Tribune*, July 8, 1923, C1.

16 "Real Estate Outlook Is Rosy for 1924," *New York Tribune*, December 2, 1923, C1.
17 "Film Folk Are Now Investing in Real Estate," *Los Angeles Times*, May 27, 1923, V8.
18 "Ruth Roland Will Open Subdivision," *Los Angeles Times*, May 7, 1923, II16.
19 "California Now Leading World in Real Estate," *Los Angeles Times*, May 27, 1923, V12.
20 "Lots Sell at Night," *Los Angeles Times*, May 20, 1923, V15.
21 "Quit Society for Work," *Los Angeles Times*, February 26, 1924, A1.
22 "Zeb Terry Peddles Real Estate," *Los Angeles Times*, February 13, 1923, III1.
23 Bernard Rosenthal, "What Investor Should Watch," *Los Angeles Times*, June 3, 1923, V2.
24 "Farm Lands Selling," *Los Angeles Times*, November 4, 1923, V11.
25 W. Franklin Burnham, "Home Building Drive Favored," *Christian Science Monitor*, May 12, 1925, 18.
26 Major William Kennelly, "1925 Promises to Be Great One for Realty," *New York Herald Tribune*, January 25, 1925, B4.
27 Kennelly, "1925 Promises to Be Great One for Realty."
28 Kennelly, "1925 Promises to Be Great One for Realty."
29 "Chamber Warns Small Investor," *Christian Science Monitor*, September 24, 1925, 4.
30 "Real Estate Development Speeds Exodus from City," *Christian Science Monitor*, November 18, 1925, 5B.
31 Joseph P. Day, "Real Estate Is Entering a New Phase," *New York Herald Tribune*, March 8, 1925, B3.
32 "$24,810,625,013 Has Been Invested in Real Estate," *New York Herald Tribune*, May 24, 1925, B1.
33 W.E. Hill, "The Real Estate Office," *Los Angeles Times*, June 28, 1925, C4.
34 "Warns against Building Boom," *Los Angeles Times*, November 22, 1925, E16.
35 "Investors Guide: Speculating in Real Estate," *Chicago Daily Tribune*, July 5, 1925, A11.
36 "Investors Guide: Speculating in Real Estate."
37 "Begin Inquiry into "Give-Away Realty Schemes," *Chicago Daily Tribune*, August 16, 1925, H26.
38 "Buy Real Estate but Buy It Carefully," *Chicago Daily Tribune*, October 20, 1925, 8.
39 "Biggest Real Estate Boom in Suburban Property for Colored People This Summer," *New York Amsterdam News*, July 22, 1925, 8.
40 "Suburban Planning Gaining Importance in Real Estate," *Christian Science Monitor*, January 13, 1926, 4B.
41 "Home Workshop for Character," *Christian Science Monitor*, March 30, 1926, 3.
42 "Real Estate Buying of Year Is Chiefly for Investment," *Christian Science Monitor*, July 28, 1926, 4B.
43 Max N. Natanson, "Real Estate Is Discussed in Every Part," *New York Herald Tribune*, January 31, 1926, B2.
44 "More People Seek Homes in Country, Realtor Finds," *Christian Science Monitor*, May 7, 1927, 4B.
45 "Store Will Sell Real Estate," *Los Angeles Times*, January 12, 1926, 2.
46 "More Than Half Country's Wealth in Real Estate," *New York Herald Tribune*, January 31, 1926, B5.
47 Robert Lord, "The Real Estate Salesman Goes Crazy," *Life*, January 6, 1927, 25.
48 Snowshoe Al, "Al Looks at Real Estate," *Chicago Daily Tribune*, May 6, 1928, I1.

49 "Home Ownership Lays Foundation towards Financial Independence," *New York Amsterdam News*, August 3, 1927, 10.
50 Donald Ogden Stewart, "The Other Day," *Chicago Daily Tribune*, September 4, 1927, Q4.
51 Real Estate Has Made Many People Rich," *Los Angeles Times*, December 18, 1929, 15.
52 Fisher P. Weaver, "National Prosperity Will Operate in Favor of Real Property," *New York Herald Tribune*, January 27, 1929, D1.

2 A Desirable Social Goal

Home ownership is a desirable social goal, and the progress of civilization is measured by the structures which men erect.

Saturday Evening Post, April 1931

A running story in Hollywood circles of the 1930s revolved around the transition New York playwrights and novelists often made after being drawn west by the promise of the big money to be made in the movie business. The writers, many of them Jewish intellectuals (think Barton Fink), would arrive with plenty of wisecracks about Los Angeles, thinking the place to be a cultural wasteland with little to offer cerebral types like themselves. They would typically live in a hotel or rent an apartment, planning to skedaddle back to Manhattan once their fat check cleared.[1]

Finding the climate and relaxed setting to their liking, however, these new screenwriters would, during their second year in Tinseltown, buy a house in Beverly Hills, justifying it as a good investment. By their third year, the once-skeptical would also own a place in Malibu and, by their fourth, a ranch in the country and/or a weekend getaway in Palm Springs. By their fifth year in Los Angeles, the writers would be selling real estate on the side, finding it to be as lucrative as scribbling fluffy romantic comedies or silly but wildly popular melodramas.[2]

The story—like the plotlines of many movies—had some basis in fact, a reflection of the key role that home ownership played in the lives of many Americans. While the 1930s got off to a very bad start, things would gradually turn around through the decade, laying the foundation for what would turn out to be a golden age of home ownership in the United States. Until then, however, it would be hard times for investors in property, as simply surviving the economic crisis took priority over realizing the dream of owning a tiny piece of the country.

The Bugaboo of Depression

Predictably, the stock market crash of fall 1929 had a direct and dramatic effect on the nation's housing market. New construction came to a virtual

DOI: 10.4324/9781003481485-3

dead stop, as the flow of money from banks, mortgage houses, and other lending institutions was reduced to a relative trickle. Between September and November of that year, the market lost more than half its value, falling from $64 billion to about $30 billion. While just 10% or so of Americans owned stocks, about a third lost most of whatever savings they had. Many jobs too disappeared as a result of the crash and the events that preceded it, notably speculation in real estate.[3] "Much of the unemployment in the United States has been due to a country-wide curtailment of residence and other construction," the *Christian Science Monitor* sadly reported in the summer of 1930.[4]

The annual get-together of the National Association of Real Estate Boards (NAREB) that year was no doubt a literally depressing affair, yet voices of optimism could be heard among the 3,000 delegates. It was true that Wall Street had "laid an egg," to paraphrase the famous headline in *Variety*, but absolutely nothing could stop the desire for Americans to own property. There was, after all, a tremendous amount of land that could be settled. In just five years, advances in air travel would lead to the creation of new suburbs one hundred miles from cities, a Chicago city planner told the group, with businessmen hopping into commuter planes rather than cars and trains to get to and from their downtown offices.[5]

In fact, it was up to the real estate industry to lead the nation back to prosperity, the members of the NAREB agreed, making it incumbent for anyone involved in the business to nurture that latent desire for home ownership. Like faster airplanes, speedier construction methods could bring about a rosy future for real estate; homes could be made in factories as automobiles were, greatly reducing their cost. A New York-based engineer claimed that a home could be constructed in three days "just as a child builds a house of blocks," good news for the conference attendees wondering if they were out of a job.[6] President Hoover himself was counting on real estate to get the country back on its feet. Many of the jobs that disappeared after the crash had to do with construction, motivating Hoover to urge lenders to offer loans to builders. Requiring less money down would also go a long way to rebooting the economy, something that leaders of the NAREB asked bankers to consider.[7]

While money was tight in 1930 and would remain so for the next few years, that didn't mean that the buying and selling of homes had come to a halt. Considerable bargains could be had on "preowned" properties, as those who couldn't keep up on monthly payments or maintenance were eager to sell before the bank grabbed them. Brokers seemed as busy as ever, showing as many as ten properties in a single day to clients. The automobile had radically changed the way that agents and brokers did business, expanding the market much like how online listings would decades later. Knowing it was a buyer's market, house-hunters became more discriminating in what they wanted in a property. "Now the buyer wants to live on the state road, a tile bath, latticed windows in the bedroom, an oil heater, a garage, electric refrigeration, and good radio location," the *Christian Science Monitor* observed.[8]

Expectantly, real estate executives downplayed the financial kerfuffle, using the media to frame the mess as just the latest example of the normal up and down economic cycle. Values had dropped but not dramatically, at least yet, and a turnover of existing inventory wasn't necessarily a bad thing.[9] It was the stock market that crashed rather than the real estate market, after all, and while the two were intertwined, they often didn't run on a parallel course. "I look for a splendid building and real estate movement during 1930," Major William Kennelly beamed in the *New York Herald Tribune* a few weeks into that year, displaying the kind of optimism that was standard in the field.[10] "There is no doubt that real estate has withstood the shock splendidly," echoed Morton R. Cross, seeing great opportunities ahead.[11]

Locating in historical context what was increasingly being recognized as a depression gave real estate people hope that the current calamity was just a bump in a very long road. Denying that the country was in quite a pickle would be a mistake, but real estate had always bounced back from economic crises. From this perspective, things weren't really that bad, as there had been much worse real estate busts in American history and the long view showed a long-term trend in property appreciation. New York City, most notably, had experienced one following wild speculation in 1868 but had obviously recovered nicely. (Lots on Fifth Avenue at 59th Street in Manhattan could be had for $6,000 in 1858.) "Land has gone up in the past and will go up in the future," I. Jerome Riker assured readers of the *New York Herald Tribune* in 1931, words of comfort to those thinking they may be facing financial ruin.[12]

In fact, those who had weathered the storm by avoiding stocks were putting everything they could into discounted property, believing the good deals would likely not last long. (A literally valuable lesson could be learned from John Jacob Astor who, during an economic panic of the early 19th century, invested heavily in real estate, making a fortune in the process.) William P. Maurer of Los Angeles was on such a tear; the man who already owned more than 5,000 parcels in the county had recently added 180 more to his portfolio. It was believed that Maurer already owned more property in the county than any other individual, but that wasn't stopping him from grabbing parcels that he felt were undervalued. "This is the best buyer's market I've seen in twenty-two years," he told the *Los Angeles Times* in 1931, advising others to get a piece of the action before prices went back up.[13] The real estate board of Maurer's home state also remained bullish about the opportunities to be had based on the still rising population, adopting "Buy California" as its slogan.[14] "Timid investors should not be frightened by the bugaboo of depression," added James L. Davis, real estate editor of that newspaper.[15]

Some owners of property in the early 1930s were essentially forced to sell in order to remain afloat, making those parcels the ones investors like Maurer were most keen on. A guessing game of sorts was being played by those in the latter fortunate position, as players tried to predict when prices would hit rock bottom.[16] Many families in larger cities were "doubling up" at the time, meaning sharing an apartment or house to save on rent. (Some were actually "tripling up.") At some point, however, when the economy improved, these families were likely to once again want to have places of their own. It was such faith that made investors feel good about spending their money in a down market, seeing big money to be made on rentals or sales perhaps a few years down the road.[17]

Confident there was money to be made in fall 1932, despite it being the darkest days of the depression, were agents in Washington, DC. Every two, four, or six years, newcomers arrived in the nation's capital and they all needed a place to live. Newly elected representatives and senators would come into real estate offices seeking a lease for their respective term, although more likely than not they would stay in Washington even if they didn't serve a second term. Those who bought rather than rented clearly intended to stick around for a while, not about to go back to Dubuque or some other burg after making it to the big time. DC agents were famously non-partisan, knowing they would get business whomever won.[18]

There was good news for agents across the country that fall as it became apparent that the Volstead Act was likely to be repealed. FDR had indicated that he would end Prohibition if elected, and when he won, a fair share of brokers and agents celebrated with some soon-to-be-legal beer and whiskey. Repeal meant that saloons might open back up again, expanding local commercial real estate and raising rents. Landlords with vacant space, too, were delighted, although it wasn't clear yet whether FDR would allow drinking establishments in legalizing the consumption of alcohol. Restaurateurs were also happy to see Franklin Roosevelt get into office, knowing that they too would benefit if the new president overturned the 18th Amendment.[19]

Booze or no booze, the real estate industry was more than ready to say goodbye to 1932. The future was unknown, of course, but that year did appear to be rock bottom of the economic crisis. Save for some government-backed projects, new construction was almost nil, a function of there being virtually no mortgage money to be had. An oversupply of available space made property leasing a less profitable business, and simply collecting rent had become more challenging. Vacancies had risen as tenants doubled up, making landlords lower rents in order to just cover costs.[20] Home ownership in America had reached a low ebb, but some sun was beginning to peek out behind the clouds.

Passing the Danger Point

Indeed, in July 1933 the NAREB announced that there had been in dozens of cities an increased market activity for the first time in three years. Many other cities reported there had been no drop—this too a victory of sorts given the consistent downward trend of the past few years—and the Federal Home Loan Bank Board revealed that there had been a decline in the number of foreclosures.[21] Also, the glut of single-family houses had eased somewhat, another positive sign that a rebound could be on the way. Still, mortgage money was scarce, as banks and other financial institutions were not ready to begin offering loans carte blanche to those hoping to build a new home. Existing home prices remained low, making it a good time to buy property if one could.[22]

Bargains weren't going to last long, some experts were warning, urging investors to get in now before it was too late. The panic selling had stopped, and the FDR administration was taking steps to get the nation's economy moving again. Commodity prices were up, and while one might not think there was a connection between grain and real estate, a mood of optimism prevailed in the business community, suggesting that property values (and prices) would rise.[23] It would take an extra bit of work, but buying a property carrying an "incumbrance," i.e., a defaulted mortgage or lien, could pay off nicely, some were finding. Clearing the title was the first order of business in such cases, after which the buyer might very well put it right back on the market to make a quick profit. In Los Angeles, distressed property was in fact disappearing fast as it became clear that the economy was beginning to turn around. New houses too were starting to pop up there and elsewhere as banks untied their purse strings.[24]

By fall 1933, Los Angeles bankers were reporting that prices in residential property had risen 15–20% since reaching the low point of about a year previously. Small homes were selling best, and lots that had been vacant since the crash were attracting buyers. Best of all, it was "responsible" investors (i.e., those with cash) who were examining properties rather than the speculators who populated the field in the 1920s. The worst of that sort were carpetbaggers who came to Los Angeles only to take advantage of what was, with the possible exception of Miami, the hottest real estate market in the country.[25]

Meanwhile, in Chicago, that city's leaders of the real estate industry were struggling with a different, thornier issue: Should the wives of agents be invited to the annual Chicago Real Estate Board and Cook County Real Estate Board banquet? It had never been done in forty-nine previous fetes but perhaps it was now time that members of the fairer sex be allowed to attend, some felt. Those in favor pointed out that attendance at the event over the last few years had been literally depressingly low, as why go to such a celebration when there was no business to be had? Besides helping to fill the room, women would bring a certain *je ne sais quoi* to the dull dinner. "It would add color and charm to what has always been a rather drab affair," noted Samuel E. Erickson, president of the Chicago Real Estate Board (which was merging with the Cook County Real Estate Board), adding that including wives would make dancing possible for the first time.[26]

While Chicago's male agents struggled with their dilemma (dancing with female agents legitimately invited to the event was apparently out of the question), a NAREB survey revealed that the nation's real estate scene was definitely improving in 1933. In New York City, real estate owners were paying back taxes on their properties, leading the city's Controller to announce that Gotham was "passing the danger point."[27] The only thing holding back a full-fledged rebound in the country was the dearth of mortgage money; while some had begun to flow, it wasn't nearly enough to support the number of new prospective homeowners. There was a paucity of financing available for developers as well, this too stunting the revival of real estate in the country.[28]

Conditions had improved even more by 1934, however, with all signs that the housing and the nation's economy had survived the rough patch. Encouragingly, the recovery didn't resemble at all the frenzy of the Roaring Twenties when overbuying and overfinancing led to a surge in realty prices. "There is a vast difference between a legitimate, warranted uptrend in prices, such as now seen, and boom-hysteria inflation," Charles C. Cohan wrote in the *Los Angeles Times* that year, thinking the current valuations were "right and desirable."[29]

All involved were happy to see the passage of the National Housing Act by Congress in 1934. A big piece of FDR's expanding New Deal, the Act was designed to boost the residential real estate market and promote home ownership, each seen as a means to get the country out of the Depression. Along with the Act came the creation of the Federal Housing Administration (FHA), which offered a federally guaranteed mortgage insurance program. The program—something that leaders of the real estate industry had for years urged the government to establish—made it possible for banks to grant discounted loans, making it possible for more Americans to buy homes. (50% down and full repayment of a loan after just five years were the standard terms at the time.)[30]

Although the housing market and overall economy had improved by the passage of the Act, foreclosures had been in freefall through 1932 and 1933, leading the administration to take action. Knowing that the government would guarantee or insure loans, banks were incentivized to not only offer more of them but make the terms much friendlier—usually just 20% down with a full payment in twenty to thirty years. The Act would prove to be effective, although African Americans and other minorities were excluded from the program due to virulent redlining in the suburbs.[31] Segregation in many cities across America was as bad as ever, with local real estate boards and chambers of commerce working together to contain African Americans in certain areas.[32]

Funds made available through the National Housing Act could also be used for repairs and improvements to existing properties. Permits for doing so were expected to at least double as owners of both homes and businesses "modernized" their properties, something much needed after putting off patch-ups or renovations that had been neglected for years. Bankers, builders, and city planners were encouraging residents to take advantage of the loans, knowing that the flow of money would stir up local economies. Committees were formed to inform residents about the program, with newspapers and radio used to get the word out. Committee members were also going house to house in neighborhoods to let homeowners know they could finally fix their roof or add an extra room.[33]

The effort to repair or improve what must have been millions of structures—houses, apartment buildings, stores, office buildings, factories, warehouses, and farm buildings—was a massive one. For those with a reasonable credit history, up to a $2,000 loan at 5% interest was provided, with equal monthly installments paid between one and three years. Those considering a loan were advised to first call a contractor or architect to get an estimate, a smart move lest the $2,000 (about $46,000 today) not be enough to do the job.[34]

We Believe in America

It was unlikely for any of the Hollywood set to apply for an FHA-backed home loan. The film industry had done well in the early 1930s despite the Depression, as going to a movie was a cheap form of entertainment and an enjoyable if brief escape from the moribund mood of the nation. The list of industry people who had recently invested in real estate by purchasing properties, whether to occupy, rent, or both, was a long one. Silent film stars Harold Lloyd and Charlie Chaplin had each put a portion of their piles of dough into houses, the former a Beverly Hills estate and the latter a beachfront retreat in Playa del Rey. Ruby Keeler and Al Jolson had also invested wisely in property—a good thing now that talkies had put a damper on their careers—and Joan Crawford and Norma Shearer had each bought a number of places. Top producers Carl Laemmle and Irving Thalberg as well as studio head Jack Warner each had income properties, the former located at, naturally, Hollywood and Vine.[35]

Real estate was at the heart of a celebrated legal case of 1934 involving Mary Pickford. The star was attempting to recover $25,000 that she had invested in a property venture, and she appeared in person in a Los Angeles court to testify. A representative for the defense, a realty company, claimed that he had only dealt with Pickford's (now deceased) mother and the actress's manager in the deal, and thus there was no case. Pickford had filed nine additional suits against other brokers she believed had swindled her, trying to get back another $150,000 she had invested in deals gone bad.[36]

Ordinary investors, meanwhile, were looking to real estate to serve more modest ends. As the economy improved, inflation was rising, impelling more Americans to look to property as a way to protect their assets. Those of a certain age remembered what had happened in Germany before the Great War, when the currency of that country became virtually worthless. While things in the United States were going in the right direction, the future was uncertain, with another, even worse collapse of the economy in the realm of possibility. Brokers, bankers, lawyers, and insurance executives were waiting to see how FDR's New Deal would affect the real estate industry. So far, with the notable exception of the National Housing Act, the administration had largely left real estate alone, something that couldn't be said to now very regulated labor, business, and agriculture.[37]

Despite the greater scrutiny from the federal government, the business community was excited about the opportunities to be had in real estate in the mid-1930s. Some saw another boom ahead, but one that was grounded in sound business practices and could be sustained. With the economy back on track, it was foreseeable that rents would rise, and new construction would take off due to a shortage of homes. "We believe in real estate because we believe in America," stated Edward D. Duffield, president of Prudential Insurance, in 1935, predicting that the next two years would be very good ones for his company, the real estate industry, and the country as a whole.[38]

The NAREB's annual survey of the national real estate scene that was released a few months later suggested that such optimism was warranted. More mortgage money was being made available to borrowers in 1935, good news to those whose dreams of a new home had been put on hold through the early 1930s. Rents were indeed rising, and Corporate America was investing more of its capital in real estate just as business executives had indicated. Still, many banks across the country were not following the guidelines of the National Housing Act, being not quite as generous as the administration had hoped they would be in making loans. While the economy had improved, unemployment levels remained relatively high, making lenders reluctant to dish out financing like they did in the Roaring Twenties.[39]

Based on the overt discrimination of the times against people of color, African Americans would have an even slimmer chance of walking out of a financial institution with a loan to build a new house or modernize an existing one. Through their race-based policies and practices, bankers and builders were largely ignoring what was in fact a significant market; Blacks reportedly owned $750 million worth of real estate in 1935, according to a study published in the journal *Domestic Commerce*. If just $50 per house (or farm) was spent on improvements or repairs, some $37,500,000 would pour into the nation's economy, suggesting that the business community was not as patriotic as they liked to believe.[40]

The 1936 NAREB survey was even more encouraging, with real estate conditions better than they had been since the high point of 1926. Values and rent were each up over the previous year, and the demand for property was continuing to rise. "The upward march of real estate and building is in progress," a *New York Herald Tribune* article read, with very few "steals" now to be found. Both central and outlying business property in many cities was particularly strong, the survey showed, as companies leased out more office space downtown and in the suburbs.[41]

The annual convention of the NAREB in 1936 was a festive one, and not just because it happened to be held in New Orleans. "Whipped to a spirit of exhilaration, the gay realtors from New York to California, Canada to Hawaii...celebrated the onrush of prosperity," M.V. Casey, real estate editor of the *New York Herald Tribune*, told his readers after witnessing firsthand the exultation of the group. More of everything related to real estate—rent income, residential properties, apartment buildings, factories, and, most important, investors—was indeed reason to celebrate. Capital normally didn't like government to interfere with its operations but, knowing what could happen with unchecked growth, the attendees welcomed the administration's oversight. In fact, Stewart McDonald, Federal Housing Administrator, traveled from Washington to speak at the conference, ensuring that the government was deeply committed to having real estate lead the nation's economic recovery.[42]

FDR himself, as well as Alf Landon, Governor of California, made that clear in the run-up to the 1936 presidential election. The Democratic incumbent was running for his second term while the Republican Landon was basing much of his platform on lowering taxes. The candidates agreed on the importance of real estate to the economies of California and the country, however; each man sent a letter to the California Real Estate Association a few weeks before the election to get support (and votes). "The security of our social and economic system rests upon having millions of individual farmers and homeowners," Landon's letter read, crediting them with guiding "our spirit of independence as a nation." Roosevelt, meanwhile, congratulated California agents and architects on the emphasis they had placed on the "planning of homes and neighborhoods," something he felt brought "increased value and security" to the state and nation.[43]

The election turned out to be a landslide for FDR (he won every state except Maine and Vermont, giving him more than 98% of electoral votes), a solid endorsement of the president's New Deal program. That real estate conditions had improved tremendously over the course of his first term likely played a part in his popularity. Interest rates had fallen, and investors were confident that realty values were going to continue to rise. Those who would have been happy to sell their house for half its previous value in the early 1930s were now holding on to their property, assured that the market would only get better. Housing was believed to have actually decreased over those years, as the number built was less than the number that was torn down, destroyed by wind, fire, or flood, or simply became uninhabitable. Add that to an increase in population and couples waiting longer to marry and cohabitate, and one can see why there was so much optimism for real estate.[44]

Perhaps the most impressive thing about the late 1930s upswing was that there was no wild scramble for property, no bubble to be popped as in so many expansions of the past. Most new building was for occupancy rather than speculation; this is the key difference that assured investors that they would not lose the money they had gained. A gradual advance may not deliver the overnight profits that wildcatters were after, but it was just fine for those looking for a safe place to put their money with the knowledge that it would almost certainly appreciate over time.[45]

Still, it didn't hurt to give renters a bit of a nudge. That's what the California Real Estate Association did in the spring of 1937 via its "Buy a Home First" campaign. The association, which comprised realty firms in more than 200 cities and towns in the state, had quite a few arguments in support of the wisdom to invest in property rather than make landlords wealthy. One was "It's a natural instinct and will haunt you until you fulfill it," another one being "Your fondest dreams center about the new home." If instincts and dreams didn't work, there was always the do-it-for-your-country angle. "Home ownership is the best defense against the 'isms' that threaten the stability of our country," the association informed Californians in its campaign, drawing on the assumption that those with a white picket fence were unlikely to engage in subversive activities.[46]

The Quarrel among the Nations of Europe

Given the trends in real estate in the country, flaunting the benefits of home ownership was icing on the cake. Armed with the knowledge that there would be more prospective buyers than in a decade, brokers braced themselves for what would be a busy fall of 1937. Many new houses were completed during summers because of the weather and due to the fact that those with money tended to travel that season of the year. But that all changed every September, when the phones of real estate offices began to ring. And unlike now, apartment leases typically expired October 1 or November 1, meaning the rental side of the business picked up as well.[47]

Just like now, however, a big part of agents' and brokers' job was trying to figure out how to match their clients' wishes with a particular piece of property. No matter how much input a client provided, the process could be a frustrating one for each party. There were an infinite variety of intangibles, and something completely out of left field could be the x factor for the client to make an offer. A certain kind of flower that happened to be growing in the backyard of a house might be the motivator, for example, despite the client having made it clear that it was location or size that was the most important criterion. Others were known to pull out their checkbooks as soon as they saw what they wanted most, not even bothering to see the rest of the house.[48]

Agents were also finding that it was details that often sold a property, something automobile dealers had learned long ago when selling cars. Things like a laundry chute from upstairs to the basement, closet lights that flicked on automatically when the door opened, or telephone plugs in every room of the house could do the trick. (Phones used to have to be plugged into the wall, younger readers may not realize.) A particular doorbell chime was another minor but surprisingly important detail for some, as was an adjustable shower head. Tubs with straight backs and armrests were just the thing for those wanting a more comfortable bathing experience.[49]

Successful agents also had to be able to work with both men and women. It was believed that women held title to 40% of all the real estate in America, a figure that would have come as a surprise to many. They were also reported to own two-thirds of all the savings accounts in the country, possess a good chunk of stocks and bonds, and be the beneficiaries of 80% of life insurance policies. "In an economic sense, our country is a matriarchy," Herbert U.

Nelson posited in the *New York Herald Tribune*, adding that "in no other nation known to history have women owned or controlled so much of the wealth and this tendency is growing." The implications for agents were clear. "In the selling and financing of real estate, the preferences of women must be given a very considerable, sometimes a controlling weight," Nelson wisely advised.[50]

Regardless of gender, fewer fussy buyers or those with smaller pocketbooks were opting for one of the prefabricated houses that were becoming popular in the late 1930s. Assuming one had a place to put it, one could be a homeowner in just two or three weeks and for around $5,000 ($106,000 today), a miracle of the modern age. Some of these relied on cheap materials or cracker-box construction, but others did not reveal that the sections—walls, floors, and ceilings—were produced in factories and then assembled like a jigsaw puzzle.[51]

$5,000, in fact, was a figure that President Roosevelt had recently mentioned in a December 1937 speech about housing. Like many at the time, FDR envisioned the techniques of mass production that had greatly advanced between the world wars to be applied to homes. The administration wanted more Americans to own homes for a variety of reasons, and the "traitor to his class" was fully aware that not everyone could afford to live in an estate like his at Hyde Park.[52]

In addition to prefabricated houses that could be had for five grand, there was always the possibility of buying a fixer upper. Some clever, cost-conscious contractors were in fact specializing in salvaging run-down places that appeared better suited for the wrecking ball. Such houses, some of them a century or even more old, could be made not just livable but entirely presentable at not a great cost.[53] For just $3,000, for example, the owners completely altered the external appearance of their six-room bungalow in Beverly Hills and added an extra bath and an air conditioning system, more than doubling its rent.[54]

With the housing shortage not yet resolved and financing still not readily available, "used" houses of all kinds were being sought by those with modest incomes. Many foreclosed properties remained, an ideal opportunity for first-time homeowners. A preowned property, likely "reconditioned," could be had with a small down payment and terms of $20–$40 a month, a good deal that some banks were promoting in order to get the "distressed" assets off their books.[55]

Buying an existing home could be a simple thing—a phrase agents liked to say—but having one built was usually something quite different. Going back and forth among the array of contractors, subcontractors, and accessory manufacturers was a daunting process, and in fact served as a primary obstacle in more Americans becoming homeowners. Estimates for materials and labor from local builders varied widely, even within the same geographic area, and there could be dozens of wholesalers and retailers to choose from. There were no national manufacturers as there were in the automobile industry, making the whole endeavor a confusing enterprise perhaps better forgotten.[56]

The decision to build a home would soon become a moot point. War had broken out in Europe in September 1939, and there was a possibility that the United States would enter it at some point. Those connected to real estate began to ponder over the effects another world war would have on the industry, some of them old enough to look back on events of twenty years past. Should the United States get involved, there would be a population shift from rural areas to cities, if World War I history was an accurate measure, and rents would rise due to a greater demand for housing. Bankers anticipated higher interest rates, but there would likely be little building because of a lack of materials. "Virtually every material going into home construction also goes into the making of war materials," Philip W. Kniskern noted in *Bankers' Magazine* a month following the start of the European war. The president of Philadelphia-based First Mortgage Corporation recalled that the cost of building materials rose tremendously during the Great War, making new construction unviable until peace was declared. The price of copper had already risen sharply, a sign perhaps of bigger things to come.[57]

Although the United States was remaining neutral for the time being, it was natural to wonder what the future held for home ownership. "Already communities have begun to answer for themselves the question 'How will war in Europe affect real estate here?,'" Herbert U. Nelson observed in the *Washington Post* in October 1939. A war of a year or so, assuming we stayed out of it, probably wouldn't do much in terms of prices, the executive vice president of the NAREB mused, but a long one would likely bring "controls of various kinds that would be unfavorable." Major wars tended to trigger inflation, he noted, a positive thing in terms of real estate values, and as yet new construction wasn't being slowed down in any measurable way. "1940 as a building year will about repeat 1939, which now promises to be the best year since the depression," Nelson reported, predicting that "1941 should be even better."[58]

Despite such attempts to look on the bright side, the annual convention of the NAREB in October 1939 was a decidedly somber affair. Home ownership had risen over the last few years, but this new war threatened to erase all the gains that had been made since the terrible days of the Great Depression. "If America enters the quarrel among the nations of Europe," Holman D. Petitbone told the 1,300 delegates who had gathered in Los Angeles, "private enterprise as we know it today will cease to exist." The president of the Chicago Title and Trust Company believed that real estate, like all businesses, would come under the jurisdiction of the federal government should there be a Second World War. This would magnify the sizable power that the FDR administration wielded over the business, he fretted, reminding attendees that Washington already determined the interest rate on mortgage money, dictated house construction standards, and even had a say in property values. War would only further tip the scales toward government intervention, putting real estate people on the sidelines for months, possibly years.[59] It was clear that home ownership in America was at a major juncture in its turbulent history, its future as uncertain as ever.

Notes

1 Edwin Schallert, "Hollywood Bug Gets 'Em All," *Los Angeles Times*, September 14, 1932, 11.
2 Schallert, "Hollywood Bug Gets 'Em All."
3 https://pressbooks-dev.oer.hawaii.edu.
4 "Suburbs Places 100 Miles Out Within 5 Years?," *Christian Science Monitor*, July 9, 1930, 2.
5 "Suburbs Places 100 Miles Out Within 5 Years?."
6 "Houses Built in 3 Days, Aim of Realty Men," *Christian Science Monitor*, July 10, 1930, 6.
7 "Hoover Urges Home Building Fund Provision," *Christian Science Monitor*, July 31, 1930, 5.
8 "Real Estate Shopping—Then and Now," *Christian Science Monitor*, August 2, 1930, 18.
9 Alexander M. Bing, "Operators and Brokers Confident Year Will See Revival of Interest in Realty," *New York Herald Tribune*, January 26, 1930, E2.
10 Major William Kennelly, "Metropolitan Area Preparing for Population," *New York Herald Tribune*, January 26, 1930, E3.
11 Morton R. Cross, "Public Demands Too Much from Real Estate," *New York Herald Tribune*, March 9, 1930, E2.
12 I. Jerome Riker, "'76 Real Estate Recession Seen as Lesson to '31," *New York Herald Tribune*, August 23, 1931, E12.
13 "'Buy Real Estate Now,' Advises Owner of 5682 Parcels in County," *Los Angeles Times*, May 3, 1931, D1.
14 "'Buy California,' Slogan," *Los Angeles Times*, May 6, 1931, 10.
15 James L. Davis, "Survey Shows Realty Status," *Los Angeles Times*, July 5, 1931, D11.
16 Charles J. Quinlan, "Good Bargains in Real Estate Held Plentiful," *New York Herald Tribune*, January 31, 1932, D2.
17 "Real Estate Transactions in City and Suburban Fields," *New York Herald Tribune*, February 6, 1932, 30.
18 Genevieve Forbes Herrick, "New Crop of Dignitaries About to be Elected; So Washington's Real Estate Dealers are Now All A-Quiver," *Chicago Tribune*, October 30, 1932, G2.
19 Al Chase, "Beer is Pot O' Gold for Real Estate Rainbow," *Chicago Tribune*, November 12, 1932, 25. See John C. Gebhart, "Prohibition and Real Estate Values," *Annals of the Academy of Political and Social Science*, September 1932, 105.
20 "Real Estate at Low Ebb During the Year 1932," *Christian Science Monitor*, January 4, 1933, 8.
21 "Foreclosures on Real Estate Show Decrease," *Christian Science Monitor*, August 30, 1933, 13.
22 "Real Estate Market Gain Noted for First Time in Three Years," *Christian Science Monitor*, July 22, 1933, 3.
23 "Buyers' Market in Real Estate Fading as Business Rises, Says Banker," *Los Angeles Times*, May 7, 1933, 19.
24 Charles C. Cohan, "'This Real Estate Works This Way, My Friend': 'You're Telling Me!' He Said, 'I Bought Some!,'" *Los Angeles Times*, June 25, 1933, 17.

25 "Real Estate: Today's Best Investment!," *Los Angeles Times*, September 3, 1933, 15.
26 "Woman Question Still Rages in Two Real Estate Boards," *Chicago Tribune*, January 1, 1933, 9.
27 "Real Estate Owners in N.Y. Paying Back Taxes," *Christian Science Monitor*, April 20, 1934, 11.
28 Al Chase, "Real Estate Throughout the Nation at Last Takes Upward Trend," *Chicago Tribune*, July 23, 1933, B10.
29 Charles C. Cohan, "New Uptrend Disclosed Gives Encouragement," *Los Angeles Times*, February 25, 1934, 23. See Elmer R. Coburn, "The Real Estate Boom—And After," *Current History (1916–1940)*, August 1933, 559.
30 Adam Hayes, "National Housing Act: Overview, Impact, Criticisms," June 20, 2022, www.investopedia.com/terms/n/national-housing-act.asp. See *Well Worth Saving* for more on "how the New Deal safeguarded home ownership." A HUD report from 2006, "Evolution of the U.S. Housing Finance System," is good reading for those particularly interested in the financing of home ownership, specifically as related to the changing structure of the home mortgage. That report, which is intended to offer lessons for emerging (international) markets, was ironically issued just as our system blew up. https://www.huduser.gov/publications/pdf/us_evolution.pdf.
31 Hayes, "National Housing Act: Overview, Impact, Criticisms." See Trevor M. Kollmann and Price V. Fishback, "The New Deal, Race, and Home Ownership in the 1920s and 1930s," *American Economic Review*, May 2011, 366.
32 "Blame Real Estate Board for Segregation in St. Louis," *Chicago Defender*, April 21, 1934, 13.
33 "Home-Repair Plan Begins," *Los Angeles Times*, September 7, 1934, A1.
34 "Guide to Real Estate Modernization and Repair," *Los Angeles Times*, September 16, 1934, 15.
35 Alma Whitaker, "Celebrities of Screenland Like and Acquire Southland Realty," *Los Angeles Times*, September 23, 1934, 18.
36 "Screen Star Deals Told," *Los Angeles Times*, November 10, 1934, A12.
37 Al Chase, "New Deal is Driving Investors to Real Estate, Says Pettibone," *Chicago Daily Tribune*, May 27, 1934, 22.
38 "Greatest Building Boom in History Seen by Authorities on Real Estate," *Christian Science Monitor*, May 4, 1935, 11.
39 Al Chase, "National Real Estate Outlook Best in Several Years, Survey Shows," *Chicago Tribune*, August 18, 1935, A12.
40 "Colored People Said to Own $750,000,000 in Real Estate," *Baltimore Afro-American*, February 2, 1935, 3.
41 "National Survey Records Vast Improvement in Real Estate Conditions," *New York Herald Tribune*, August 16, 1936, I1.
42 M.V. Casey, "Real Estate News in City and Suburbs," *New York Herald Tribune*, November 19, 1936, 42.
43 "Landon and Roosevelt Laud Real Estate Men in Messages," *Los Angeles Times*, October 8, 1936, A2.
44 Al Chase, "Real Estate Market is Believed Entering Long Upswing," *Chicago Tribune*, May 31, 1936, C10.
45 "Real Estate Prices and Rents Throughout the Nation Climbing," *Christian Science Monitor*, February 4, 1937, 13.
46 "'Buy a Home' Facts Given," *Los Angeles Times*, May 23, 1937, F4.
47 W. Clifford Harvey, "Real Estate Men Study Trends in Homes," *Christian Science Monitor*, September 3, 1937, 10.
48 Harvey, "Real Estate Men Study Trends in Homes."

49 Harvey, "Real Estate Men Study Trends in Homes."
50 Herbert U. Nelson, "Women Control Held Increasing in Realty Field," *New York Herald Tribune*, August 15, 1937, D6.
51 W. Clifford Harvey, "New Pre-Fabricated Houses Go Up Like Mushrooms," *Christian Science Monitor*, November 19,1937, 13.
52 W. Clifford Harvey, "Remodeling of Old Houses Opens New Field to Builders," *Christian Science Monitor*, December 17,1937, 13.
53 Harvey, "Remodeling of Old Houses Opens New Field to Builders."
54 "Remodeling Shown as Means to Increase Real Estate Value," *Los Angeles Times*, October 31, 1937, E3.
55 W. Clifford Harvey, "'Used House' Buying Era Forecast," *Christian Science Monitor*, February 4, 1938, 11.
56 W. Clifford Harvey, "Housing Guild Tries to Make Building a Home as Easy as Buying a Car," *Christian Science Monitor*, August 19, 1938, 11.
57 Philip W. Kniskern, "Real Estate Trends in War Time," *Bankers' Magazine*, October 1939, 361.
58 Herbert U. Nelson, "Home Prices Firm as Result of War Start," *Washington Post*, October 1, 1939, R2.
59 M.V. Casey, "Banker Visions War as Menace to U.S. Business," *New York Herald Tribune*, October 25, 1939, 43.

3 A New Order

The real estate business isn't what it used to be.

Carleton Hunneman, former president of the Boston Real Exchange Association, after riding his bicycle to work in August 1942

Agents in Washington, DC had no doubt been looking forward to their annual midsummer outing in 1942. For many years, the members of the city's Real Estate Board had attended the festive event at the Manor Country Club in Rockville, Maryland. In May, however, news came that there would be no such celebration that summer. America was at war and there was a shortage of tires and gasoline, leading the program committee to decide to cancel the outing in order to conserve the much-needed resources.[1]

Such was the state of home ownership in the early 1940s when events overseas took precedence over the buying and selling of property. While the pursuit of owning a home by no means came to a halt during the war, it experienced a number of major changes that turned it into something much different than it had been. Home ownership would bounce back nicely in the latter part of the decade, however, buoyed by a robust postwar economy and ideal conditions for white, middle-class Americans. Despite fighting the war in the name of democracy, many African Americans would be denied the opportunity to own their picket fence, a glaring contradiction of the nation's proud claims of justice and equality for all citizens.

Slow, Substantial, and Sound

War might have been raging across the Atlantic, but prospects for home ownership in America were as good as ever, as the *Christian Science Monitor* noted two weeks into the new decade. "The business of building, selling, and renting the structures in which the people of the Nation live and work is in the strongest position in its history as the New Year opens," the publication emphatically stated. Builders, bankers, and brokers were all optimistic about the future based on the fact that the foundation of the real estate business was "slow, substantial, and sound," with none of the undisciplined

DOI: 10.4324/9781003481485-4

speculation that had fueled some previous growth periods. Not just sales, rentals, and construction were healthy but all the other factors that went into residential housing—occupancies, market activity, availability of mortgage money, interest rates, and building costs—were positive as well, good reason to be happy about where things were and appeared to be going.[2]

Especially good news was that construction of single-family houses had reached the level achieved in 1929, immediately before the stock market crash dramatically reduced the money available to be lent for building and buying. Such construction had peaked in 1925 and leveled off until the onset of the Great Depression brought things to a virtual standstill. New construction began to improve in 1934, however, and now in 1940 was where it was when Wall Street laid its giant egg.[3] Reducing the cost of construction represented a prime opportunity to create more homeowners and was something that the FDR administration was proactively pursuing. The Federal Housing Administration was backing the production of a $2,500 house so that those with low incomes could also plant their roots in the American soil. There was a vast market for such a house, builders agreed, assuming it was possible to make such a thing.[4]

Yet more reason to be bullish on real estate in 1940 was national defense. The federal government was preparing for possible war in many ways, one of them being housing for what would certainly be an expansion of the military and greater need for civilian personnel. The administration had recently formed a National Defense Commission composed of notable businesspeople charged with figuring out how to most efficiently manufacture the materials for war, should that come to pass. Enlarging industrial plants without disrupting residential construction was a key consideration.[5] Until then, however, it was mostly business as usual. "The building of homes goes on despite echoes of world upsets," W. Clifford Harvey noted, with a conscious effort seemingly being made to forget that a war of considerable magnitude was taking place in Europe.[6]

The 1940 edition of the NAREB's annual survey reflected this sanguine attitude while at the same time recognizing "war jitters." Things were currently stable but could change at any minute, the poll of members of local real estate boards revealed. "The preparedness program is the cue for the next act," as a journalist summarized the results of the survey, with most attention being devoted to the possible effects of increased industrial activity. Some members believed there could be a severe housing shortage if things sharply escalated although there was no cause for alarm, at least yet.[7]

One good thing coming out of the gradual ramping up of defense was a noticeable revival of inner cities. Through the 1930s, there had been a steady drift of both residents and businesses to the suburbs, a result of overcrowded and increasingly rundown urban neighborhoods. "With the stepping up of industrial production, the older sections of these larger cities are taking new life," Herbert U. Nelson of the NAREB observed, with defense-related workers moving into the grittier sides of town to be close to the plants (especially shipbuilders and airplane manufacturers). Long term, this could have a major effect on the population distribution of metropolitan areas, perhaps stemming the flight to the suburbs and maintaining the value of real estate near factories.[8]

It was the eleven-year high construction of single-family houses that was getting the most attention in real estate circles in 1940, however, a fact that was spun into powerful rhetoric by those with a vested interest in such matters. "Americans are coming to realize that no matter what happens, a home of your own is one of the best safeguards against an uncertain future," an article in the trade journal *American Builder* read, especially if said home included "a plot of 'good earth' for a garden." As in the past, real estate was favorably compared to stocks and bonds; the latter were "only pieces of paper" while a home was "a useful, livable, life-supporting investment that is good under any form of social order or political condition." Such language was designed to counter the usual objections to investing in property, i.e., high taxes, an economic slide, or massive unemployment, and was thus good ammunition for builders to use if a situation called for it.[9]

In many communities across the United States, however, both developers and real estate agents were doing everything they could to prevent African Americans from becoming homeowners. Restrictive covenants—leases, deeds, or other legal agreements or contracts that placed limitations on residents, often with regard to race—not only were common but had been effectively endorsed by the federal government. The Federal Housing Administration had published a guide called "Outline of Protective Covenants" which advised real estate agents to include race-based restrictions in their contracts when seeking mortgage loans insured by the agency. The FHA claimed to have removed the restrictions from the guide but was still backing loans in communities that barred African Americans from buying homes in the area. In 1940, Thurgood Marshall, then special counsel for the NAACP, wrote a letter to the FHA protesting the agency's guaranteeing loans to real estate agents in Salinas, California, where race-based restrictive covenants were in place.[10]

The administration's #1 priority in terms of housing was, however, for developers to build more homes and as fast as possible (the smaller and more affordable the better to accommodate defense workers and their families). Doing so would help the nation's defense program that was escalating as it became more likely that the United States would have to enter the war at some point. In April 1941, Defense Housing Coordinator Charles F. Palmer joined FHA Administrator Abner H. Ferguson and Philip W. Kniskern, now president of the NAREB, on a coast-to-coast radio broadcast urging builders to speed up their projects and exhorting brokers to sell them post haste. Beyond production and sales, the real estate community could contribute via a myriad of other ways including providing the FHA with accurate listing information, performing fair appraisals, modernizing run-down properties, and avoiding the temptation to raise rents should even greater shortages develop in a wartime economy.[11]

That no such data existed in any coherent form reflected the fragmented and regional nature of the real estate field. Nobody could say for sure how many houses were being built in the country, what the inventory of building materials was, or who possessed the materials. When a rumor began circulating in November 1941 that the federal government was going to order all home construction for civilians to soon shut down so that builders would focus exclusively on defense housing, John Mowbray of the Home Builders Institute requested that information be gathered before such a decision was made. Government contracts were certainly nice, but builders were understandably nervous that their normal business would completely disappear for who knew how long. Agents were even more worried, as it was the selling of residential homes that put food on their tables.[12]

On December 5, 1941, Kniskern appeared in Atlantic City to ease the concerns of New Jersey agents. Sales of homes across the nation had risen consistently through the year, he told members of that state's real estate boards, with no break in the ascendant pattern that had existed since the mid-1930s. "There is every indication that the upward movement will continue," Kniskern pronounced, confident that the outlook for home ownership in America was a bright one. Something much different lay in store, however.[13]

The Influence of War

Just two days later, the Japanese bombed Pearl Harbor, immediately after which the United States entered the war. The surprise attack made all citizens, including builders and brokers, readjust their priorities, as winning the war took precedence over everything else. Kniskern said as much in a telegram that he sent to President Roosevelt on Christmas Eve of 1941. The members of the nation's 480 local real estate boards volunteered their services "in any and every way," the telegram read, adding that the realtors "stand at your command."[14]

1941 had been a good year for real estate in America, as builders figured out ways to keep their businesses going in what were unusual times. Now, however, with America at war in a major global conflict, there was, according to the *Christian Science Monitor*, "a new order." Some in the field believed that a significant part of the new order involved wealthy European refugees buying large tracts of land in the United States on which to live and, perhaps, farm or ranch. This wasn't pure speculation; Prince Alexander of Hohenlohe (Poland) had in fact purchased a 600-acre farm in Maryland, and Pierre Matisse (son of the famous French painter) had bought a 65-acre farm in New Jersey. Also, requests for information about property in the United States had come into realty offices from Havana, Cuba, the Virgin Islands, the Panama Canal Zone, and various South American countries, more indication that foreigners with substantial assets were looking to America as a good place to settle, at least during the war emergency.[15]

While rich foreigners wanted to live in the country, Rosie the Riveters and their male equivalent were likely to seek housing in cities. The trend toward centralization (or de-decentralization) had begun in the defense buildup, and now it had become a defining component of the wartime real estate scene. With gas rationing, a tire shortage, and a ban on new automobile sales, the ability to walk or bike from home to work was of paramount importance. In the 1930s, car ownership had contributed to a decline in metropolitan real estate values as taxpayers moved out of cities, but the war had reversed this population shift. How long it would last was unknown, but city planners welcomed the unexpected development, having been unable to come up with any effective idea on how to stem the suburban tide.[16]

With the immediate trend toward centralization, some expected the war to ultimately serve as a catalyst of greater decentralization. (As soon as the nation entered the war, in fact, much pondering was devoted to the postwar future, a period of time that was consistently portrayed as being filled with prosperity and technological wonders.) Airplanes were being extensively used during the war, of course, and it was imagined that in peacetime they would be put into service by veterans to commute to and from work. Such a scenario had been predicted in the 1920s, but planes had come a long way over the past generation, it was said, making personal air travel more possible. Revolutionary changes in real estate development and urban planning could be on the horizon, proposed Carlton Schultz, who presented his thoughts in the trade journal *The Mortgage Banker*. "Vertical landings will probably be common," he forecast, allowing planes to take off and land without the need for a long runway.[17]

Until then, however, the world of real estate was being shaken up in more practical ways. As with virtually all occupations, many agents and brokers had immediately enlisted after December 7, leaving the field with fewer people to sell property. But a fair number of those whose businesses were slowed down or completely stopped by the conditions of war—car salesmen, tire store operators, and appliance retailers, notably—were taking real estate classes and taking the required exams to get a license in the field. This was especially true in Southern California, where thousands of new residents were headed to take high-paying jobs in war-related industries. "Defense subdivisions"—clusters of small houses built quickly for workers in those factories—were springing up all over the region, an opportunity for agents to make sales and earn commissions.[18]

By the summer of 1942, however, even the flurry of defense housing could not prevent a drop in the nation's real estate business. "Realtors are beginning to feel the influence of war," economist James C. Downs wrote in the *National Real Estate Journal*, noting that there had been an overall dip in both home sales and mortgages. The slide was especially pronounced in smaller communities where there was no production of war-related materials. Given the administration's looming mandate to stop construction of residential housing during the emergency, the drop was hardly surprising.

Vacant lots were not being sold to developers as the shutdown neared, and relatively few new houses were being sold to prospective homeowners. Thankfully (unless one was a landlord), rent controls imposed by the Office of Price Administration were allowing many to stay in their apartments until the federal government allowed the normal transfer of residential property.[19]

The topsy-turvy state of real estate during the war years could be seen in other ways. Since the early 1920s, women had comprised a significant portion of agents and brokers, a reflection of the generally independent nature of the job. Just as those whose livelihoods had been curtailed due to restrictions and shortages were entering the field, more women had hung out a shingle as a agent to handle the booming rental business. Men were continuing to be called into military service as the war escalated in 1942, depleting their numbers in offices of all kinds. "It's a field that lends itself to the part-time talents of married women as well as a potential career field for all women with a flair for business," Carleton Hunneman, the Boston real estate executive, noted.[20]

To his surprise, Hunneman was finding his bicycle to be a great way to see downtown properties, appreciative also of the exercise he was now getting. The man (who was himself on call for service) recognized the value his new employees were bringing to his firm. "We are finding it profitable and convenient to take on more and more women for realty sales," he told the *Christian Science Monitor*, thinking that "most of them will stay on when the war is over to take care of the postwar business expansion."[21]

The fact that great numbers of Americans were in the fall of 1942 changing residences (reportedly more than any previous time in history) was yet more reason to have good agents on staff. Families were migrating from one place to another for various purposes, often crossing state lines to take advantage of the job opportunities to be had in industry. Leases were terminated *en masse* on October 1 of that year, with easy commuting distance of defense plants taking priority over the usual wish of a nice garden and lawn. Renting had become a much more popular choice than buying in choosing a new home, with the dream of owning a place deferred until peacetime. Some were taking up residence in attics and trailers if the place was walkable to the factory, the #1 real estate criterion of "location" perhaps never more important.[22] The administration had put in place a national program converting private homes to wartime housing, increasing the chances to rent a room near one's job.[23]

The 1943 NAREB survey was an upbeat one despite the vast changes to the industry as a result of the war. In areas where defense work was active, the markets for both residential and industrial real estate were strong, so strong in fact that they were each near maximum occupancy and capacity. (The same could not be said to be true in areas where there was no factory work to be had.) Simply put, real estate had been reimagined from being principally about the buying and selling of property to determining how to use property to best serve the interests of the country while it was at war. Like equipment and people, in other words, real estate was perceived as an asset that could help lead the United States to victory. All agreed that the fundamentals remained healthy despite the shock of war, and that the markets would be better than ever in peacetime.[24] The lack of home construction during the war would make the demand that much greater, it was commonly believed, a golden age of real estate beckoning.[25]

A Reconverted Chicken House

Wartime patriotism, much of it rooted in the rhetoric of democracy, could not always overcome the evils of racism and greed, however. In segregated Atlanta in 1944, for example, unscrupulous agents (both white and Black, reportedly) had taken to defrauding homeowners in white residential neighborhoods by telling them that the areas had been "rezoned" for African Americans. The goal was to get the homeowners to sell their property at less than full value before prices really plummeted. The scam was actually working, motivating the mayor of the city, William B. Hartsfield, to try to stop it. If one homeowner sold, his or her neighbors often did likewise, causing a ripple effect throughout the neighborhood. To his credit, Hartsfield made it clear that no such "rezoning" was in effect. In fact, he added, the U.S. Supreme Court had decided that defining areas by race was unconstitutional, and that homeowners should not be persuaded otherwise.[26]

With the rhetoric of American democracy cast against Nazi racist dogma during the war, businesspeople were essentially forced to address blatant discrimination within their industries. Leaders of the NAREB did just that in 1944 by recommending to the nation's 600 local real estate boards that they put in place programs to provide better housing for African Americans. The housing shortage was particularly acute for people of color who were often "contained" in specified areas of a city and not permitted to live in white neighborhoods (despite having the money to buy or rent a place). Some 20,000 real estate firms and individual agents in 46 states belonged to the NAREB, giving the organization considerable power in leveling the playing field in terms of race. Wisely, the NAREB presented the initiative as an economic opportunity for agents, fully aware that there would be resistance against it where restrictive covenants were firmly in place.[27]

The invasion of Normandy or D-Day had been a turning point in the war, stimulating further attention to the projected postwar landscape of housing. There was a consensus that a home building boom was looming due to an unprecedented set of social, economic, and political conditions that were becoming plainly evident as the end of the war drew near. "G.I. Joe is going to move into his postwar house without having to wait until he accumulates a down payment," W. Clifford Harvey reported in the *Christian Science Monitor* in July 1944 after Congress passed the Serviceman's Readjustment Act (or "G.I. Bill"). Not just housing but college education and unemployment insurance were included in the act, making it a piece of legislation that would reshape the contours of American society for decades to come.[28]

In terms of home ownership, the act provided the opportunity for honorably discharged veterans who could demonstrate "reasonable" ability to meet mortgage payments to immediately purchase a property. It could be seen how with such a program much more housing would be needed, generating a surge in construction activity that would have a ripple effect throughout the nation's economy. Banks would loan billions of dollars, with those secured through the FHA fully guaranteed. About a million "G.I. Joes" had already been discharged and tens of thousands more were entering civilian life every month, the makings of an enormous market for homes of all kinds.[29]

The market for existing small- and medium-sized homes was already booming. A house sold in April 1944 for $7,000 was worth $10,000 just six months later as well-paid veterans and war workers outbid each other. What was driving this desire for white picket fences? "As birds instinctively build nests, so married couples like to have a home," explained entrepreneur and economist Roger W. Babson, his meaning being that large numbers of men and women with cash in their pockets were finding connubial bliss as peacetime approached.[30] News that the War Production Board had issued an order allowing new homes to be built was certainly welcome, although the relaxation on restrictions on construction was quite limited due to the lack of materials and labor.[31]

Despite widespread discrimination, African American war workers and military personnel had benefited from the good money to be made in the early 1940s. One real estate developer had estimated that the nation's Blacks had accumulated $18 billion in savings by March 1945, allowing many in theory to move out of the crowded urban areas in which they had been forced to live. Rents were typically high in these areas as landlords took full advantage of the local redlining policies and practices, making home ownership even more desirable if it was made possible.[32]

Given all the factors involved, it was perhaps inevitable that the legality of restrictive covenants be addressed on a national basis. In May 1945, the U.S. Supreme Court took up the issue, specifically whether private parties could deny people of color the right to own, occupy, convey, lease, rent, or receive as a gift property. The specific case involved a judgment by the United States Court of Appeals for the District of Columbia. A property in which a race-based restrictive covenant was in effect had been conveyed to Clara I. Mays of Washington, DC but the woman had not been awarded the deed because of her being African American. The higher court's decision obviously would be an important one, likely to affect the lives of millions of American citizens (many of whom had fought in one or possibly two world wars).[33]

A month after the U.S. Supreme Court took the case, the Georgia Supreme Court upheld the legality of such covenants, finding them not to be in violation of the Fourteenth Amendment to the United States Constitution (which granted all citizens, including former slaves, "equal protection under the laws").[34] Ultimately, it would not be the Mays case but a 1948 U.S. Supreme Court case that settled the issue, at least in legal terms. In Shelly v. Kramer, the Court ruled that restrictive covenants in real estate deeds prohibiting the sale of property to non-Caucasians unconstitutionally violated the equal protection of the Fourteenth Amendment.[35] While the decision did prove to strike a blow to the covenants, enforced segregation in housing would continue for decades (and is still around today).

Jim Crow attitudes notwithstanding, the much-predicted postwar housing boom was becoming a reality. By the summer of 1946, billboards for new suburban developments could be seen on highways across the country as builders, often backed by investor syndicates, got back to business. Subdivisions with bucolic names were popping up like daisies in what would one day be called the crabgrass frontier. In the Northeast, a good number of lots had been geometrically plotted after a developer had acquired a large estate, some of them dating back to colonial times. Land costs were already rising and, with OPA restrictions no longer in place, could go as high as the market dictated. Materials and labor each remained tight, however, limiting the amount of actual construction that could actually proceed. Many were buying a lot before prices skyrocketed, however, confident that their dream home would be built at some point in the future.[36]

Although there was a slowdown in activity in most cities in the fall of 1946 due to "buyer resistance" (too high prices), it was full steam ahead in Washington, DC and San Francisco. "How much longer a reconverted chicken house would be able to masquerade as a palatial estate for the wife and kiddies is anybody's guess," observed a reporter for the *Washington Post*, noting that open houses in the nation's capital were as busy as ever.[37] Things were also humming along in Miami Beach, which had been invaded by scads of military personnel during the war who took up residence in beachfront hotels and private homes. Transactions over the first half of 1947 were close to what they had been shortly before Pearl Harbor, due much in part to soldiers who had been stationed there staying true to their vow that they would return after the war to make the tropical paradise their home.[38]

A Master-Race Theory

Meanwhile, developer extraordinaire William Levitt and his sons were building a community that for many would come to define the American dream. Levitt had already been in the business for a couple of decades, along with others blazing the suburban trail of Long Island. ("We think Long Island is God's country," Levitt had once remarked.) By 1948, his Manhasset-based firm and that of Gross-Morton had risen to the top of home building on the island. There was much snow on the ground in February that year, but Levitt's construction projects continued, their foundations having already been prepared. There were many developers on Long Island, but Levitt and Alfred Gross approached the business not unlike Henry Ford had done with automobiles. Continuous large-scale operations were the key to efficient, mass-produced building, they knew, distancing themselves from the rest of the pack and making a huge amount of money in the process.[39]

On a number of levels, Long Island developers like Levitt and Gross had an advantage over most others in the United States. Beyond having a large continuous spillover of potential buyers from the country's most populous city just to the west, the land of Long Island was ideally suited for development. Alongside urban decentralization, there were sizable flat stretches on which to build, particularly in the center of the island, and the sandy soil made it easy for steam shovels to dig into the earth. Unlike in many other parts of the country, Long Island builders' bulldozers and trenchers effortlessly chewed up tree roots and granite ledges. Farmland was quickly turned into neatly arranged suburban landscapes, geographical or topographical confirmation that—for large-scale housing development, at least—Long Island was indeed God's country.[40]

While Levitt was about to take the business model to a new level, it had actually been Alfred Gross who pioneered the concept of "whole community" (versus individual house) development. Between the late 1920s and early 1930s, Gross built about 2,500 houses in Laurelton, Queens, to create what many agreed was the nation's largest community of moderately priced homes. The formula consisted of acquiring lots of land at reasonable prices, purchasing materials at a bulk rate, using mass production principles to build the houses, and offering easy financing or credit for buyers. In 1948, Gross was using that same formula to build a 3,800-unit garden apartment community in Glen Oaks Village, Queens, while Levitt was focusing on Nassau County. In addition to taking a systematic planning approach to building, Levitt included appliances and other extras in the cost of a house, a brilliant marketing move that was said to win many housewives over.[41]

Levittown, as it was called, was initially a rental housing community designed for war veterans. Despite a record snowfall in early 1948, Levitt kept building, as demand remained strong. (He was, however, unable to keep up his thirty-houses-a-day pace.) Two thousand houses had already been built, and another four thousand were on the way, which would bring the population of the town to twenty-five thousand by the end of the year. The American Legion had formed Levittown Post 1711, which was said to already have the most members of any post in New York State and possibly the nation. Two weekly newspapers were being published, adding to the community feel of the mass-produced town.[42]

By March that year, the snow was beginning to melt, allowing Levitt to gear up to full speed, which would be six hundred houses a month (each renting for $65 per month). The numbers associated with a fully completed Levittown were staggering. The community would have more than one hundred miles of paved roads, Levitt announced, and over two hundred miles of sidewalks and curbs. Three large shopping centers were planned, the biggest to cover twenty acres along Hempstead Turnpike and the others twelve acres each north and south of the turnpike.[43] Levittown was well on the way to becoming the country's largest single postwar housing development and biggest rental project ever undertaken.[44]

Levitt was hardly done making his town bigger and better, however. There would be six swimming pools (one for each thousand families) as part of a new park district to be built, he revealed in August 1948, all at no additional charge to residents.[45] A week later, Levitt had more news: his firm had purchased an additional adjoining five hundred acres of land, which would enable two thousand more houses to be built. Levittown would consist of eight thousand houses by the end of 1949, he told the media, although these two thousand new houses would be for sale rather than rent. With this addition, the population of Levittown would be thirty-two thousand, placing it among the largest localities on Long Island.[46]

Unable to rent a Levittown house, even if they had served in the war, were African Americans (and, presumably, Asian Americans). Like his Strathmore development, Levittown was redlined, as a clause in a rental prospectus for the development made clear. ("No dwelling shall be used or occupied except by members of the Caucasian race," Clause 25 read, although non-Caucasian "domestic servants" were permitted.) The FHA tried to eliminate the clause to resolve what was overt race discrimination, but the agency lacked the power to do so (even though Levittown was an FHA-backed project). In March 1949, a number of groups, including the NAACP, the American Jewish Congress and the American Jewish Committee, condemned not just Levittown's rental policy but also the FHA's inability to do anything about it.[47]

Two months later, however, and clearly under considerable pressure, Levitt dropped the clause from the leases. (No such clause had been in sales contracts, meaning that for a couple of months, African Americans, Asian Americans, and other racial minorities could buy but not rent a Levittown house, rather oddly.)[48] Levitt still had the right to choose to whom he'd sell or rent a house, however, meaning the race issue wasn't completely resolved.[49]

Despite the Supreme Court cases in play, Levitt's stance on race was not unusual for the times. In 1947, the NAACP urged Congress to initiate "a searching investigation of real estate and mortgage investment interests of this country" based on abundant evidence that there was widespread discrimination against African Americans with regard to housing. President Truman himself had recently suggested as much, telling Congress that the real estate industry was "one of the most stubborn obstacles in the way of any constructive program."[50]

Such critiques were certainly justified given the intersection of race relations and home ownership in Detroit. That city was among the most redlined in the nation, with African Americans barred from all parts of town except the East Side. Kenneth Draper, president of the Detroit Real Estate Board, made his thoughts on the matter clear in 1947, freely admitting that living space in the city was and should be restricted based on race. In defense of his position, Draper claimed that most Americans, including Black people, wanted to live among themselves, framing segregation as a natural and good thing.[51]

A judge in Los Angeles saw things quite differently. Restrictive covenants singling out African Americans were grounded in "Nazi race theories," Superior Judge Stanley Mosk stated in a courtroom when presented with a case involving three Black families (including those of well-known actresses Hattie McDaniel and Louise Beavers) who had not been allowed to live where they would have liked because of the color of their skin. "This court feels that there is no more reprehensible un-American activity than to attempt to deprive persons of their own homes on a master-race theory," Mosk added.[52]

Things were not much better in the nation's capital for African American residents. Unlike in most American cities, many Blacks and whites had for decades lived alongside each other there with relatively little friction, but African Americans were increasingly being segregated in certain neighborhoods in the late 1940s. The bullish real estate market in Washington, DC for more affluent whites had something to do with it (Georgetown was becoming exclusively white) but it was the development of highways, parks, and public buildings that was primarily responsible for the pushing out of Black people into crowded slums. Beautifying the city was all well and good but it was coming at the expense of African Americans, an ironic thing given the rhetoric of democracy against Communism being spouted by politicians at all levels in the capital. Also, restrictive covenants were common in Washington (Jews were sometimes included), this too incongruous given the debate on the issue taking place in the Supreme Court Building.[53]

The revelation that the NAREB lumped Negroes together with bootleggers, gangsters, and madams as real estate "blights" served as additional proof that the cards were stacked against African Americans in housing. "No reputable broker" should introduce people of those persuasions into a respectable neighborhood, the association's official policy declared in its "code of ethics," a troubling fact uncovered by the NAACP. Not surprisingly, given that kind of guidance, not just race-based covenants but discriminatory rental and selling practices were the norm across the country, as was the reluctance of local banks to offer mortgage loans to Blacks.[54]

Given all this, the Supreme Court's 1948 (unanimous) decision that property-related restrictions against minority groups were unconstitutional was, needless to say, welcome news to the African American community. The evidence cited in the Court was startling; it was reported that forty million houses and apartment buildings held such covenants against Blacks, Jews, Mexicans, and other minority groups. 90% of new housing being put up in the United States enforced the restrictions, this too shocking. Most telling, perhaps, was the fact that three justices of the Court—Wiley Rutledge, Robert H. Jackson, and Stanley P. Reed—lived in areas where there were covenants, requiring that they disqualify themselves from the ruling on its legality.[55]

Following the ruling, agents from coast-to-coast huddled together to decide how to implement the Court's decision in their handling of properties. Passing a law was one thing but following it was quite another, something Paul Robeson knew quite well. In July 1948, Robeson, the celebrated singer, actor, and activist, showed up without fanfare at the annual NAREB convention in Atlantic City to urge members to enforce the ban against restrictive covenants. Fight for "complete human dignity," he beseeched the real estate group in his address, after which he sang and recited an excerpt from *Othello*, the Broadway production for which he was most famous.[56] While one hurdle for equality in housing had been cleared, another one—slum clearance, under the guise of urban renewal—was just around the corner, signaling a new chapter in the history of home ownership in America.

Notes

1 "Real Estate Board Outing Canceled," *Washington Post*, May 24, 1942, R1.
2 "Real Estate Sees Big Year Free of Speculative Boom," *Christian Science Monitor*, January 13, 1940, 2.
3 "Production of One-Family Homes Back at 1929 Rate," *Washington Post*, March 3, 1940, R1.
4 W. Clifford Harvey, "So This is the $2,500 Home," *Christian Science Monitor*, March 8, 1940, 15.
5 "Defense Work to Aid Building, Smith Asserts," *Washington Post*, June 2, 1940, R1.
6 W. Clifford Harvey, "Building of Homes Goes on Despite Echoes of World Upsets," *Christian Science Monitor*, June 28, 1940, 14.
7 "Real Estate Market Stable, with Slight Upward Trend," *Washington Post*, July 7, 1940, R1.
8 Herbert U. Nelson, "Defense Program May Change Pattern of Cities, Nelson Says," *Washington Post*, August 4, 1940, R1.
9 "War Found to Bolster Public Interest in Home Ownership," *Washington Post*, September 1, 1940, R1.
10 "Housing Covenants Approved," *Pittsburgh Courier*, November 30, 1940, 5.
11 "Speed Urged in Building Projects," *Washington Post*, April 18, 1941, 19.
12 Thomas M. Cahill, "Real Estate Boards to Fight to Build More Civilian Homes," *Washington Post*, November 6, 1941, 24.
13 "Kniskern Sees Outlook Bright for Real Estate," *Washington Post*, December 6, 1941, 23.
14 "Real Estate Boards Pledge War Service," *Christian Science Monitor*, December 24, 1941, 17.
15 "Extensive Real Estate Progress Throughout Nation Reported for 1941," *Christian Science Monitor*, January 2, 1942, 5.
16 W. Clifford Harvey, "Real Estate Trend Pauses as War Makes Auto Travel to Suburbs Uncertain," *Christian Science Monitor*, January 30, 1942, 3.
17 "Airplane Likely to Affect Real Estate," *Christian Science Monitor*, May 6, 1942, 22.
18 Rodney L. Brink, "Salesmen in Curtailed Fields Turn to Real Estate Market," *Christian Science Monitor*, April 8, 1942, 15.
19 "Real Estate Activity Drop Due to Times," *Christian Science Monitor*, August 5, 1942, 19. See Daniel K. Fetter, "The Home Front: Rent Control and the Wartime Increase in Home Ownership," *Journal of Economic History*, December 2016, 1001.

20 W. Clifford Harvey, "War Brings Many Adjustments in Conduct of Boston Real Estate Business," *Christian Science Monitor*, August 14, 1942, 5.
21 Harvey, "War Brings Many Adjustments in Conduct of Boston Real Estate Business."
22 W. Clifford Harvey, "Record in Family Migration in the N.E. Area in Next Three Months Forecast," *Christian Science Monitor*, September 18, 1942, 5.
23 W. Clifford Harvey, "1,000 Family Dwellings in Connecticut Being Converted to Wartime Housing," *Christian Science Monitor*, November 6, 1942, 5.
24 "War Shock Fails to Cause Much Injury to Real Estate," *Washington Post*, October 10, 1943, R5.
25 W. Clifford Harvey, "Big Decline in Home Building Forecasts Vast Postwar Boom," *Christian Science Monitor*, December 17, 1943, 5.
26 "Defraud White Homeowners by Negro Scare," *Norfolk New Journal and Guide*, May 27, 1944, A2.
27 "National Real Estate Industry Urges Better Housing for Race," *Norfolk New Journal and Guide*, June 17, 1944, p. 4. See Helen Humes and Bruno Schiro, "Effect of Wartime Housing Shortages on Home Ownership," *Monthly Labor Review*, April 1946, p. 560.
28 W. Clifford Harvey, "No Down-Payment on Homes for Veterans Has Bank Backing," *Christian Science Monitor*, July 28, 1944, 2.
29 Harvey, "No Down-Payment on Homes for Veterans Has Bank Backing."
30 Roger W. Babson, "Real Estate Boom," *Washington Post*, October 2, 1944, 11.
31 W. Clifford Harvey, "You Can Build—If You Get Materials," *Christian Science Monitor*, October 20, 1944, 2. See Richard U. Ratcliff, "Notes on the Recent Decline in Home Ownership," *Journal of Land & Public Utility Economics*, November 1944, 373.
32 "Negroes Ready, Able to Buy Homes, National Real Estate Survey Shows," *Chicago Defender*, March 10, 1945, 6.
33 "Supreme Court Asked to Settle Real Estate Bias," *Cleveland Call and Post*, May 12, 1945, 11B.
34 "Ga. Court Upholds Real Estate Bias," *Baltimore Afro-American*, June 16, 1945, 10.
35 www.law.cornell.edu/wex/shelley_v_kraemer_(1948).
36 W. Clifford Harvey, "New Signs Point Path to Coming Realty Boom," *Christian Science Monitor*, August 6, 1946, 5. See John P. Dean, *Home Ownership: Is It Sound?* (New York: Harper & Brothers, 1945).
37 Post Reporter, "Real Estate Booming Here Despite Drop in Other Cities," *Washington Post*, September 25, 1946, 13.
38 "Miami Beach Real Estate Sales Near Prewar Rate," *Christian Science Monitor*, July 16, 1947, 14.
39 Frederick Gutheim, "Mass Building Pattern Is Set on Long Island," *New York Herald Tribune*, February 8, 1948.
40 Gutheim, "Mass Building Pattern Is Set on Long Island."
41 Gutheim, "Mass Building Pattern Is Set on Long Island."
42 "Large Demand for Homes in Levittown, L.I.," *New York Herald Tribune*, March 7, 1948.
43 "Large Demand for Homes in Levittown, L.I."
44 "Financing Completed on 4,000 Remaining Levittown Houses," *New York Herald Tribune*, May 16, 1948.
45 "Six Swimming Pools Planned for Levittown," *New York Herald Tribune*, August 8, 1948.
46 "Levitts Purchase 500 Acres to Expand Home Development," *New York Herald Tribune*, August 15, 1948.

47 "FHA Can't Prevent Negro Housing Ban," *New York Times*, March 19, 1949.
48 "Race Ban Dropped from Leases on Rented Homes in Levittown," *New York Herald Tribune*, May 29, 1949.
49 "650 Ex-GI's Sign Up for Levitt Housing," *New York Times*, August 17, 1949; Levitt maintained his blatant racist policies by not only refusing to sell houses to African Americans but also putting covenants in buyers' contracts not permitting them to resell their houses to Black people.
50 "Real Estate Probe Urged by NAACP," *Chicago Defender*, July 26, 1947, 8.
51 "Real Estate Head Says Most People Want Segregation," *Michigan Chronicle*, October 18, 1947, 4.
52 "Los Angeles Judge Bars Housing Covenants," *New York Amsterdam News*, November 8, 1947, 15.
53 "Discrimination in Capital's Schools, Housing Disgraceful," *Baltimore Afro-American*, December 20, 1947, 5.
54 "Real Estate Body Fastens Blight on Race," *Norfolk New Journal and Guide*, January 31, 1948, 11.
55 "Realty Ghetto Pacts Ruled Unconstitutional," *New York Amsterdam News*, May 8, 1948, 16.
56 "Paul Robeson Urges Real Estate Brokers to Fight for 'Complete Human Dignity,'" *Baltimore Afro-American*, July 31, 1948, D4.

4 The World's Best Buy

Thousands of young American couples are getting in on what some investment men think is "the world's best buy"—a home in the United States.

Fred L. Chapman, 1953

In 1955, *Life* magazine had five "regional rooms" constructed where they would be on display at Chicago's Merchandise Mart for a few months. "Style in architecture and furnishings is the creation of a region, shaped by its climate, by the background and customs of its inhabitants and by its raw materials," editors for the magazine explained in a February issue of that year. Distinguished members of the American Institute of Decorated had created the rooms, which included the Southwest (expansive and masculine), the Northeast (cosmopolitan and worldly), the Midwest (warm and rich), the South (elegant and charming), and the West Coast (Oriental). But rooms in any house could be inspired by tastes from other parts of the country, the magazine told its many readers. "Today the U.S. ferries regional styles at will from coast to coast and plunks them down anywhere," the article stated, making architecture and furnishings an eclectic, aesthetic grab bag.[1]

From such pleasing features, it was evident that the American home had come a long way by midcentury, a reflection of the prosperity that had arrived for many after the thrift required during the Great Depression and sacrifices associated with World War II. By 1950, more than half of all Americans owned their homes for the first time in the history of the nation, largely a function of a robust job market and easy credit for veterans. African Americans remained largely excluded from this rise in home ownership, however, as a pervasive "gentleman's agreement" between private and public interests blocked racial integration in the burgeoning suburbs. As well, as demand for housing increased so did prices, a hint of where things were going in home ownership.

For Sale

With 1950 being the midpoint of the 20th century, it was natural to both take a look back at the past and anticipate what may lie ahead. Those who

DOI: 10.4324/9781003481485-5

had served in the military but had not taken advantage of the home purchasing incentives offered by the GI Bill were reminded to consider doing so. The law was in effect through 1956, and there remained thirteen million veterans who had yet to make use of the low-cost mortgages and low-cost loans that were available to servicemen and servicewomen. (Qualified women and African Americans were legally entitled to the benefits but actually receiving them was another matter.) Getting more Americans to own homes was not just something sought by brokers but was still an important goal of the federal government, especially as the Cold War intensified and fears of communism in the United States ran rampant.[2]

While investing in a home was perceived as a kind of patriotic act, many at mid-century wanted their piece of the American dream to offer more than basic shelter. The American home of 1960 should include a host of amenities that were not commonly available in 1950, a survey of agents by the NAREB revealed, an indication of how houses were expected to evolve. Home buyers of a decade hence will want appliances like refrigerators, washing machines, television sets, and dishwashers to be standard equipment, according to the study, with a deluxe version throwing in radiant heat, radar cookers (microwave ovens), visaphones (video phone booths), deep freeze units, central air conditioning, and clothes dryers. House design was also expected to improve, with homeowners of the future desiring larger lots, more bathrooms, more insulation, and bigger windows.[3]

Rather than in Orbit City, however, such Jetsonesque houses (a visaphone was actually featured in one of the episodes of the original animated sitcom that ran between September 1962 and March 1963) would more likely be set in the American suburbs. Urbanites were continuing to flock to outlying metropolitan areas where easy credit for the white middle class made home ownership an attractive proposition. Marriage and birth rates were each high, and a single-family house on the crabgrass frontier promised a host of advantages over living in a small apartment in an increasingly crowded (and racially and ethnically diverse) city. The opportunity to build equity versus making one's landlord rich (or getting the super to fix that annoying leak) was yet more reason to invest in property, even if it did mean the family breadwinner having to commute to work downtown.

Sensibly, retail, including large department stores, was following this migration to the suburbs, as new homeowners, especially those producing the children to be one day known as baby boomers, made ideal consumers for many marketers. The demographic shift presented major potential implications. If people lived and shopped in the suburbs, some wondered, would working there be next? Stephen G. Thompson, the real estate editor for the *New York Herald Tribune* in 1950, raised that very question, fully aware that the answer was critical to the livelihood of downtown building owners and managers. "Will urban decentralization eventually include the construction of spacious office buildings in association with outlying shopping centers," he asked, seeing a possible "exodus of tenants" on the horizon.[4]

While such musings were certainly worthwhile, it was more the present that real estate people had on their minds in the early 1950s. The Korean War was in full swing in 1951 and, while its effects were not as sweeping as those during World War II, the housing industry was feeling the pinch. New houses were indeed rising on lots across the country, but a decided slowdown could be detected when compared with the building and buying frenzy of the immediate postwar years. Government restrictions on home construction had again gone into place, as materials needed for war—steel, copper, and aluminum—were prioritized for the military. Experts were predicting another housing shortage, something that would stall the steady growth the industry was enjoying. Builders felt such controls were unfair, as no such production limits were placed on cars or other consumer goods.[5]

The dip in new construction was not necessarily bad news to companies involved in what we call today home improvement. Soon after the end of the war, large, well-attended home shows appeared in various cities, running parallel with the mass migration to the domestically oriented suburbs. The 1952 Home Show Festival in Washington, DC was an especially festive one, timed with the annual April blooming of the city's beloved cherry blossom trees. For nine days, thousands of local residents and tourists cruised through the National Guard Armory to see the latest trends in home building and decorating. Modern kitchens and room stylings were featured, of course, and attendees were excited to see General Electric's latest "House of Magic" (demonstrations of the company's research lab developments that had debuted at the 1933 Century of Progress in Chicago). With building a new home currently a challenge because of the materials shortage (and higher cost), tips on remodeling were not surprisingly a main part of the show.[6]

One wouldn't know there was a materials shortage or sensitivity to price in certain parts of the American West. In states where land was plentiful and relatively cheap, real estate could operate on a much larger scale than in the denser Northeast. In Nevada or Texas, for example, one could buy a lot bigger than Rhode Island, a roomy spread for even the biggest of ranchers. And while William Levitt went for economy, Dallas developer Howdy Howard was going for luxury. The latter was in 1952 building a community with homes priced at a whopping $69,500 ($805,000 today), an exorbitant sum at the time. One got a lot for his or her money, however, as new homeowners would find groceries in the pantry, food in the refrigerator, prime steaks in the freezer, and, as a topper, a Cadillac in the garage.[7]

In going after the upper end of the market, Howdy Howard was certainly going against the grain of the times. Agents attending the 1952 NAREB convention in Miami agreed that the postwar boom had ebbed, with housing permits down and buyers now more discriminating and cost-conscious. New houses priced under $12,500 still flew off the shelves, but it was much tougher to move those costing anything more than that. "For Sale" signs typically hung outside older homes for months, and fewer retailers were renting space downtown. New shopping centers were springing up in many suburban areas, taking considerable business away from stores that may have thrived for decades.[8]

While agents grumbled about how it had become tougher to make a sale, they no doubt shared war stories about more difficult buyers and sellers. Home shoppers who were late to showings or never arrived were a definite annoyance, as time was money. Another less desirable group were those who asked to see homes that were way beyond what they could afford, and then there were the buyers who had hired multiple brokers. ("Oh, I've already seen this house" was a common refrain from that sort.) Buyers who didn't reveal that they intended to wait a year or more before actually purchasing anything were yet another type that brokers would rather not have as clients.[9]

For every difficult buyer, however, there was an equally challenging seller. (Brokers of course worked both sides of the fence.) Not informing the broker that one wanted more or would settle for less than the listed price for one's property was certainly irritating, as such news would come as a surprise when negotiating with buyers. Other less than welcome sellers were those who didn't reveal (or actually hid) flaws in their house, a source of considerable embarrassment when said flaw was discovered by the buyer upon inspection. Finally, and perhaps most irksome, were the sellers who not just wanted to be present at showings but insisted on doing all the talking. "The broker is a professional salesman and knows his business," John C. Tysen of Previews, Inc. advised buyers and sellers, recommending that a form of "etiquette" be followed in the exchange of real estate.[10]

Democracy in Housing

Such rules of etiquette were hardly needed in the rush to the suburbs in the early 1950s, however. Seeing the demand and money to be made from them, many more Levittown-style communities appeared in the United States through the decade. Millions of Americans called such places home, with the thinking being that a fair share of them would eventually move up from such middle-class developments to more luxurious ones as their incomes rose. Critics were not quite sure what to make of this new model of suburban housing, however, as there had never been anything quite like it.[11] After reading Harry Henderson's recent article, "The Mass-Produced Suburbs," in *Harper's*, Richard B. Lyman of the *New York Herald Tribune* addressed this peculiar and wildly popular way of living:

> The mass community has neither history, tradition, nor established structure, no inherited customs, institutions, socially important families, or big houses. Also, practically speaking, there are no rich or poor, and the large-scale projects started out with no older people, teenagers, in-laws, family doctors, "big shots," organizations, or local governments.[12]

In writing his piece, Henderson had visited six such mass communities, the largest one being Levittown and the second largest Lakewood, California (near Long Beach). Because the houses were so similar on their exterior, Henderson found, much effort was given to interior decorating to personalize them. The communities were highly social, and their commonality along social lines (class, age, race, and education level) encouraged shared points of view on many subjects. Much thought to neighborhood planning had negated urban problems like traffic jams inside the communities (outside was a whole other matter), and previous apartment dwellers were still getting used to not bumping into each other while moving from room to room. (Crime also was virtually nonexistent.) The only thing William Levitt and his competitors had not carefully orchestrated was dogs, which brought a singular form of chaos to the otherwise startling sense of calm. Considering a dog as the final piece to the suburban lifestyle, many new homeowners had immediately acquired a puppy, which soon proceeded to race across lawn and backyards, knock down children, wreck gardens, howl and bark at all hours, and bite the occasional mailman or deliveryman.[13]

Henderson's piece, which relied on a social or cultural anthropological research approach somewhat reminiscent of the Lynds' *Middletown* study, was truly remarkable, as the man recognized the significance of this new postwar suburban model as it was emerging. Towns and cities had historically developed gradually, and relied heavily on local trade of some sort, but such instant communities did not. Also, older suburbs had ringed an urban area, but places like Levittown sprang up on open farmland, almost independent from their host city. Most importantly, perhaps, the marketing of these houses relied on the kind of mass production and consumption formula that had been perfected in the first half of the 20th century. A variety of powerful social and economic forces including the baby boom, easy credit, and the expansion of the middle class fueled the commodification of the suburbs, in the process changing much of everyday life in America and eventually the world. Levittown and its siblings were "a new generation's version of the 'American way,'" Henderson wrote, entirely in-sync with their time and place.[14]

A different kind of American way was taking place in the Hollywood Hills. Given the business to be had, agents covering that area of Los Angeles were likely to put up with the most difficult of clients. Since the film industry had moved out west, movie stars were known to be extremely fickle when choosing where or where not to live. Careers in that business were often a rollercoaster ride where income rose or dropped precipitously, for one thing, and film folks were known to get married and divorced multiple times. Those factors, in addition to having certain whims regarding plumbing or any other element of a house or apartment, were a dream come true for agents like Al Herd, house seller to the stars. "Out here, people swap houses the way they change hats elsewhere," he gleefully told the *Saturday Evening Post* in 1953, considering Holmby Hills, Bel-Air, Brentwood, Pacific Palisades as well as Beverly Hills "a real-estate paradise."[15]

No such paradise awaited aspiring African American homeowners, however. In most cities (Baltimore and Atlanta were the notable exceptions), it was difficult or impossible for Blacks to get house loans, as financial institutions more often than not claimed that they didn't meet the economic qualifications for a mortgage. (Lower income whites were also commonly turned away.) In the fall of 1953, African American brokers presented President Eisenhower with a blueprint to achieve "Democracy in Housing," urging that federal action be taken to even the playing field in home ownership in terms of race.[16]

As the civil rights movement heated up in the early 1950s, Black activists were less willing to wait for the president to discourage discrimination in real estate. In many areas of the country, there were "gentlemen's agreements" in place to keep African Americans confined to what were sometimes referred to as "Black belts." It was such agreements that activists strongly objected to in their national campaign to realize "open occupancy" (housing made available to anyone, without regard to race, ethnicity, religion, or any other social division). The U.S. Supreme Court's decision banning restrictive covenants was naturally viewed as a major victory, but there was considerable resistance against it, even in less racially divisive cities such as Cleveland and Atlanta. In the latter, Black brokers were being intimidated for showing African American buyers in "white folks" neighborhoods. (The licenses of two such brokers had actually been suspended by the local real estate board on charges of "unethical practices.") This was just the kind of thing that had to be stopped to realize democracy in housing, activists made clear.[17]

One sign of progress was the decision by publishers of three Philadelphia newspapers—the *Bulletin*, *Inquirer*, and *Daily News*—to stop designating real estate ads by race. It had been common for an ad to state something like "This house is particularly for colored buyers" or "The neighborhood is colored." (Areas were also often defined by religious makeup, e.g., Catholic or Protestant.) After the urging of local Black brokers, however, such race-based specification ended, a move to which many white brokers objected under the (false) premise that property values dropped with the arrival of African American residents. Philadelphia was in fact becoming more racially diverse. "Negroes are now buying homes in all parts of the city, and, after the first shock, a sufficient number of whites usually remain to make the neighborhood mixed," the *Pittsburgh Courier* observed in 1953.[18]

Democracy in housing meant more than the ability for all Americans to live where they wanted, however. Owning property was a prime avenue to building or at least preserving wealth, raising the stakes of equal opportunity in housing. If nothing else, real estate was a reliable hedge against inflation, a key concern in the 1950s. (Purchasing power in the United States had been almost halved between 1940 and 1953.) Homes and income property usually retained their value over time despite changes in economic conditions, making real estate a protective form of investment.[19]

If both brokers and builders had their way, houses would be "traded in" much like cars were, with their appraised value used as a down payment on a newer (and usually better) model. Such a plan was being seriously considered as millions of couples outgrew the houses they had purchased soon after World War II. Those couples might have had a child but now, almost a decade later, it wasn't unusual for them to have two, three, or four. Material possessions had also amassed over those years, more reason to trade up if it was at all possible. The fly in the ointment was the difficulty in selling a pre-owned home, but the FHA had recently approved "modernization" loans to contractors. There was an enormous market of used houses, and it was becoming clear that money could be made after investing in some repairs and improvements. A new kitchen, an additional bathroom, or an updated heating system could dramatically raise the marketability of older homes, something more contractors were discovering after getting a loan to do the work.[20]

A Non-criminal Co-conspiracy

By 1954, however, more sweeping changes were seen as needed to modernize the landscape of housing in America. Certain neighborhoods were being alternatively labeled "slums," "ghettos," "blight," or simply "unfit housing conditions" by city officials as the impetus for what would be considered urban renewal. Local governments in Chicago, Dallas, Ft. Wayne, Houston, Memphis, Milwaukee, Omaha, Providence, and Tacoma were among no less than 173 cities taking some sort of action through code enforcements and regulations regarding neighborhood conservation. Mostly ignored ordinances referencing standards of safety and sanitation for housing were being put into effect, in other words, a program that the NAREB branded as "Build America Better." "Housing code enforcement is a basic tool in this vigorous new war on slums," Ronald J. Chinnock, the current president of the NAREB, stated, calling for everything from replanning and rezoning to demolition to solve the problem.[21]

What Chinnock didn't mention was that an overhaul of hundreds, perhaps thousands of neighborhoods across the country would benefit all parties except residents. Communities of color often sat on or near central downtown property, making it in the best interests of those who bought and sold property to increase its value. The real estate lobby had for years opposed federally funded public housing for low-income members of a community, making it no surprise that it was in favor of "renewing" existing, undervalued neighborhoods. Public housing was perceived as eliminating private housing, making it a lost financial opportunity given that land was in limited quantity.

The "Baltimore Plan," as urban renewal was called in that city, was proving to be a model for other communities in the country to follow. More people from the South, Black and white, had migrated to Baltimore as agricultural mechanization eliminated many farm-related jobs. Crowded slums were being cleared block by block to make room for thousands of units in public housing alongside two private redevelopment projects. In addition to rewriting the city's housing code, bolstering the housing bureau, and setting up a housing court, a million feet of rotting fences were taken down and 24,000 outside toilets removed. (Baltimore had the dubious distinction of having more of the latter than in any other city.)[22]

It was unclear whether urban renewal had anything to do with it, but 1954 was turning out to be a record year for residential real estate transactions in the United States. While production of new houses was still lagging somewhat, more homes were being bought and sold that year than any other. Americans were also going into deeper debt than ever before, with the volume of mortgage loans forecast to break the $20 billion mark. Two million new and old houses would be bought, according to government housing statistics, in part a function of easy credit terms, i.e., the need to put less cash down in exchange for bigger loans that could be paid over a longer period of time. That year's National Home Week, an annual event sponsored by the National Association of Home Builders (NAHB) in which model homes could be toured, was also busier than ever. "More people saw more houses, bought more houses, and learned more about new houses than ever before," an NAHB spokesperson reported.[23]

Older homes too were selling relatively briskly, however, particularly if they had been modernized in some way. While selling an existing home was easier than it once had been, those who went through what could be an exhausting and frustrating process were ready to share tips on how to get it done. "Older homes are like mothers-in-law," observed Paul F. Healy in the *Saturday Evening Post*, adding that "almost everybody likes to visit one, but hardly anybody is anxious to acquire one permanently." Healy knew that he had two main selling points to unload his decidedly dated 1920s bungalow—value and architectural charm. After receiving a long list of stern do's and don'ts from a broker, the man from Chevy Chase, Maryland, decided to go it alone although he did allow brokers to show the house to potential buyers. After 78 stressful days (he had to take possession of another home in 90 days), the house was sold (for $1,500 less than his $19,950 ask).[24]

Figuring out what a house was worth was then, like now, an inexact science. Hiring a professional appraiser was highly recommended, whether one was selling or buying. If considering remodeling, it was also good to have an estimated "as is" value before putting more money into a place. But even the most methodical of appraisers were unable to say with any precision what a property was worth to a specific individual. "Their judgments are subject to the tastes and whims of unusual buyers," Tysen of Previews, Inc. remarked of appraisers, a particular architectural feature—that gargoyle, say—able to sway someone on the fence to either sign (and even overpay) or walk away.[25]

Tysen was one American who went to Vienna, Austria, to attend the annual meeting of the International Real Estate Federation in 1956. (His company was described as "the world's only international clearinghouse for real estate," making it a kind of stock exchange for global properties.) The brokerage business was becoming increasingly international as buyers looked beyond their own countries to invest in real estate. Americans were looking to Europe and Europeans to the United States, a function of a generally robust global economy. In his address to the group, Tysen not surprisingly boasted of the activity taking place in his country; Southern California, New York City, Boston, and Florida were experiencing especially lively demand for residential property. Not just residential but commercial property was selling well, notably timberland in the Carolinas and Georgia and office buildings in Denver. Tysen was also there to sell the American way of life during the Cold War. "It is such case histories of America's success under a free enterprise system which stimulate foreign countries to break away from governmental restrictions and strive for the free economy which can be the foundation of real prosperity," he told the attendees.[26]

William H. Oliver, Co-Director of the Fair Practices Anti-Discrimination Department of the UAW-CIO-AFL, did not share Tysen's patriotic and some would say propagandist spirit. He had recently spoken at the Detroit Real Estate Brokers Association in that city which was well known for having particularly Draconian redline practices. "There are no free markets in real estate financing as far as minority groups are concerned," the union man alleged, no doubt making the agents squirm a bit in their seats. Black Detroiters could not buy homes in suburban areas of the city, Oliver stated, claiming that "a non-criminal co-conspiracy" existed among the FHA, Veterans Administration, and many in the real estate business (notably brokers and bankers).[27] Oliver was clearly referring to the "gentlemen's agreement" between the private and public sectors that was in place in many cities to contain African Americans in designated areas due to racist attitudes and fears that property values would fall should Blacks move into white neighborhoods.

Economists and sociologists were in fact at the time studying what effects, if any, the presence of African Americans had on property values. In a 1957 article published in *The American Journal of Economics and Sociology*, Thomas L. Gillette examined what took place in the Santa Fe district of Kansas City, Missouri, after a number of Black families moved in. Bombings had occurred in the early 1950s when some crossed the designated color line, the product of white neighbors who considered their move an invasion and threat to the value of their homes. Still, the area became more racially mixed, leading Gillette to discover if the concerns of the white residents were justified. After tumbling the numbers, he determined they were not. "The results indicate that prices in this particular neighborhood were enhanced rather than lowered through Negro entry," Gillette concluded, believing that his evidence "refutes the idea held by many that Negro invasion must result in a drop in property value."[28]

Beyond the fundamentally faulty economic assumption that informed Jim Crow policies and practices in housing, there was the additional fact that the

African American market was sizable and largely untapped, particularly with regard to preowned homes. New construction was still sliding somewhat in 1956 as the GI Bill benefits expired but because of the trend to bigger, more expensive houses, builders were not overly concerned. With fewer new home buyers, however, some brokers were paying more attention to what was being called "trade-in" housing. The situation was analogous to what took place in automobile sales in the late 1920s, when car dealers realized that they would have to take trade-ins as the used market (mostly Model-Ts) ballooned. The FHA estimated that perhaps sixty million Americans wanted to move but had concerns that they wouldn't be able to sell their house. The agency had begun offering a financing program allowing brokers and developers to obtain FHA mortgages on trade-in homes, liberating them from having to carry the debt on less than desirable properties until a buyer came along.[29]

Borrow, Borrow, Borrow

African Americans represented another major market for preowned homes, but rampant segregation in housing across the country was thwarting potential sales. Civil rights activism was becoming aggressive in the late fifties, with discrimination in housing one of the key battlegrounds. The issue was raised at the 1957 National Housing Conference, with civic leaders, housing experts, brokers, and builders discussing what to do about the problem with regard to minorities and lower-income groups. Eight years had passed since Congress passed the Housing Act of 1949 whose main objective was to make possible "a decent home in a suitable living environment for every American family." It was clear that that objective had not been achieved, the group agreed, with the federal government complicit in the failure to provide equal opportunity for home ownership. A number of resolutions were passed in the hope that the country had moved closer to realizing the goal in another eight years.[30]

Public housing was serving as an especially passionate point of contention with regard to the racial dynamics embedded in real estate. Whenever such a project was announced by city officials, protests and demonstrations by white residents almost inevitably followed. "Not in my backyard" or words to that effect, they would declare, fearing not just a loss in the value of their property but crowded schools and a rise in crime. Although Blacks and whites were evenly represented in some urban developments, "public housing" equated to "minority housing," making race the key issue, the kicker being that the projects would come at the taxpayer's expense. Congress had authorized Federal aid for 35,000 new public housing units for the fiscal year 1956–1957 but not one was under construction due to what Howard H. Thomas of the *Philadelphia Tribune* called "non-receptive" residents.[31]

Non-receptive residents could certainly be found in the Bucks County, Pennsylvania Levittown, William Levitt's second titular development.

A group there calling itself the "Levittown Betterment Committee" was attempting to keep their community redlined, urging that the kind of restrictive covenant outlined in Clause 25 of the original Levittown rental contracts be applied. The Myers, an African American family, had moved into a home in the Pennsylvania Levittown, causing the committee to make their feelings on the matter known. Howard Thomas stated that their effort would be "as futile as the efforts of the Confederate Army during the Civil War," however, noting that the vast majority of the community's residents had expressed their disfavor with what they considered an act of bigotry.[32]

It was believed that at least six Black families called the original Levittown on Long Island home in 1957, although no one knew the exact number. (The geographic borders of Levittown itself were unclear.) While African Americans represented a tiny fraction of the community that now consisted of an estimated 65,000 residents in 17,500 homes, there were reportedly no tensions or problems in terms of race. Betsy Yaller, who had served as executive director of the Committee to End Discrimination in Levittown, described relations between Black and white families as "most pleasant." Children played and went to school together regardless of their skin color, she maintained, and racial differences were no barrier to friendships among adults.[33] "We'd like everybody to know that Levittown does have successful integration," she told the *New York Amsterdam News* when hearing about the Myers incident, adding that the few Black families who did live in Long Island's Levittown had homes scattered around the development rather than lived in a particular section.[34]

With Levittown No. 3 in New Jersey, however, Levitt's good luck would run out. In 1959, Levitt was building a 16,000-home development near Burlington, New Jersey, and he publicly stated that he wouldn't sell houses to African Americans there, just like at the first two Levittowns. (Green Fields Farm, another New Jersey builder, shamefully echoed Levitt.) A 1957 amendment to a New Jersey housing law barred discrimination in federally guaranteed loans, however, ruining Levitt's and Green Fields' plans. Seven Black families now lived in the Long Island Levittown and one in the Pennsylvania Levittown (having purchased their homes from white residents), but it appeared that there could be many more in New Jersey given that state's progressive law.[35]

Rather unexpectedly, Levittown soon played a role in international politics when President Eisenhower mentioned that he wanted Russian Premier Nikita Khrushchev to see the new Pennsylvania development as a model "workers town." (Levitt had chosen its location primarily because it was near United States Steel's Fairless plant.) But even African American employees of that plant were not allowed to purchase homes in that Levittown, something that Roy Wilkins of the NAACP pointed out as Khrushchev's trip to the United States neared. "Levittown, Pa. has become known the world over as the town where a single Negro family had to fight off a mob in order to occupy a modest home," he wrote in a telegram to Eisenhower, recommending that the President steer the Soviet leader away from any Levittowns. "Levittown in Long Island, N.Y. was built as a lily-white community," he added, thinking that the Russian would "score a telling propaganda point" should he be shown "almost any new housing anywhere in America."[36]

While undeniably heavily freighted with racism, real estate was without doubt a good way to make money and even get rich. That was becoming increasingly clear near the end of the 1950s, when ordinary investors shifted more of their assets to property as their values continued to rise. "How-to's" had long been written with regard to stocks and bonds, but now real estate was becoming a popular subject for authors wanting to show others how to invest wisely and profitably. Any homeowner was an investor in property, of course, but such books were targeted more to those who purchased houses, other buildings, or land to generate income and capital gains.[37]

Two such books were *How to Retire on Real Estate Profits* and *Rental Housing: Opportunities for Private Investment*. The former, published by the editors at Harian Publications, argued that investing in real estate was a much better choice than anything the stock market had to offer. There was more money to be made in property in both the short and long term, the authors maintained, and best of all it was most often inflation-proof. The latter book, authored by Louis Winnink, made a strong case for rental housing, an investment that had declined in recent decades as more Americans sought single-family homes. (Apartment building construction had peaked in the 1920s.) Winnink predicted that there would be a back-to-the-city movement as the suburbs became more crowded, as their tax burden rose, and as homeowners aged—all things that would happen beginning in the 1990s as the principles of New Urbanism gained traction.[38]

That real estate could be a great source of wealth for anyone with a little extra cash and time on their hands appeared to be becoming a literary genre all its own. In his *How I Turned $1,000 into a Million in Real Estate—in My Spare Time*, William Nickerson showed how he had parlayed a small investment into a big pile of dough while keeping his day job at a telephone company. The secret was to start small and continually trade up to larger properties, with good money to be made from both rentals and building appreciation. (Fred F. French, one of the biggest real estate operators in the 1920s, had followed this same formula.) Improving run-down properties was an excellent way to raise rents and increase values, Nickerson explained, happy to be able to now work for himself.[39]

Nickerson's book was timely. "No book has enlarged the fantasy life of Americans more dramatically this season," *Time* observed, noting that "more than 100,000 readers have broken open this fortune cookie." 10,000 copies a week were being sold, in part because the publisher promised a full refund to readers who did not earn a million dollars in real estate after ten years. While most believed that the three most important things in the business were "location, location, location," Nickerson insisted it was "borrow, borrow, borrow," as that was the way to leverage gains into bigger ones.

A little luck certainly helped, but virtually guaranteed population growth meant that more people would need places to live. When advertising rental property, he advised, "redecorated" and "spacious" were keywords to use, as was "manager" (over "janitor"). Avoid at all costs the "L" word (as in landlord), Nickerson wrote, as that term had become a dirty word during the thrifty 1930s.[40]

Considerable success could also be made by selling real estate, of course, regardless of one's gender. Since the 1920s, many women had worked as agents, finding it to be one of the few occupations in which results mattered more than anything else. Josephine Schaefer told her extraordinary story in the *New York Herald Tribune* which perhaps served as inspiration for many other women considering careers in real estate. Divorced and with a young son to support around the time of the 1929 market crash, Schaefer, a New Yorker, weighed her job possibilities, which she considered to be acting, buying for a department store, and getting into the real estate business. She chose the latter, first learning typing and shorthand and then sending a letter to Douglas Elliman who hired her as a secretary. "I badgered them to let me sell and finally, after four years, I was allowed to go out," Schaefer explained, doing well enough to eventually become a broker and an officer with the company. The woman was in 1959 selling co-op apartments, likening her job to that of a psychiatrist because of the need to understand people.[41] Schaefer's skills would have been useful in the decade to come, as a new set of challenges altered the trajectory of home ownership in America.

Notes

1 "Cross-Country Roundup of U.S. Homes," *Life*, February 21, 1955.
2 Howard Adams, "Real Estate for Veterans," *Philadelphia Tribune*, July 15, 1950, 8. See Daniel K. Fetter, "How Do Mortgage Subsidies Affect Home Ownership? Evidence from the Mid-Century GI Bills," *American Economic Journal: Economic Policy*, May 2013, 111.
3 Richard B. Lyman, "Houses of '60 Will Be Sold with More Equipment," *New York Herald Tribune*, October 10, 1950, 37.
4 Stephen G. Thompson, "Offices May Follow Stores to Outlying Sites," *New York Herald Tribune*, October 18, 1950, 36.
5 W. Clifford Harvey, "House Output Slows Down Due to Curbs," *Christian Science Monitor*, June 1, 1951, 17.
6 W. Clifford Harvey, "Show Grows into Full-Blown Pageant," *Christian Science Monitor*, April 18, 1952, 8.
7 The Real Estate Editor of the Christian Science Monitor, "Real Estate is Big Business—Way Out West," *Christian Science Monitor*, October 31, 1952, 16.
8 "Past the Peak," *Time*, November 24, 1952.
9 John C. Tysen, "Buying or Selling Your Home," *New York Herald Tribune*, May 31, 1953, 2C.
10 Tysen, "Buying or Selling Your Home."
11 Richard B. Lyman, "'Levittowns' Set New Urban Pattern," *New York Herald Tribune*, November 6, 1953, 31.
12 Lyman, "'Levittowns' Set New Urban Pattern."
13 Lyman, "'Levittowns' Set New Urban Pattern."

14 Harry Henderson, "The Mass-Produced Suburbs," *Harper's*, November 1953, 25.
15 Frank J. Taylor, "He Sells Houses to the Stars," *Saturday Evening Post*, July 25, 1953.
16 "Real Estate Man to Seek 'Democracy in Housing,'" *Baltimore Afro-American*, September 26, 1953, 19.
17 "Real Estate Meet Studies Restrictions," *Philadelphia Tribune*, October 6, 1953, 8.
18 "Drop Racial Tag in Real Estate Ads," *Pittsburgh Courier*, November 7, 1953, 14.
19 Fred L. Chapman, "Can You Make Money in Real Estate?," *Better Homes & Gardens*, October 1953, 48.
20 Herb Bailey, "We Traded in Our Old Home for a New Model," *Better Homes & Gardens*, February 1954, 36.
21 "Gain Seen in Cities' Attack on Slums," *New York Herald Tribune*, April 13, 1954, 34.
22 Mary Hornaday, "What Citizens Can Do About Their Slums," *Christian Science Monitor*, July 23, 1954, 9.
23 William Kerwin, "1954 Most Active Year in U.S. Real Estate History," *Norfolk New Journal and Guide*, October 16, 1954, 11. See William I. Greenwald, "The Actual Costs of Home Ownership," *Southwestern Social Science Quarterly*, March 1954, 45.
24 Paul F. Healy, "So You're Selling Your House!," *Saturday Evening Post*, November 5, 1955, 38.
25 John C. Tysen, "Buying or Selling Your House," *New York Herald Tribune*, December 25, 1955, 12C.
26 The Real Estate Editor of the Christian Science Monitor, "Global Real Estate Federation Meets in Vienna for Seventh Congress," *Christian Science Monitor*, June 15, 1956, 16.
27 "No Free Markets in Real Estate, Oliver Charges," *Michigan Chronicle*, April 7, 1956, 6.
28 Thomas L. Gillette, "A Study of the Effects of Negro Invasion on Real Estate Values," *The American Journal of Economics and Sociology*, January 1957, 151.
29 "Trade-in Housing," *Time*, July 30, 1956.
30 Howard H. Thomas, "Chief Topic at Meeting," *Philadelphia Tribune*, June 29, 1957, 4.
31 Howard H. Thomas, "Housing Code Designed to Protect the Public," *Philadelphia Tribune*, August 3, 1957, 9.
32 Howard H. Thomas, "Full-Scale Integration Only a Question of Time," *Philadelphia Tribune*, August 31, 1957, 9.
33 Tom Barrett, "Negroes Integral Part of the L.I. Levittown," *New York Herald Tribune*, August 21, 1957, A1.
34 James Booker, "New York's Levittown Has No Trouble Now!," *New York Amsterdam News*, August 24, 1957, 1.
35 "Levitt Loses Housing Bias Case in N.J.," *New York Herald Tribune*, July 23, 1959, 9.
36 Charles Loeb, "World View: Best Keep Mr. Khrushchev Away from Levittown," *Cleveland Call and Post*, August 22, 1959, 3_C.
37 Ralph W. Porter, "Real Estate Investment Aired," *Christian Science Monitor*, January 21, 1959, 13.
38 Ralph W. Porter, "Real Estate Investment Aired," *Christian Science Monitor*, January 21, 1959, 13; The Editors of Harian Publications, *How to Retire on Real Estate Profits* (Greenlawn, NY: Harian Publications, 1959); Louis Winnink, *Rental Housing: Opportunities for Private Investment* (New York: McGraw-Hill, 1959).

39 Ralph W. Porter, "Real Estate Bonanza Told," *Christian Science Monitor*, March 25, 1959, 12; William Nickerson, *How I Turned $1,000 into a Million in Real Estate—in My Spare Time* (New York: Simon & Schuster, 1959).
40 "Bestseller Revisited," *Time*, July 6, 1959.
41 Guin Hall, "Real Estate: A Woman's Business," *New York Herald Tribune*, May 21, 1959, A2.

5 The Threshold of the Good Life

"House, be not sad that we decline your elegance and grace of line. Someone will come and find you right for need of day and deed of night."
Edsel Ford, "On Saying 'No' to a Real Estate Man"

In 1962, the NAREB partnered with the Bureau of Land Management (BLM, part of the Department of the Interior) on a nationwide search to promote the anniversary of each organization. The BLM sought to celebrate the 100th anniversary of the Homestead Act, which had been signed by President Lincoln on May 20, 1862. The NAREB, meanwhile, wanted to recognize National Realtor Week, which also took place in late May.[1]

The search involved finding the oldest homesteader in the nation, i.e., the (still alive) individual who could claim possession of the longest continuously held title to a particular piece of land. It was a big country, making finding that person no easy task. Each organization put its resources to work (there were 71,000 members of the NAREB) and, after an intensive search, the individual was found. She was Mrs. Bertha W. Ingalls of Colorado Springs who in 1893 had homesteaded a property thirty miles south of Wray, Colorado. Now ninety-four years old, Ingalls had settled into a sod house built by her husband when there were more wolves and coyotes in the area than people. Ingalls displayed her original title (called patent then) that had been granted by the U.S. Government and dated March 3, 1893. The still "alert and active" woman was honored at a gala luncheon in Denver, marking the anniversary of the Homestead Act through which millions of acres of public land had passed to private ownership.[2]

Homesteading, if it could still be called that, had come a long way since the turn of the 20th century, but its foundation—to own a tiny slice of the nation—remained essentially the same. Home ownership in the United States had risen to 62% by 1960 and was continuing to grow as "white flight" to the suburbs accelerated. The postwar economic machine would run out of steam in the latter part of the decade, however, bad news for those hoping to realize their domestic American dream. Also, race-based discrimination in housing would crash head on with the civil rights movement of the sixties, making it a defining theme of home ownership during the turbulent decade.

DOI: 10.4324/9781003481485-6

Typically American

To that point, some steps had been taken by state governments and realtor organizations to end or at least lessen discrimination against minorities in housing, but there remained a very long way to go. Glaring demonstrations of bias were taking place at the local level, with each case attracting the attention of elected officials. In 1960, for example, it was revealed that brokers and property owners in Grosse Pointe, Michigan, were using a "point system" to screen prospective purchasers of homes in the affluent Detroit suburb. Buyers were rated on criteria such as nationality, "color" (race), accent, "way of living," occupation, "complexion" (something apparently considered different than "color"), dress, education, "grammar," and whether they were "typically American." Michigan officials were moving to pull the licenses of brokers who vetted buyers on their race, religion, or nationality.[3]

Some in pursuit of equal opportunity in housing were not waiting for politicians to take action. In July 1960, what was reported as New England's first sit-in took place by members of the Boston chapter of CORE. The group appeared at the sales office of a developer who was building a community in Woodvale, a northern suburb of Boston, and announced they wouldn't leave until they had the chance to complete a purchase agreement. "The agents dropped everything, fled from the office, and beat a speedy retreat by car," as the *Philadelphia Tribune* described the scene, puzzling the fifty other prospective buyers who showed up that day to review plans for the development.[4]

For years, discriminatory practices within the housing market had been a main topic of conversation at the NAREB annual convention, and the 1960 meeting in Cleveland was no exception. In many areas of the country, brokers simply refused to show African Americans properties, and mortgage bankers often displayed a similar attitude when considering loans. Black developers were fully aware of these restrictions and knew that getting people of their race into houses they built was a big challenge. Even African Americans with excellent credit were more often not refused financing, the result being that renters in Black neighborhoods could not become property owners.[5]

There was no doubt that the housing industry remained both an enabler and an enforcer of race-based segregation in America in the early 1960s. Most local real estate boards had codes of ethics that prescribed open housing, making these a viable point of attack for those attempting to change the system. Trying to skirt their code, some agents were approaching homeowners near a house for sale and urging them to put pressure on the seller to choose "someone you would want as a neighbor," omitting references to race. Short of a state-by-state or federal fair housing law, more progressive communities were disseminating facts that challenged the commonly assumed, entirely negative changes in a neighborhood when people of "other" races, ethnicities, or religions moved in. Property values didn't drop, the neighborhood didn't physically deteriorate, public school standards were not lowered, and crime didn't increase, the data showed, countering popular belief.[6]

Brokers continued to pressure white homeowners in some areas to sell their houses cheap under the pretense that Black people were moving into the neighborhood and property values would soon plummet. Such "panic selling" resulted in lower than fair value prices, meaning a big gain awaited the broker when he resold the house to another white family. In Philadelphia, a city commission advised homeowners who were approached in such a way to write "Return to sender" if sent a letter or, if contact was made by phone or a personal visit, to say that that kind of solicitation was unwanted and objectionable. (Just asking the broker if he was licensed usually instantly ended the conversation.)[7]

Smart tactics, but history showed that more robust enforcement was required to transform the way things were done in the world of real estate. By 1961, six states—Colorado, Massachusetts, Oregon, Ohio, California, and Connecticut—were moving toward passing laws or strengthening existing Fair Housing Practices statutes against racial discrimination in housing. Local court cases had prompted state legislators to act, with the Civil Liberties Union sometimes filing a "friend of the court" brief in support of the law being considered. In one case, developers had signed a contract with a woman who was or appeared to be white only to cancel it upon learning that her husband was Black.[8]

Brokers who "broke" or "busted" blocks (sold houses to African Americans in white neighborhoods) could receive unwanted attention in a community. When Walter Loving did just that in Richmond, Virginia, in 1961, local newspapers ran articles about the sale, and who was responsible. Loving, a Richmond native who happened to be Black, was blazing the trail of integrated housing in the city and was proud to be doing it. Loving didn't approve of the term "block busting," however, thinking it was simply a matter of helping people who faced obstacles in obtaining decent housing. "My concern is to find homes to supply this need," he told the *Baltimore Afro-American*, adding that he was "not concerned about the race and color of the residents in the neighborhood, nor of the buyer or seller."[9]

Likely hearing about the dramatic effects of the Boston sit-in, Brooklyn-based CORE members decided to hold their own the following year. A thirty-four-year-old African American widow had tried to sign a lease for an apartment on Union Street in that borough but repeatedly got the "brush-off." The woman appealed to CORE for help and, rather cleverly, the group had a white Brooklyn College student visit the real estate office to say that his sister would like to rent the three-room flat. The broker told the student that the apartment was available and to bring his sister to the office to sign the lease. The "sister" turned out to be the widow, who again was denied the apartment because of her race. A 25-hour sit-in was soon underway in the office (six to twelve CORE members alternated), resulting in the woman getting the apartment.[10]

Such activism was certainly helpful in leveling the playing field of housing, but it was more likely the workings of capitalism that would truly transform it for the better. A study published in 1962 revealed that there was "a vast Negro market" for homes, a function of the emergence of a large Black middle class. While discrimination in employment was rampant, many African Americans had benefited from the healthy postwar economy. In fact, according to the study of the minority housing market completed by the Detroit-based Advance Mortgage Corporation, there were fifteen times the number of middle- and upper-income Black families in America than there had been a decade earlier.[11]

As such statistics became more widely known, developers were coming around to the fact that there was indeed a sizable market of potential homeowners that was being overlooked because of prevailing racial attitudes. Many in this untapped market were currently renting apartments that were well below their financial means and not buying property only because of the barriers that were in place in many urban areas. In much of the country, particularly the Midwest, little integration had taken place in housing, with white families tending to move out if Black families moved in. That would change over the next decade, predicted the president of Advance Mortgage, if only because too much money was being left on the table through broker and lender bias.[12]

It was ironic that such a study would have been completed by a company based in Detroit, which was, again, one of the most segregated cities in the country. Pontiac, a city twenty miles north of downtown Detroit, had been notorious for redlining, making it a logical place for James Del Rio to begin his campaign of integration. Del Rio, an African American real estate broker in Detroit, realized considerable success in Pontiac, where most of the latter city's 13,000 Black residents were sardined in a forty-square-block "ghetto." Four years after he had opened a branch office in Pontiac, some of them were living happily alongside whites in Herrington Hills, a subdivision of medium-priced houses, with Del Rio having served as the agent of record for the African American homeowners.[13]

How had he achieved such a thing? Del Rio pressured the Veteran's Administration to provide "open occupancy" listings of repossessed homes in all neighborhoods rather than just Black ones, which, as a federal agency, it was essentially forced to do. His target now Detroit, he next approached the FHA, which had an even bigger list of repossessed homes, and repeated his formula in that city. There was of course a long way to go, but by 1963, Del Rio had earned the reputation as "Michigan's Ghetto Buster," on a mission to integrate the entire state block by block.[14]

Progress was made that year in another Midwestern city as the civil rights movement gained additional traction. (It was the year of the March on Washington for Jobs and Freedom, in which more than 200,000 demonstrators made their presence and feelings known. Martin Luther King closed the rally with his "I Have a Dream" speech.) In Chicago (home of the NAREB), the previously all-white Chicago Real Estate Board admitted an African American. Not just one but four Blacks were accepted to the

79-year-old organization, making the decision a true breakthrough. The Mayor's Commission on Human Relations had pressured the board to do the right thing for the past two years, and the powerful group finally relented.[15]

A Giant Machine

Alongside the struggle for racial equality in the early 1960s, fundamental issues relating to housing continued to percolate. One of the most basic was the decision to rent or own, with adherents to each school convinced that they had chosen wisely. In 1962, a woman from Brookline, Massachusetts, was pitted against one from Medfield and, although they lived within an hour's car ride of each other, their views on the matter couldn't be any different. Mrs. Adam Orzechowski of Brookline argued that while apartment preferers like herself were in the minority, she felt strongly that owning was wasting good money. "There are so many things that can go wrong in a house," she explained, an expensive and time-consuming proposition given that her husband had no home repair skills whatsoever. Orzechowski spent her time on more pleasurable activities than mowing a lawn, painting the kitchen, or putting a new tile floor in the playroom and spent her money on traveling instead of plumbing or roof repairs.[16]

Jane P. McCarty of Medfield, however, felt the time and money invested in a home of one's own was more than worth it. Her three-year-old child now played in a grassy backyard rather than in a cement playground in the city where they had rented an apartment, and they certainly didn't miss the walking up and down the four flights of stairs. McCarty's husband found chores like building a fence or planting shrubs not at all disagreeable, the knowledge that one was improving one's property deeply satisfying. Going to her first New England town meeting turned out to be a meaningful experience, with animated discussions on zoning, taxes, and schools offering the sense that one was part of a real community.[17]

If one wanted to be a homeowner but liked apartment life, there were in many areas of the country cooperative apartments, which had been around for decades. In a typical co-op, occupants owned shares in a corporation or association that owned the land and the building. A rather new thing was appearing in the early 1960s, however, and getting a mixed reception. "The condominium, young cousin to the cooperative apartment, is treated like an uninteresting stranger in some American cities and feted like a hero in others," the *Christian Science Monitor* observed. In a condominium, residents owned their apartment and also owned a share in the common facilities (e.g., land, parking, elevators, and the building itself). The condominium concept was included in federal housing legislation in 1961, and the first one to be built with FHA mortgage insurance was Park Layne Towers in Hallandale, Florida. More were being built across the country, but so far only older couples with significant assets seemed interested, as co-ops were a better value and offered more flexibility.[18]

In his 1963 article "Condominium: Home Ownership for Megalopolis?" published in the *Michigan Law Review*, John E. Cribbet took a deep dive into the history and potential future of that form of home ownership. Could broad ownership of condominiums be the solution to the problem of home ownership in America, i.e., that not everyone could afford a single-family house? It was currently a particularly tense moment in the Cold War, the reason why Cribbet, a professor of law at the University of Illinois, considered the question in relation to the ownership of property in Russia. "A society which fails to provide satisfactory housing for its citizens has stubbed its toe at the threshold of the good life," he wrote, seeing the issue as going well beyond the discriminatory practices against African Americans.[19]

Cribbet had keen insights into the challenges facing what he termed "the Western yearning to have an individual castle." There was little prime land left to develop in most urban areas, he held, and suburban sprawl was making life more inconvenient and costly for many homeowners. Commuting distances and time had increased significantly from decades of development, leading Cribbet to think there could be a mass migration back to inner cities. That meant more apartment living could be in store for millions of Americans, making condominiums a logical alternative to the single-family houses in the suburbs. Renting, he posited, just wasn't in our individual or collective DNA despite the kind of sentiment expressed by Mrs. Adam Orzechowski of Brookline, Massachusetts. "The tenant half of the landlord-tenant relationship runs counter to a deep strain in the American psyche," Cribbet concluded, with even the prospect of a hefty, lengthy mortgage not daunting enough to discourage the desire to have a home of one's own.[20]

As home ownership continued to grow in the 1960s, advice of all kinds poured out of the popular media to help readers wade through the complexity of buying or selling a property. *Better Homes and Gardens* was not surprisingly a major voice of domesticity, offering all kinds of valuable advice related to being the queen of one's castle. In addition to offering guidance on things like creating a patio that would be the envy of neighbors and growing blue-ribbon begonias, the magazine ran a series of articles under the umbrella of "Family Money Management." "Should you shop for a new home before you sell your old one?" the magazine asked in 1963 in the first of the series, the answer being, "Yes—but only if you can be sure that you won't find yourself paying for two homes, with two sets of bills for taxes, mortgage, interest, insurance, and maintenance."[21]

The second question *Better Homes and Gardens* posed in a subsequent issue was, "Should you trade your home in on a new one?" Many Americans were indeed "trading in" their current house for a just-built one for a variety of reasons, including greater size. (The baby boom was still booming in the early 1960s, making many families long for more space.) The market for older houses remained soft, however, meaning the spread between what one got for the old and had to spend for the new would be significant. Better build in the broker commission when doing the math, the magazine added, lest one be in for an unpleasant surprise when closing the deal.[22]

Some months later, the question the magazine asked and answered was, "How should you list your home when you sell it?" There were three options, the first one being an exclusive listing, in which the seller worked with just one designated broker. One theoretically received preferred attention and a concentrated effort with an exclusive, but it came at the cost of limited exposure. Open listing allowed any and all brokers to sell one's house (and even oneself, eliminating a commission) but be prepared for an intense, likely chaotic experience as brokers battled each other for the sale. Finally, there were multiple listings, in which a single broker posted the listing on the Multiple Listing Service (MLS, whose origins dated back to the late 19th century). Multiple listings offered the best of both worlds of exclusive and open, but it was available in just 45% of the country in 1965.[23]

The question and answers in *Better Homes and Gardens* kept coming, suggesting there was a real need for advice on all things home in the mid-1960s. "How should you handle your home if you're transferred?," the magazine asked readers, congratulating them if they were in such a position as it usually meant a promotion or raise. The good news was that companies often guaranteed employees they were transferring that they wouldn't lose money when selling their house (which typically happened with haste, as that lucky manager might have to report to his or her new post in just two or three weeks). The bad news was that more stingy companies based the sale on the original cost of the house, ignoring any appreciation that had likely occurred.[24]

Many readers no doubt wondered "What's the best way to rent a home?," which was the next article in the series. One would have to pay a broker 50–60% of the first month's rent but it was worth it, the magazine counseled. Brokers not only vetted candidates but were good at setting the price, writing the ad, and composing the lease.[25] Finally, there was a thorny one: "Who pays when a visitor gets hurt on your property?" The short answer was that it depended on who the visitor was and what, if anything, the owner did to protect him or her. Owners did have a legal responsibility to ensure the safety of guests or workers, but uninvited trespassers were a different matter. Even then, however, many states made property owners liable should an injury or death occur under the "attractive nuisance" rule. Also, reasonable care had to be taken to make sure the milkman would not get bitten by Fido and that even the most annoying insurance salesman didn't slip on an icy path.[26]

Such nuts-and-bolts information about acquiring, managing, or selling a domicile was certainly useful, but it was the future of the home that was most intriguing. "A new type of push-button home is emerging from the developing use of electronics and automation," proclaimed W. Clifford Harvey of the *Christian Science Monitor* in 1964, foreseeing a Jetsonesque world on the horizon. "The housewife who controls her automobile automatically, opening and closing windows, raising and lowering tops, wiping windshields electrically, now envisages her home as a giant machine doing most of the chores 'on its own,'" he wrote. Architects, engineers, and manufacturers shared this forward-looking view, believing that new construction methods and appliances would make the house of tomorrow a wonderful thing, offering greater comfort and convenience.[27]

All Shapes and Sizes

The home of the future played a prominent role in the 1964–1965 New York World's Fair that ran from April 1964 to October 1964 and again from April 1965 to October 1965. The nation's postwar obsession with domestic life was on proud display at the fair in Flushing Meadows-Corona Park (the same site as the 1939–1940 New York World's Fair), often a backward-looking perspective that presented the home as a self-contained bunker offering sanctuary from a dangerous world. Filled-to-the-gill model houses seemed to be everywhere one looked, many of them described as utopian paradises or, in real estate lingo, dream homes. "American model houses at the World's Fair come in all shapes and sizes, above and below ground," noted George O'Brien of the *New York Times*, all of them generously stocked with the consumerist trappings linked to the American dream.[28]

Fittingly, *Better Homes and Gardens* made an appearance. Six "space-saving" model rooms created by designers the magazine commissioned were on display, as was the full-sized, seven-room Westinghouse "Dream House," where predictions about the future of the kitchen were offered. There were in fact no fewer than twenty-nine kitchen exhibits at the fair, displaying what *Look* magazine described as "the greatest concentration of take-home planning ideas ever presented." Leading appliance manufacturers presented ranges, refrigerators, ovens, freezers, dishwashers, and sinks in pastel and primary colors and in a global potpourri of styles including Early American, International Modern, Oriental, and Latin-American. General Motors' exhibits included a Frigidaire Kitchen Idea Center, offering "clever decorating ideas from all over the world" as well as "revolutionary appliances" such as the Imperial refrigerator-freezer and the world's first Jet Action Washer.[29]

At the world's fair's House of Good Taste pavilion, three more model homes—Traditional, Contemporary, and Modern—presented "the latest ideas in comfortable living" under the slogan, "The World of Tomorrow Today." The traditional house was an updated version of a New England farmhouse, complete with a white (and plastic) clapboard, sewing nook, fully equipped nursery, and indoor barbecue. Rooms in the Cleaveresque traditional house included a "Dining Room for Irenne Dunne" and "Study for Douglas Fairbanks, Jr.," evoking the tastes of stars whose heydays were closer to the last New York fair than this one. The contemporary house, with its Asian-inspired décor, incorporated reflecting pools, sliding glass walls, and a skylight window in the living room. Rooms in the *Brady Bunch*-like contemporary house included a "Family Room for Anita Bryant," she then known more as a singer than orange juice shill (or homophobe), and a Finnish sauna. With privacy as its central theme, the modern house was "inward-looking," best exemplified by its indoor garden under a big glass dome. Rooms in the modern house, "a house for the sophisticated and young at heart," included a "Kitchen for Joan Crawford" and "Dining Room for Kitty Carlisle," two other stars of yesteryear.[30]

As the names of its rooms perhaps suggested, the architects and designers for these model homes were not chosen by professionals but by one Lady Malcolm Douglas-Hamilton, head of the aptly named American Institute of Approval, which was responsible for organizing the exhibit. Members of the Institute of Approval were women prominent in their community, with no professional design experience required. Another literally big-as-a-house exhibit was the Formica World's Fair House, a seven-room model home which made extensive use of plastics. Designed with an emphasis on "care-free" living, the Formica House would be the very first to use "wipe clean" laminated plastic for all interior and exterior walls. A sweepstakes to win a complete $50,000 (upped to $100,000 in 1965) version of the house (lot included) to be built anywhere in the country was offered, along with 2,500 other prizes, including automobiles, stereos, and furniture.[31]

Not surprisingly, critics were less than impressed with the amateurs' choices. "By and large, the buildings are disappointing, and do not begin to indicate the current thinking and planning of American architects and interior and furniture designers," said one reporter for the *New York Times*. Another one from that newspaper added that "The House of Good Taste exhibit is in quite good taste, which is to say it neither excites nor offends." "A wonderful opportunity to show the world what America is capable of in housing has been missed," the architectural critic concluded. A Swedish architect was less kind, thinking that "they all look about twenty years behind the times."[32]

Critics were largely missing the point of the House of Taste (named by the public relations person for the fair, Thomas Deegan), however. The purpose of the pavilion was not to display leading-edge architecture and design but to sell existing furnishings and appliances, all of which were readily available in stores across the country. The pavilion was sponsored by scores of building, decorating, and housewares companies, with manufacturers paying $5,000 to a whopping $100,000 to display their appliances and furnishings in the homes. One towel manufacturer gladly shelled out $20,000 to have its products in the bathrooms of the three homes, a good indication of how big a sales opportunity some companies viewed the House of Good Taste.[33]

The Pavilion of American Interiors, co-sponsored by Du Pont and the American Institute of Interior Designers, was another blatantly commercial enterprise, with manufacturers also ponying up to show their wares. The four-story, two-wing pavilion stretched two city blocks, as more than 120 exhibitors displayed furniture, floor coverings, fabrics, tableware, paints, decorations, and lighting fixtures. In addition to a number of do-it-yourself exhibits, inside were fourteen model rooms, including two Leisurama houses.

(In 1959, a prototype of the Leisurama house became a weapon in the Cold War when it was shown off as a typical American home at a trade show in Moscow, sparking the famous "kitchen debate" between Vice President Nixon and Soviet leader Nikita Khrushchev.) The most interesting space in the pavilion, however, was the "Moon Room," featuring a clear plastic table and chairs that floated in the air, suspended from the ceiling.[34]

Despite this bit of futuristic whimsy, *Time* considered the pavilion to be simply "a big furniture showroom that charges 50 cents admission." O'Brien was especially critical of the pavilion's heavy representation of contemporary furnishings, considering "contemporary" to be "a polite word for anonymous design" and saying that the furniture would "probably look more at home in a motel." The home furnishings editor for the newspaper was particularly disappointed that the Pavilion of American Interiors failed to show what the American home furnishings industry was truly capable of, seeing it as nothing more than a "paid advertisement." Visitors apparently agreed with O'Brien, as the pavilion went bankrupt during the fair's second season.[35]

Unquestionably the oddest model home at the Fair was the Underground World Home, an "ultramodern" ten-room house built fifteen feet below the Earth's surface. The house and its patio were contained within a specially designed concrete shell under two million pounds of topsoil. Windows looked out onto a mural of trees, grass, and sky, while in the garden lay a bed of plastic flowers. Not subject to the whims of nature, lighting could be set for daytime or nighttime (starry sky or glowing moonlight), offering the happy subterranean owner "summer in winter" and "midnight at noon." With its steel double door and "quadruply filtered" air, the home offered complete privacy, acoustical and climate control, and protection from noise, pollution, inclement weather, and, oh by the way, radioactive fallout. Curiously, the house was not positioned as a fall-out shelter but rather as "a way to save space above ground" (begging the question, "Was there a shortage?"). Underground living was presented by guides as less expensive, healthier, and "more fun" than above ground, with a no-joke-intended side benefit of 100% security against Peeping Toms. The house's snack bar sold, appropriately enough, "crab burgers."[36]

The designer of the underground home, Jay Swayze, was clearly convinced that appealing to a mass market meant staying away from the unpleasantness associated with nuclear war. Swayze cited solid research to pitch his house to fairgoers, including a study he conducted showing that people didn't look out their windows 80% of the time and of the 20% of the time they did, half the time what they saw was "undesirable." "I aim to give people views that are equal to or better than what they see ordinarily," said Swayze, who lived with his family in such a house in Plainview, Texas, saying that they much preferred living underground.[37]

Although the designer preferred to focus on the superior quality of life of a mole-like existence, some visitors could not help but view the home as a bunker, albeit a plush one. *The New Yorker* considered the home to be "the ultimate article in fallout shelters ... combining the small, familiar pleasures of the hearth with the headier excitements of Doomsday." The only real flaw with the house seemed to be that there was no way to tell what was going on above ground, i.e., whether the radioactive smoke had cleared or not. The magazine, tongue in its cheek, recommended that Mr. Swayze add a "good working periscope, so that mistakes can be avoided" in this regard.[38]

Absolutely Essential

While through 1964 and 1965 tens of millions of people looked at homes, both those intended to be above ground and under it, African Americans continued their decades-long struggle for "open housing." By 1966, the "conspiracy" between local real estate groups and elected officials to keep people of color out of neighborhoods primarily populated by whites was public knowledge. If there was any doubt about that, Attorney General Nicholas Katzenbach dispelled it in his testimony to the Senate Constitutional Rights subcommittee (part of the administration's civil rights bill) in July of that year. Katzenbach insisted that including fair housing in the bill was "absolutely essential" to getting rid of the ghettos in urban areas, a response to some opposition from Senate Republicans.[39]

The FHA was also leveraging its power to end Jim Crow practices in housing. Many brokers were still refusing to sell FHA-insured properties to Blacks, something that was in violation of the executive order on equal opportunity in housing that had been in effect since 1962. Any and all housing programs sponsored by the federal government could not discriminate on the basis of race, the order made clear, but that hardly meant the law was followed. In early 1967, FHA Commissioner Philip Brownstein sent a letter to all of the agency's offices that asked the directors to make sure that local brokers were aware of the non-discrimination policy. Also, advertisements had to include the following language: "FHA properties are offered for sale to qualified purchasers without regard to the prospective purchaser's race, color, creed or national origin."[40]

Meanwhile, an experiment in "instant rehabilitation" was underway in New York City courtesy of the Department of Housing and Urban Development (HUD) along with a private foundation. This was a new kind of attack on slums as an alternative to the traditional method of urban renewal—demolish a building and put up a new one commanding rent that the previous tenants couldn't afford. While residents were placed in a nearby hotel, new walls, appliances, and plumbing were installed in each apartment in a building on Manhattan's Lower East Side in just forty-eight hours (the rats decided to relocate). The goal was to preserve an existing neighborhood and at the same time save money (restoring a building cost half of erecting a new one). There were said to be five million "substandard" homes in urban areas of the country, making slum rehabilitation a potentially huge market for companies wanting to get in the federally financed business.[41]

Alongside such federally sponsored efforts to improve the housing situation in America was the pursuit of a national fair-housing law. Such a bill had not been passed in 1966 but now a new one championed by Senator Walter Mondale (D-MN) was in play in the Senate Banking and Currency Committee which was holding hearings on housing legislation in August 1967. Racial unrest in American cities had escalated, much of it grounded in conditions in Black neighborhoods and overt economic and employment inequalities, leading Mondale and others to urge that action be taken on the issue. Attorney General Ramsey Clark agreed, stating that, "Sooner or later we must manifest our national commitment to open housing and act on that commitment."[42]

It was perhaps beside the point and quite obvious, but analysts pointed out that civil disorders (riots, more commonly) decreased the value of both residential and commercial property in those neighborhoods. The 1966 riots in the Watts area of Los Angeles had done just that (10% and 20%, respectively) according to a report called "The Impact of Civil Disobedience on Property Values" produced by the Los Angeles-based Shattuck Company. If it was any consolation to those who owned property there, the value of commercial property on a portion of the city's Sunset Strip had fallen 30% as a result of what the *Philadelphia Tribune* called in 1968 "the disruptive behavior of 'hippie' concentrations."[43]

If only because of its economic consequences, widespread urban unrest appeared to be acting as a wake-up call for the federal government to permanently end discrimination in housing. George Romney, secretary of HUD in 1969, was a loud voice of open housing, this despite his usually conservative ways. "The Number One need of this country today is housing," the Republican and businessman told the 300 African Americans attending a conference of the National Housing Producers Association that had been organized by the NAACP. Romney was launching something called "Operation Breakthrough," a program designed to make race-based restrictions in housing a thing of the past. Romney had hired two African Americans, Sam Simmons and Sam Jackson, to help lead the program, as "only from the Black experience can minority problems be met."[44]

Few people more than Father Theodore M. Hesburgh, president of the University of Notre Dame and chair of the U.S. Commission on Civil Rights, would agree that a breakthrough was required to turn history around regarding the nation's problematic housing situation. The cards were stacked not just racially but economically, he told the Subcommittee on Housing of the House Committee on Banking and Currency in 1969, as the poor were being denied the basic American right of choosing where to live through exclusionary practices. Only a major federal housing policy effort was capable of stopping lingering redlining, Hesburgh insisted, as too many suburban communities had a not-in-my-backyard resistance to low- and moderate-income housing.[45]

The challenges were indeed great but, as the tumultuous decade of the 1960s drew to a close, there was reason to believe things were headed in the right direction. E. Washington Rhodes, the publisher of the *Philadelphia Tribune*, took a little space in his newspaper to report the economic progress African Americans had made in Philadelphia, hoping perhaps to bridge the racial divide that had become great in recent years. Ghettos had come to largely define Black urban areas in the nation and, while the City of Brotherly Love certainly had its share of them, it didn't tell the whole story. A full third of Philadelphians were African American, Rhodes pointed out, and they spent $700 million a year as consumers (and paid their taxes). Home ownership among Black Philadelphians was "spiraling" (upward), he maintained, adding that, "property values go up, not down, when Negro homeowners move into a hitherto all-white neighborhood."[46] Everything that Rhodes wrote was true, but the next chapter of home ownership in America had yet to be written, and it would turn out to be an interesting one.

Notes

1 "Homesteader of 1893 Acclaimed," *Christian Science Monitor*, May 25, 1962, 15.
2 "Homesteader of 1893 Acclaimed."
3 "Michigan Fights Real Estate 'Point System,'" *Baltimore Afro-American*, June 11, 1960, 2.
4 "Housing Sit-In Amazes Real Estate Customers," *Philadelphia Tribune*, July 26, 1960, 9.
5 "Bias in Real Estate Topic at NAREB Meet," *Chicago Defender* September 24, 1960, 4.
6 "HRC Chairman Says Real Estate Industry Encourages Segregation of the Races," *Pittsburgh Courier*, October 8, 1960, 5.
7 "Methods of Fighting Real Estate Pressure Tactics," *Philadelphia Tribune*, November 1, 1960, 15.
8 "Six States Act Against Discrimination in Housing," *Norfolk New Journal and Guide*, April 22, 1961, 20.
9 Samuel Hoskins, "Why One Real Estate Dealer Wars on 'Exclusive' Housing," *Baltimore Afro-American*, September 23, 1961, 8.
10 "25-Hour Sit-In in Brooklyn Gets Apartment," *Philadelphia Tribune*, November 7, 1961, 8.
11 W. Clifford Harvey, "Vast Negro Home Market Sighted," *Christian Science Monitor*, December 7, 1962, B28.
12 Harvey, "Vast Negro Home Market Sighted."
13 "Michigan's Ghetto Buster," *Ebony*, February 1963, 55.
14 "Michigan's Ghetto Buster."
15 "Chicago Real Estate Board Admits Negros," *Chicago Daily Defender*, February 19, 1963, 3.
16 "Do You Prefer Apartment or House?," *Christian Science Monitor*, May 18, 1962, 11.
17 "Do You Prefer Apartment or House?"
18 The National Association of Real Estate Editors, "Condominiums Get Mixed Reception," *Christian Science Monitor*, April 5, 1963, 15.
19 John E. Cribbet, "Condominium: Home Ownership for Megalopolis?," *Michigan Law Review*, May 1963, 1207.
20 "Condominium: Home Ownership for Megalopolis?"
21 "Should You Shop for a New Home Before You Sell Your Old One?," *Better Homes and Gardens*, August 1963, 7.

22 "Should You Trade Your Home in On a New One?," *Better Homes and Gardens*, September 1964, 11.
23 "How Should You List Your Home When You Sell It?," *Better Homes and Gardens*, May 1965, 140.
24 "How Should You Handle Your Home If You're Transferred?," *Better Homes and Gardens*, July 1965, 8.
25 "What's the Best Way to Rent a Home?," *Better Homes and Gardens*, August 1965, 6.
26 "Who Pays When a Visitor Gets Hurt on Your Property?," *Better Homes and Gardens*, October 1965, 8.
27 W. Clifford Harvey, "Push-Button Home," *Christian Science Monitor*, June 12, 1964, 13.
28 George O'Brien, "Model Homes at Fair," *New York Times*, April 23, 1964, 30.
29 William Nickerson, *1965 Official Guide: New York World's Fair* (New York: Time Incorporated, 1965), 68; J. Peter, "New Cook's Tour," *Look*, September 8, 1964, 28; "Material Relating to Homes," F128T793/H7, New-York Historical Society (N-YHS); "Material Relating to Home Furnishings," F128T793.H75, (N-YHS).
30 *1965 Official Guide*, 88; "Model Homes at Fair."
31 "Material Relating to Homes."
32 *1965 Official Guide*, 88; "Model Homes at Fair."
33 Martin Tolchin, "Big Companies Pay for Plugs at Fair," *New York Times*, May 25, 1964, 29; Rosemarie Haas Bletter, "The 'Laissez-Fair, Good Taste, and Money Trees: Architecture at the Fair," in Robert Rosenblum (ed.), *Remembering the Future: The New York World's Fair from 1939 to 1964* (New York: Rizzoli, 1989), 124, 128.
34 *1965 Official Guide*, 98.
35 "The World of Already," *Time*, June 5, 1964, 83; George O'Brien, "Contemporary Dwelling is Built Around Courts," *New York Times*, May 20, 1964, 46; George O'Brien, "History, Bit of Future Part of Fair Exhibition," *New York Times*, May 9, 1964, 18.
36 "Model Homes at Fair"; *1965 Official Guide,* 210.
37 "The Fair," *The New Yorker*, May 2, 1964, 40.
38 "Notes and Comment," *The New Yorker*, July 18, 1964, 40.
39 "Open Housing Law Called 'Absolutely Essential,'" *Baltimore Afro-American*, July 30, 1966, 13.
40 John Pierson, "Jim Crow Real Estate Brokers Jolted by FHA," *Norfolk New Journal and Guide*, January 7, 1967, 16.
41 "Out of Slums into Instant Homes in 48 Hours," *Life*, May 12, 1967.
42 Lyn Shepard, "Backers Seek Speed for Fair-Housing Bill," *Christian Science Monitor*, August 24, 1967, 10.
43 "Riots Cause 20% Drop in Real Estate Values in Watts," *Philadelphia Tribune*, May 14, 1968, p. 24.
44 Romney Hails Blacks' Efforts in Solving Housing Problem," *Chicago Daily Defender*, May 17, 1969, 14.
45 "Housing Pattern So Strong That Major Effort Required for Change," *Louisville Defender*, June 19, 1969, A3.
46 E. Washington Rhodes, "Negro Home Ownership Spiraling," *Philadelphia Tribune*, November 18, 1969, 22.

6 America's Biggest Business

"Do you have any nice, one-bedroom $350-a-month apartments?," a woman asks.
"Sure, lady," replies the agent, "we got a lot of $350 apartments. But we're getting $600 for them."

1979 joke

In 1978, Diane Loercher told her personal American home story, one that likely resonated with many other new homeowners. "When I was in my 20s, I used to listen with incomprehension and faint scorn as my 'older' friends in their 30s went on and on about houses, the houses they owned or the houses they hoped to buy," she wrote in the *Christian Science Monitor*, considering this obsession with home ownership "a most peculiar one." These thirtysomethings once had "loftier ambitions," Loercher explained, but now they were entirely content with things like planting shrubs or installing a new bathroom, happy to spend much of their time and money on such seemingly prosaic domestic affairs.[1]

Although Loercher, then living in a Manhattan studio, swore to "never succumb to such a mediocre fate," the inevitable of course took place. While writing her piece, she and her husband were suburban homeowners, and the urge to get out of the city was too great to be ignored. The couple had a longing to "nest," she explained, to have, in Loercher's words, "a home of our own." Armed with the *New York Times* Sunday Real Estate section, the newlyweds journeyed through New York, New Jersey, and Connecticut to find the perfect house in the perfect neighborhood in the perfect town. They found it, or something as close as possible to it, near Trenton, New Jersey, of all places, now understanding her older friends' preoccupation with houses, real or imaginary.[2]

Given the plethora of economic challenges of the 1970s—the energy crisis and stagflation, to name just a couple—making a home of one's own a reality represented an ambitious enterprise for many Americans. Having one's money in real estate was a far better choice than having it in the flailing stock market, however, and there were other sensible financial reasons to buy property assuming one could afford it. The median price of a home more than doubled over the course of the decade, and simply paying the bills had

DOI: 10.4324/9781003481485-7

become no easy task for the middle class. Still, despite or perhaps because of the obstacles, the dream of owning a home appeared to be as strong as ever, and it was clear that Americans had no intention of giving up on it.

One of the Essentials of Human Life

For Richard A. Nenneman, editor-in-chief of the *Christian Science Monitor*, the decade was not off to a good start in terms of housing in America. "No area of the economy is a bigger disaster today than housing," he wrote in the publication just seven weeks into 1970, firmly convinced that "something's got to be done—now." Other social ills—crime and drugs, specifically—were making the headlines, but Nenneman held that housing presented the larger challenge. It had been two years since Congress had passed the Fair Housing Act of 1968 which called for the construction or rehabilitation of 26 million housing units over the next decade, but housing starts and permits were actually falling instead of rising. Some believed that new construction would kick in when inflation slowed or when the Vietnam War drew to a close, as each discouraged developer investment. Nenneman, however, argued that "action is needed now," as shabby housing and crowded conditions in urban America were major contributors to the social problems that got more attention in the news.[3]

Nenneman's strong feelings about housing were rooted in his broader understanding of what could be interpreted as the American way of life. "For many an American, home ownership is still the only way he sees himself personally benefiting from the capitalistic system," he continued, as the deduction of property taxes and mortgage interest from income tax served as a powerful incentive to own versus rent. Owning was simply beyond the reach of many, however, making the possibility of renting a decent house or apartment an important thing to strive for. "It is hard to see why there isn't a greater sense of urgency about one of the essentials of human life." Nenneman concluded, thinking that federal legislation equivalent to that enacted during the New Deal was required to confront the issue.[4]

Ultimately, however, it was up to individuals to make the dream of home ownership a reality. It may have been a rather square notion in the groovy 1970s, but experts advised that the best way to make it happen was to save money. More young couples were thinking it might be nice to move out of their fourth-floor walkup in a bad neighborhood even if it did mean life in the bland suburbs. Growing up in what John Kenneth Galbraith had called "the affluent society," however, it was not instinctive for such folks to put money away for the proverbial rainy day. Twentysomethings could have as many as a dozen credit cards and charge accounts, according to the Investors Mortgage Insurance Company, making them a much different kind of generation than their parents who might have been raised during the Great Depression. A meeting with a banker could thus often be a shocking affair for those whose vocabulary didn't include the word "thrift"; the size of the down payment typically needed was 30% of the cost of a house with a conventional mortgage, well beyond what the couple could likely afford.[5]

Data from the 1970 Census revealed, however, that more Americans were moving to the suburbs, many of them to a single-family house despite the pile of dough that was required at purchase closings. Given the social unrest in American cities during the 1960s, there was considerable interest in the racial dynamics of this migration to the suburbs. While a significant number of African Americans had moved to the suburbs over the course of the decade, more whites did, making the gain of the former minimal. Blacks' presence in the suburbs went from 4.2% in 1960 to 4.5% in 1970, hardly the shift that some were hoping for. More than twelve million whites had left the inner city, resulting in the number of African Americans rising from 18% to 23% of the country's urban population.[6]

Although the vast majority of its residents remained white, suburbia was for *Time* in 1971 "the new American plurality." Seventy-five million people now lived in the 'burbs, according to the latest Census figures, exceeding the combined number of urbanites and rural folk. With that many people occupying a wide range of communities, the popular image of the classic suburbanite—martini-drinking, commuting men and station-wagon-driving, shopping women—was now a cliché, the magazine maintained. Fiction by postwar novelists such as Sloan Wilson, John Marquand, Max Shulman, Peter De Vries, and John Cheever had reinforced that stereotype, but it was now as dated as a 1958 Edsel. Findings from a recent *Time*–Louis Harris survey revealed as much. Suburbanites circa 1971 tended to stay put versus move every couple of years, were more Democratic than Republican, were not particularly affluent, and were unlikely to commute to work. Still, noted sociologist Herbert Gans, most Americans wanted to be a suburbanite. "The one-family home is something everyone aspires to, and the best place to get it is in the suburbs," the author of *The Levittowners* explained.[7]

Not everyone would agree with that assessment, however. After almost a decade of continual development, condominiums were becoming an ever-more popular form of home ownership. "Can home ownership mean apartment dwelling?" Josephine Ripley asked in the *Christian Science Monitor* in 1971, the short answer being yes. Like owning a house, a condo or a co-op offered refuge from the tyranny of rent but without having to mow a lawn, shovel snow, or the task of finding a plumber when a pipe exploded. (Monthly payments on a condominium were comparable to that of rent.) Buildings in which tenants owned apartments also tended to be in better shape than rentals, another reason to choose a condominium if one could afford the down payment. And just like a house, property taxes and mortgage interest could be deducted from income tax, yet more incentive to invest in an apartment if one didn't mind sharing walls with a neighbor. Condos were selling from $15,000 to $100,000, the sweet spot of those with middle incomes.[8]

It was well known that rents could be particularly egregious in Black communities, as landlords took advantage of redlining. There had been much study of the issue, but it remained unclear whether African Americans actually overpaid and, if so, by how much. In their 1972 article "Housing Market Discrimination, Home Ownership, and Savings Behavior" published in the *American Economic Review*, John F. Kain and John M. Quigley reported that, based on empirical evidence, "Blacks must pay between 5 and 10 percent more than whites in most urban areas for comparable housing."[9] In his edited 1972 *Tenants and the Urban Housing Crisis*, Stephen Burghardt showed how renters were fighting such discrimination in housing as a "tenants' rights" movement emerged in these activist times.[10]

More research was also being dedicated to another key dimension of African American housing—how a predominantly white urban neighborhood transitioned when Blacks moved in. Charles M. Barresi, a sociologist at the University of Akron, used Buffalo, New York, for his case study, generating interesting findings. "It starts with the sprinkling stage," he wrote in *Growth and Change*, during which trailblazers moved into a previously all-white area. These "initial in-movers" typically purchased large, rundown houses, but if renting, the landlord was usually an absentee owner. "Sprinkling" referred to the fact that the new residents were not concentrated on a particular block, as that occurred in the second stage, which Barresi called the "block strip invasion." This was when more white residents left and were replaced by African Americans, who either purchased or rented the houses from the previous owners. As this "invasion" gained momentum, the third and final stage, "filling-in," took place. That was when the last white residents abandoned the area, leaving the neighborhood predominantly or entirely African American.[11]

Some of the houses which African Americans took over were no doubt foreclosures or what were sometimes called "Sheriff sales." Overzealous buyers, Black or white, would frequently face foreclosure themselves, however, and for a number of reasons. These included purchasing a house whose monthly payment was beyond the means of the owner; not realizing how much it cost to run a house; owners learning that their dream house was less than a dream, meaning it or parts of it might fall down at any minute; and that the neighborhood was not a good one. Brokers, usually Black if the buyer was, were known to push their clients to sign, both to make a sale and, as Ed. R. Harris of the *Philadelphia Tribune* put it, "to see his fellows move up in the economic world and establish security for themselves and their families."[12]

Even if they were making their payments on time, African American homeowners might very well learn that the city had decided to seize their house so that the land they occupied could be used for what was sometimes referred to as "higher and better" purposes. This, more often than not, turned out to be an expressway, as for decades city planners looked first at "slum" areas upon which to build a speedy route through the metropolis. In his 1972

Black Home Ownership: A Sociological Study of Metropolitan Jacksonville, William Stacey examined the forced displacement of low-income Blacks in that city, finding that the removal of residents went much further than having a more efficient transportation system. Such residents were determined by the powers that be to be "alienated" and "socially unadjusted," making the dislodging a step toward their achieving "a more positive orientation to society."[13]

Near Crisis

Financial security was of course one of the primary reasons to be a homeowner. *Better Homes and Gardens* continued to provide practical advice to homeowners and aspiring ones, helping readers navigate the maze of their most valuable possession. In 1972, the magazine asked, "How much is your house worth today?," an apt question given the economic turbulence of recent years. The good news was that owners would likely be surprised at how much their home had appreciated, especially if they had purchased it a decade or two ago. Just like it was a good idea for investors to check the going prices of their stocks now and then, owners were advised to occasionally hire a professional appraiser to determine the current value of their house. Knowing that number revealed how well it was doing as an investment, how much borrowing power one had, how much it should be insured for, and, if desired or necessary, how much money it would likely reap in the marketplace.[14]

With the many financial benefits of home ownership, it wasn't surprising that those who hadn't joined the club were frustrated by the obstacles facing them. Construction costs, both materials and labor, continued to rise in the early seventies due to galloping inflation, and mortgage rates were high and still rising. It was estimated that every 1% increase in mortgage interest rates—the cost of borrowing money—eliminated between three and four million potential homeowners. Thinking smaller might be the answer, some believed, with talk of mobile homes or modest manufactured houses becoming the new normal for lower- and even average-income groups. Still, even a petite prefab had to sit on a piece of land, not an easy thing to find given that the cost of that too was going up. Also, planners were more scrutinizing about creating new residential areas or expanding existing ones than they once had been as concerns of overdevelopment and environmental impact grew.[15]

Union members might have been building houses for the affluent, but it was likely they couldn't afford one themselves. For this group of Americans, housing in the nation was "near crisis," the AFL-CIO reported in 1973 after investigating the matter. The median price of a new home was $31,500 and rising, the labor organization determined, and the cost of preowned homes in good shape had jumped sharply. (Only 1% of existing single-family houses were reportedly vacant and for sale.) Rents had gone up 31% over the past five years, and the conventional mortgage interest rate of about 8% was itself a dealbreaker for those hoping to become an investor rather than a tenant. If there was any statistic that made an impact, it was that a house in Levittown, Long Island that had cost $6,000 at midcentury was now priced at $40,000.[16]

In such a climate, was it any surprise that the concept of "urban homesteading" took root? Urban homesteading allowed or even encouraged citizens to occupy and ideally rehabilitate vacant properties. Federally owned properties might be sold for as little as $1 in the program, an intriguing idea that was gaining traction on the East Coast in the early 1970s. Slowing down "white flight" from inner cities was one of the goals of urban homesteading, another being the preservation of historic (some would just say old) buildings. Wilmington, Delaware, was reportedly the first city in the country to test the concept, with Philadelphia, Baltimore, and Boston following close behind. In theory, at least, urban homesteading could make home ownership possible for many at a lower cost than renting. After moving into her fixer-upper, one Wilmington woman got a $6,000 loan from a bank, hired a contractor, and began rehabilitating, with her loan payments less than what she was giving her landlord.[17]

Not everyone had such initiative and was willing to live in a construction zone for months or years, however, suggesting that urban homesteading would more likely just make a dent in turning renters into owners. Nearly forty million Americans owned residential property in 1970, according to Census data, significantly more than the 23.5 million renters. Americans had become a mobile people, however (moving company statistics showed that the average American family moved every five to seven years), suggesting that some were open to going back and forth between the two as circumstances dictated.[18]

What factors increased the probability that renters would become homeowners? That was a question more researchers were asking, as the answer had implications for both the private and public sectors. Geoffrey Carliner did what probably was the most thorough examination of the determinants of home ownership up to that point, publishing his findings in the journal *Land Economics* in 1974. Income, race, age, marital status, family size, and location were all considered, with the results not too surprising. Ownership was correlated with being white, married, and older and having a larger family and higher income, Carliner found, confirming that such demographics were associated with the ability and inclination to invest in property.[19]

Young, middle-income couples seeking to buy their first house clearly fell outside these criteria, making it predictable that a meeting with a loan officer would be a disappointing one. Money was tight in the still recessionary mid-1970s, with the credit squeeze making low-down-payment loans the first to be scratched. The National Association of Home Builders claimed that the average price of a new home was $37,000 in 1974, making the two or three grand that a young couple had likely socked away not enough as a down payment. Also, mortgage rates were approaching double digits, putting monthly payments out of reach for those without trust funds.[20] If that weren't enough, there were commuting costs that many forgot to include in their anticipated budget. Unless one could walk or bike to work, owning and driving a car could be an expensive proposition, and the recent oil embargo made just getting gasoline an uncertainty.[21]

Time tumbled its own numbers, determining that the money required to purchase and maintain an average house in a middle-class suburb had doubled between 1968 and 1974. Although that held on a national basis, housing costs actually varied dramatically by region and by city. Prices were lowest in the South and Southwest (no need for a basement), the notable exception being fast-growing Houston, which topped the list of major cities. The usual suspects—Washington, DC, San Francisco, New York, and Boston—were also among the costliest, while cities with declining populations—Baltimore, Detroit, and St. Louis—were the cheapest to buy and keep up.[22]

By 1975, it had become clear that the market was ready for an economy model home analogous to the AMC Gremlins, Chevrolet Vegas, and Ford Pintos that were coming out of Detroit. "The basic, no-frills house is on the way," pronounced Charles E. Dole, real estate editor of the *Christian Science Monitor*, a function of costs going one way and the economy the other. Also, many of the first wave of baby boomers had headed to college or had places of their own, making a big house unnecessary (and expensive to heat or air condition). Builders were responding to the market shift, offering cheaper houses made possible by shrinking square footage and cutting back on the amenities. Condominiums and town houses had become increasingly popular, but the overwhelming majority of Americans (93%, in fact) still preferred the single-family house, according to a survey by *Professional Builder*.[23]

The major reason Americans preferred a house over an apartment, even if the latter was owned, could be summed up in a single word: space. The average apartment had four rooms and ran about 900 square feet while the typical single-family house contained six rooms and ran roughly 1,500 square feet, quite a big difference, especially if one had a kid or two. The backyard and maybe a patio and garage were icing on the cake, and explained the deep desire for a house even if it meant going into debt for ten, fifteen, or thirty years.[24]

While owning a property was routinely labeled as a main path to financial security (and sometimes "financial freedom") and considered an excellent hedge against inflation, there were those who argued that renting was a better deal in terms of monthly living costs. This appeared to be true; on a short-term basis, renters had more cash to spend on leisure activities and such, just as Mrs. Adam Orzechowski of Brookline had convincingly argued. Over the long term, however (at least six years), owning was clearly the better deal, as long as one didn't move too often. Home ownership offered a lower cost of living in terms of dollar outflow, experts advised, yet more reason to scrounge as much money as possible even if the house in question was less than grand.[25]

An Unrealistic Goal

Even a stripped-down mini-house was beyond the reach of the economically disadvantaged, however, something that the Secretary of HUD shockingly admitted. Even if it appeared to be true, saying that some Americans did not have a chance at realizing the American dream was anathema, as it challenged one of the nation's core mythologies. "Home ownership for the poor is probably an unrealistic goal in today's economy," Carla A. Hills told members of the Washington Press Club in October 1975, who perhaps paused eating their lunches upon hearing this disturbing sentence. Even if those in poverty could somehow afford to buy a home, they couldn't afford to keep it, Hills continued. While such a claim went against the grain of popular rhetoric, the Secretary had evidence to back it up. There had been federal programs in place that had put poor people in homes but most of these recipients were ill-equipped to address the normal issues that came with home ownership, i.e., plumbing and heating problems. Some actually had abandoned the homes when major repairs were needed, leading Hills to make her stunning statement.[26]

The nation celebrated its Bicentennial in July 1976, of course, but reality set in soon after the last fireworks faded. The following month, it was reported that many Americans were simply giving up on the idea of becoming a homeowner, at least for the time being. Just 3.5% of Americans planned to buy a home in the next year, a survey by Citibank revealed, half the percentage of just five months earlier. The median price of a new home was now $43,000—twice what it had been in 1970. The fact was that fewer Americans were able to become homeowners and those that could had to use more of their income to do so. Construction costs and interest rates were, as usual, the major obstacles.[27] A 5% tax credit up to $2,000 made available by the federal government had made little impact, leading lawmakers to consider additional legislation that could possibly kickstart the moribund housing market.[28]

Even more depressing was that discrimination in home loans had hardly gone away. Congress had passed the Fair Housing Act in 1968, but three of the four federal agencies that regulate mortgage lending had never set forth antidiscrimination regulations, allowing them to continue to use race as a criterion in loaning money. All this came out in Senate Banking Commission hearings led by William Proxmire (D-WI) who called the record of these agencies (the Federal Reserve Board, the Federal Deposit Insurance Corporation, and the Comptroller of the Currency) "a disgrace." These agencies regulated themselves, so it was not surprising that zero acts of discrimination had been reported as having taken place since 1968 despite much evidence to the contrary.[29]

Not just African Americans were being treated unfairly by the federal government in real estate transactions but the poor and the elderly. Carla Hills's position on who made bad homeowners included not just the poor but senior citizens as well, alleged John Thompson, the president of the National Real Estate Broker Association. The run-up to the 1976 presidential election was approaching, and Thompson was preparing a position paper on the issue that he planned to present to both parties. The government was doing little to provide decent housing to millions of people, he asserted, hoping that at least one of the parties would adopt the problem as a campaign issue.[30]

Whether he knew it or not, John Thompson was tapping into one of the key questions of the times: How could there be such profound inequalities in what was perhaps the most prosperous society that ever existed? "The failure of advanced capitalism to eradicate the problem of poverty in an environment of affluence no doubt has helped to stimulate this latest surge of interest in distributional issues," Daniel D. Luria observed in the *Journal of Interdisciplinary History* in 1976, indirectly referencing what Thompson and others were saying with regard to the sorry state of housing for a segment of the population. Home ownership had long been promoted as a means to invest citizens with social power, and as an opportunity to become a partner in our capitalist system. Impossible to ignore inequalities contradicted that promise, however, a good example of the discord that could arise when myth bumped into reality.[31]

By 1977, America was rebounding from its economic slump defined by "stagflation," but one wouldn't know that from the news related to the housing situation. Just one family of four was financially able to buy a new home, HUD reported, the worst news being that, if current trends continued, a typical house could in four years cost a whopping $78,000. "The cost-squeeze on middle-income families is replacing the slum as the major problem in housing in this country," stated Bernard J. Frieden, one of the authors of the report. That was a debatable proposition, but there was no doubt that the wants and needs of the people were not being met in terms of where to live. There was hope that the Carter administration would take the problem more seriously than Nixon and Ford had done, but that remained to be seen.[32]

Were researchers and the media overreacting to the difficulty for average earners to become homeowners? After all, nearly two-thirds of American families did own their homes, a much higher percentage than any other industrialized country. Foreigners were amazed by how spacious and equipped houses were in the United States, another reason to think that all the griping about the cost of new homes could be based on standard American materialism.[33] Besides that, owning a home wasn't an entitlement or right that had been granted to each citizen by the Founding Fathers but (like happiness) simply a pursuit that many sought to achieve. Were Americans acting, in short, like spoiled brats, upset that the classic American dream hadn't come true for everyone?

The Carter administration, meanwhile, was focusing its attention on what was, despite Frieden's claim, the actual biggest problem—urban decline and lingering redlining. New regulations to prevent banks and other lending institutions from using race, ethnicity, or religion as a factor in mortgage money were in play, a sign that the administration was prioritizing the city over the suburbs in housing policy. An urban renaissance of sorts was taking place in the late 1970s, a backlash against suburban sprawl and the increasing recognition that automobile-centric communities were neither environmentally sound nor sustainable. Not just urban homesteaders but preservationists believed that abandoned brownstones were worth saving but banks were notoriously averse to make loans to people in "transitional" areas. A proposed Federal Home Loan Bank Board regulation would prohibit mortgage and credit practices that discriminated against older neighborhoods or buildings and mandate equal opportunity in home financing.[34]

Such a housing law was perfectly in sync with a social shift that was currently taking place. Whether called "new localism," "backyard democracy," or simply "politics of the '70s,'" a grassroots citizens' movement grounded in community activism was making itself felt. "The movement is non-ideological, racially integrated, fiercely proud, and rooted in the nation's neighborhoods," as Stewart Dill McBride of the *Christian Science Monitor* defined it in 1977. Big government had largely failed in addressing local problems, stirring citizens to take matters into their own hands, particularly with regard to home ownership. New localism was focused on the nitty-gritty aspects of an urban neighborhood—property taxes, utility bills, home mortgages, and police protection—and no doubt linked to both the concurrent "ethic revival" movement and "Roots" phenomenon.[35]

In Boston, new localism was being exemplified by a program called Urban Edge, in which abandoned houses were rehabilitated and then sold on the open market. Various public funding sources were available to complete such a worthy project, which not only saved once impressive houses but created an opportunity for those with moderate incomes to become homeowners. The quasi-private, nonprofit Urban Edge program in Boston that had begun in 1974 was centered in the Jamaica Plain neighborhood. Over four years, twenty-three single- and two-family houses had been rescued, providing homes for forty-five families who otherwise could not afford to possess a piece of the American dream.[36]

A Hugely Complicated Thing

A happy story, certainly, and one that illustrated some of the complexity of home ownership in the United States. In his 1978 book *The Builders*, Martin Mayer approached the subject head-on and revealed, should there be any doubt, that the American home was at the core of everyday life. "A home is a hugely complicated Thing," Mayer wrote, explaining that "it houses cooking, eating, washing, dressing and undressing, playing, reading, and entertaining." In 468 pages, the book traveled through what the author claimed was "America's biggest business" and, not coincidentally, the government's biggest problem. Indeed, over the decades, administration after administration had attempted to solve that problem but had, to put it generously, less than positive results. Romney's Operation Breakthrough program designed to make low-cost housing available on a mass scale had been a dismal failure, as had many other projects with good intentions but bad outcomes.[37]

The Builders was arguably the most ambitious study of the home ever written. (Mayer's focus was the United States but he also looked at housing in Great Britain, France, Denmark, Holland, and Finland.) His sweep included the more-common-than-one-might-think cases of fraud, role of unions, and influence of brokers, as well as the more pedestrian factors of land, zoning laws, and building codes. Case histories of public housing and urban renewal were typically less than sanguine affairs, the book made clear, and the fragmentary nature of the building business became readily apparent for those readers who weren't aware that it was highly regional.[38]

There were many takeaways to be had from *The Builders,* perhaps none more important than the difficulty for millions of Americans to become homeowners had seemingly made the desire to do so that much stronger. If nothing else, the appreciation of a house often kept up with inflation, which had been the scourge of the nation's economy over the past decade. Another major finding was that Americans were spending ever more of their income on housing but getting ever less for their money, a disturbing trend. Finally, despite the urban renaissance, many working-class families were moving out to the exurbs to live as a home in the suburbs became simply unobtainable.[39]

While *The Builders* made the case that a house was becoming an increasingly expensive proposition, the National Association of REALTORS® (the latter word was capitalized and registered) issued a report reassuring homeowners that they had made a wise financial decision. "A dollar invested in a single-family home in 1967 would have been worth $1.23 in purchasing power in 1977," one of the report's claims went, this 23% gain is a nice buffer against the inflation rate over the decade. Importantly, a home compared favorably to alternative investments, the NAR® pointed out. Bonds would have yielded 18%, and three other options—an interest-bearing savings account, stocks, or just keeping it as cash—would have actually made that dollar worth less ($.93, $.80, and $.55, respectively). The organization also pooh-poohed all the chatter about home prices going beyond the means of Americans with average incomes. While the cost of a home did rise, the median national income grew at the same rate, something often overlooked by critics.[40]

It was in 1978 that a switch appeared to be turned on regarding home ownership in America. Prices were continuing to go up, but more young people were buying homes, seemingly a major reversal of the tide. Industry insiders such as Joseph Benedict, vice-president of the United States League of

Savings Associations, were naturally rejoiced. Recent mortgage loan records from the organization contradicted "doomsayers who predict the end of the American dream of home ownership for all but the wealthy," the vice-president gleefully declared. 36% of all new home buyers were under thirty years old and 60% had incomes of less than $25,000, their data showed, challenging the popular belief that anyone able to afford a house in the late seventies had to be middle-aged and wealthy.[41]

That was good news, especially for those in the industry who had had a rough time of it through the 1970s. Hosea White, president of the Southwest Los Angeles Board of Realtors, certainly was thankful, as his regular "Real Estate Facts" column in the *Los Angeles Sentinel* published around Thanksgiving 1978 made clear. "The small band of colonists' dream of a new home in the land of opportunity has become a reality for millions of Americans," he wrote, believing that "their hope has become our heritage." Equating the European settlement of the New World with the ability to buy a three-bedroom ranch-style house or downtown condominium might have been somewhat of a stretch, but it was not an exaggeration to suggest that homeownership was at the heart of the American idea and experience.[42]

White also took time to point out how the percentage of homeowners in the United States exceeded that of other countries. In the United Kingdom ("the land many of the colonists abandoned," White added), just 50% of the people owned their own homes, and it was still lower in other countries like France (45%), Sweden (35%), West Germany (34%), and Switzerland (28%). That 65% of Americans were homeowners illustrated the degree to which we embraced what the colonists had crossed the ocean for. "As we gather around the table, we might remember how lucky we are that we call this nation home," White concluded, grateful that his industry appeared to be on the rebound.[43]

In an article cleverly titled "Gimme Shelter!" (after the Rolling Stones 1969 song), however, *Time* reported that while more Americans were buying homes, they were not coming cheap. "Everywhere in the U.S.—in towns and villages as well as in cities and suburbs—the cost of shelter is going through the roof," the piece began, with "runaway rents, galloping home prices and the difficulties of finding mortgages and paying sky-high interest rates" all part of the sticky situation. Between mid-1978 and mid-1979, the median price of a new single-family house rose 13% to $62,900, according to the NAR®, with no slowdown in sight. The cost of an existing house increased at the same rate over this same period of time, and mortgage interest surged by more than a percent-and-a-half.[44]

How were young couples able to buy homes in such a financial spiral? Not included in the mortgage loan records was the fact that many of the new homeowners had received significant help from their families, as without it they had little or no chance of purchasing their dream house. A good number of those less fortunate were overextending themselves by spending more than 25% of their pretax income on mortgage payments, thereby violating the commonly accepted credit rule. Simply put, the cost of a new home had in the late 1970s risen considerably faster than both personal income and inflation, leaving many Americans "house poor." A single paycheck was now often not enough to pay the mortgage and the rest of the bills, more couples were learning, with some of them deciding to postpone having children until they didn't have to worry about meeting all their expenses.[45]

Given all the sacrifices that had to be made, was becoming a homeowner even worth it, one had to ask? Perhaps and perhaps not, but another decade lay ahead that would help answer the question.

Notes

1 Diana Loercher, "And Know the Place for the First Time," *Christian Science Monitor*, June 21, 1978, 20.
2 Loercher, "And Know the Place for the First Time."
3 Richard A. Nenneman, "Action Needed Now," *Christian Science Monitor*, February 21, 1970, 14.
4 Nenneman, "Action Needed Now."
5 David R. Francis, "If You Want a House, Better Save Money," *Christian Science Monitor*, August 25, 1970, 12.
6 "A Place in the Suburbs?," *Christian Science Monitor*, February 16, 1971, B18. See George Sternlieb and Robert W. Lake, "Aging Suburbs and Black Home Ownership," *Annals of the American Academy of Political and Social Science*, November 1975, 105; Robert W. Lake, "Racial Transition and Black Home Ownership in American Suburbs," *Annals of the American Academy of Political and Social Science*, January 1979, 142.
7 "Suburbia: The New American Plurality," *Time*, March 15, 1971.
8 Josephine Ripley, "Can Home Ownership Mean Apartment Dwelling?," *Christian Science Monitor*, June 7, 1971, 14.
9 John F. Kain and John M. Quigley, "Housing Market Discrimination, Home Ownership, and Savings Behavior," *American Economic Review*, June 1972, 263.
10 Stephen Burghardt, ed., *Tenants and the Urban Housing Crisis* (Dexter, MI: The New Press, 1972).
11 Charles M. Barresi, "Racial Transition in an Urban Neighborhood," *Growth and Change*, July 1972, 16.
12 Ed. R. Harris, "On Real Estate," *Philadelphia Tribune*, July 25, 1972, 9.
13 Charles Wilder, "Review," *Social Work*, July 1973, 125; William Stacey, *Black Home Ownership: A Sociological Study of Metropolitan Jacksonville* (New York: Praeger Publishers, 1972).
14 "How Much is Your House Worth Today?," *Better Homes and Gardens*, September 1972, 24.
15 "Home Ownership Problems," *Atlanta Daily World*, August 5, 1973, 4.
16 Ed Townsend, "Labor Study Finds U.S. Housing Near Crisis," *Christian Science Monitor*, August 6, 1973, 9.
17 "'Urban Homesteading' Underway in Boston—But Some are Skeptical," *Christian Science Monitor*, January 10, 1974, 7. For more on "White flight," and its relation to home prices and income, see Leah P. Boustan and Robert A. Margo, "A Silver Lining to White Flight? White Suburbanization and African-American Homeownership, 1940-1980," *Journal of Urban Economics*, August 23, 2013.
18 Federal National Mortgage Association, *The Fannie Mae Guide to Buying, Selling & Financing Your Home* (New York: Doubleday & Co., 1973).

19 Geoffrey Carliner, "Determinants of Home Ownership," *Land Economics*, May 1974, 109; See also Raymond J. Struyk and Sue Marshall, "The Determinants of Household Home Ownership," *Urban Studies*, October 1974, 289.
20 Martin Skala, "Mortgage-Financing Squeeze Hits Young Couples the Hardest," *Christian Science Monitor*, June 12, 1974, 5.
21 Robert Edwards, "Add Commuting into House Cost," *Christian Science Monitor*, June 12, 1974, F4.
22 "Doubling the Bills," *Time*, October 28, 1974.
23 Charles E. Dole, "Hard Times Bring Back No-frill, Small Homes," *Christian Science Monitor*, April 11, 1975, 27.
24 "City Welcomes Launching of Big Chicken Balloon," *Atlanta Daily World*, August 26, 1976, 13.
25 Robert Edwards, "Analyzing Your Investments, Buying or Renting," *Christian Science Monitor*, October 6, 1976, 22.
26 "Home Ownership by Poor 'Unrealistic' Says Hill," *Louisville Defender*, October 2, 1975, A13.
27 "Slowing the Housing Escalator," *Christian Science Monitor*, August 20, 1976, 28.
28 "Housing Starts Still in Economic Basement," *Christian Science Monitor*, November 21, 1975, 6.
29 "Little Action Vs. Discrimination in Home Loans," *Christian Science Monitor*, July 21, 1975, 10.
30 "Real Estate Brokers President Assails Government' Insensitivity," *New York Amsterdam News*, August 21, 1976, A2.
31 Daniel D. Luria, "Wealth, Capital, and Power: The Social Meaning of Home Ownership," *Journal of Interdisciplinary History*, Autumn 1976, 261.
32 "One Family in Four Able to Buy a New Home Now," *Christian Science Monitor*, March 16, 1977, 20.
33 "Housing: Its Outasight," *Time*, September 12, 1977, 50.
34 "Erasing 'Redlining,'" *Christian Science Monitor*, November 14, 1977, 32.
35 Stewart Dill McBride, "Little Guys Unite in 'New Localism,'" *Christian Science Monitor*, November 18, 1977, 16.
36 Jack Miner, "Urban Edge Fixes Houses, Helps Home Buyers," *Christian Science Monitor*, November 25, 1977, 12.
37 Charles E. Dole, "Housing: The Biggest Business—and Problem," *Christian Science Monitor*, May 3, 1978, 15; Martin Mayer, *The Builders* (New York: W.W. Norton & Co., 1978).
38 Dole, "Housing: The Biggest Business—and Problem."
39 Dole, "Housing: The Biggest Business—and Problem."
40 Hosea White, "Real Estate Facts," *Los Angeles Sentinel*, May 11, 1978, D8.
41 "Many Young People Now Buying New Homes," *Christian Science Monitor*, May 24, 1978, 12.
42 Hosea White, "Real Estate Facts," *Los Angeles Sentinel*, November 16, 1978, D7.
43 White, "Real Estate Facts."
44 "Gimme Shelter! But Where?," *Time*, July 23, 1979.
45 "Gimme Shelter! But Where?"

7 A Fading Fantasy

"Home ownership is a symbol of the family unit and neighborhood and is essential if we're to have social and economic stability in our land."

Ronald Reagan, 1981

In its September 1984 issue, *Redbook* magazine offered readers to take a quiz in order to determine their "financial personality," something that would help them decide whether to keep renting or try to become a home buyer. The five multiple-choice questions related to how one would handle a drippy faucet, the likelihood of a job transfer, relative attachment to a particular neighborhood or community, how much money one had saved, and the degree to which tax breaks would be of benefit.[1]

After taking the short quiz (which had been provided by Manufacturers Hanover Trust, a bank), readers learned what their score meant. Readers scoring six to eight were "ready to own your own home both psychologically and financially," while those with a score of nine to eleven were advised to "take more time to rethink your needs." Those scoring twelve to fifteen, meanwhile, were told that "home ownership isn't for everyone, and it looks as if your priorities lie elsewhere."[2]

Although it was standard women's magazine fluff, the pithy *Redbook* quiz nicely illustrated that it was a critical juncture in the history of the American home. Through the early 1980s, the American dream of home ownership seemed to be all but disappearing due to the high prices of houses and steep mortgage interest rates. As the economy recovered in the latter part of the decade, however, it was for some a return to the glory days of the post-war years, evidenced by the increasing number of McMansions appearing on Main Street, USA. For many others, however, home ownership remained a major struggle, a reflection of the growing divide between the haves and have-nots in the country.

The Orgy Is Over

As the Reagans moved into the White House, most Americans were hesitant to invest in a new home, and with good reasons. In fact, just a couple

DOI: 10.4324/9781003481485-8

of weeks into the new decade, it was reported that the Federal National Mortgage Association, the largest supplier of mortgage funds in the country, was planning to launch the first advertising campaign in its forty-two-year history. Fannie Mae, as it was commonly called, was experiencing a drop in mortgages due to the current slumping housing market and hoped that a campaign designed to, as the *New York Times* expressed it, "stimulate the idea of home ownership and how to attain it" might incentivize renters to talk with a banker or other lender. Putting $1 million into newspapers and magazine ads would be money well spent, top officials of the Washington, DC-based, federal government-backed organization believed, although having to convince Americans that owning a piece of property was certainly an unusual thing.[3]

Given the depth of the situation, however, a million dollars may not have been nearly enough. "The housing crisis for millions of Americans, color no matter, is becoming worse and worse," an editor for the African American *Chicago Defender* wrote, thinking that the amount of money now needed to buy a house (new or old) was beyond most of the middle class. The price of condominiums too had jumped, making that option untenable for those with average incomes or borrowing power. Only the well-to-do, or perhaps their children who had found a very nice gift under their Christmas tree, would be able to get the kind of mortgage that Fannie Mae would soon be advertising.[4]

Happily, some local communities were recognizing the problem and taking action. A program called "inclusionary zoning" was gaining traction which enabled low- and moderate-income families to buy a home in a new development for half or even less of the market price. Developers, in exchange, got fast-tracked through the usual red tape and were granted more lenient building standards, a welcome thing that was worth the discounting. A number of states on both coasts were offering the program, although it represented just a drop in the bucket of what many agreed was a true housing crisis.[5]

Indeed, the costs of getting a mortgage at the time were so high that *Time* declared that the roof of the nation's housing had "caved in." "The all-American dream of home ownership is turning into a black nightmare," the magazine stated as new housing starts dropped precipitously. The numbers were the worst since those of the 1970s recession and permits were falling still further, suggesting that things were gettting only worse. The Federal Reserve's credit squeeze was mostly to blame, experts held; most prospective home buyers simply didn't have enough money to borrow what was being required by lending institutions and, even for some of them, the rates were too high to make the monthly payments.[6]

In an article published in the *Journal of Consumer Affairs*, Mary Winter found hard data to support the other evidence that young families' pursuit of their American dream had become, in her words, "increasingly difficult." An owner-occupied, single-family detached home was in the United States a prescription for "cultural norms," according to Winter, with many studies over the years backing up that claim, regardless of one's age, class, race, or ethnicity.[7]

If the media were to be believed, however, that staple of the American experience was on the brink of becoming something of the past. The median price of a new home more than doubled through the 1970s, and the median prices of existing housing had risen by more than 50%. Paradoxically, perhaps, home ownership in the country had never been higher, with about two-thirds of Americans still prescribing to that "cultural norm." The Iowa State professor found that among young families, it was higher income (either through both spouses working or one with a high-paying job) that made it possible to own property.[8]

While the desire to own a home cut across all social divisions, including race, the fact was that "the probability of home ownership is considerably lower for Blacks than it is for comparable whites throughout the United States." That was the conclusion of Mary R. Jackman and Robert W. Jackman who published their findings in the journal *Social Forces*. The professors (she of the University of Michigan and he of Michigan State) also found in their study that outside the South, African American owner-occupied homes were valued considerably less than those of comparable whites. "Home ownership is an intrinsic part of the American dream," they began their article, ending it by stating that "the cumulative constraints facing Blacks in the housing market constitute a serious impediment to their participation in the mainstream of American society."[9]

Although it was clear that the cards were stacked against them in housing, African American homeowners were often blamed for bringing down real estate values and for not properly maintaining their properties. Ted Baker, a top developer based in Los Angeles, objected to such accusations, insisting that Blacks did indeed have pride in home ownership. Baker, who was Black, cited research that revealed why urban African Americans were getting what he called a "bum rap." Housing designed for this market were poorly constructed compared to that intended for white homeowners in the suburbs, making it not too surprising that they were worth less and appeared shabby. Developers commonly bought up abandoned buildings on the cheap and then dressed them up a bit for resale, but the improvements were only cosmetic (leaky pipes were usually left untouched). "Pride in home ownership fades as the victim realizes that he is unable to secure the funds needed to really put the house in livable shape," Baker explained, with the owner having little choice but to walk away from the property.[10]

Buying a used home and hoping for the best was the only real option for those renters without a lot of money in the bank. By 1980, the median price of all homes had surpassed $60,000, with just a third selling for under $50,000. An accepted guideline was to designate one week's pay per month as the share of the family budget for housing costs, with mortgage lenders generally using about $30,000 in annual income to qualify for a $50,000 house. Just a quarter of American families made that much money at the time, however, explaining why there was so much discussion about the American dream now being in the nation's rear window. The percentage of African Americans earning $30,000 a year was only 12%, making the dream that much more elusive for them.[11]

Based on such figures, it was understandable how those with some grasp of the history of housing in America argued that it was the end of an era. During the Great Depression, the federal government had put in place an array of successful measures, including more affordable and insured mortgages with longer repayment periods and the savings and loan association, to protect Americans from losing their homes and allow others to buy new ones. Turning the country into "a nation of homeowners" carried an economic, social, and political agenda grounded in providing a sense of security for middle-class (and white) families. Although such programs were designed to promote democracy (and discourage subversive activity), homeowners quickly realized that owning real estate was a great way to make money. Property became viewed as not just a place to live but as an alternative investment to the up-and-down stock market, with appreciation almost guaranteed due to inflation.[12]

That model appeared to be broken, however, as Karen W. Arenson observed in the *New York Times* in 1981. "It was an orgy, and the orgy is over," she declared, with high interest rates and, ironically, galloping inflation, putting an end to the wild party. "It marks the end of a golden era of housing," Arenson continued, the once efficient system of lending money to hopeful homeowners now a mess in an era of severe financial constraints. For the white middle class, the half-century run was by all measures an amazing one—the envy of the world, in fact—but the workings of the banking business had changed dramatically over the years. The federal government was showing all signs of prioritizing industry rather than housing, leaving citizens to fend for themselves in a daunting marketplace.[13]

A Quiet Revolution

If there was any good news to be found in this rather bleak picture, it was that home ownership was increasingly crossing gender lines. Single, professional women making good money were buying condominiums in significant numbers, and for the same reasons that buyers had always considered. "I bought it for investment, for a tax break, and for the pleasure of owning a home," said one Chicago woman after purchasing a condo, adding that she was "sick of throwing money away on rent." Never married, divorced, and widowed women accounted for a third of condominium sales and a tenth of the house sales in the nation in 1981, according to the NAR ®, and represented the fastest-growing segment in the housing market.[14]

Similar numbers were reported for cooperative apartments in New York City, with a major shift in the gender split having taken place there since the mid-seventies. It was then that federal laws had been passed banning gender-based discrimination in lending and home buying, and the feminist movement no doubt also played a part in balancing out the historically male-dominated real estate market.[15]

Media targeted to women took note of the trend. "Yes, you can buy a home!" exclaimed Leah Fletcher for *Essence*, thinking that "a quiet revolution" is going on in the housing market." In 1966, just 15% of women who were heads of families owned a home, according to HUD. But a decade later, 48% did, a huge leap in a relatively short period of time. Women had always played a major, often leading role in the acquisition and maintenance of a house; "our intuitive nature is an asset in selecting and buying property," Fletcher proposed. Now with equal access to credit, at least legally, more women were taking advantage of the benefits of home ownership, i.e., the building of equity, financial credibility, provision of a tax shelter, buffer against inflation, and the ability to plant roots in a community.[16]

With homes costing too much for the majority of Americans, however, alternatives to the traditional single-family dwelling were being sought. If it really was the end of an era, as many experts were saying, a new and different kind of residential landscape would have to emerge. Because of the money crunch, along with more women working and there being fewer children in households, some were predicting that the two-family house would serve as the new model. "Older people in big suburban houses are teaming up as housemates, both for splitting costs and for company," Marshall Ingwerson wrote for the *Christian Science Monitor* in 1981, thinking, "the grass may be greener if it's shared." Denser living arrangements made sense not just for economic reasons but for social ones, sociologists were pointing out, as feelings of isolation were not unusual in the sprawling burbs.[17]

Could the classic version of the American dream based on Jefferson's independent farmer be replaced by one that seemed more, well, foreign? Perhaps, especially if one looked at the latest data on home ownership costs across the nation provided by the NAR®. San Francisco, Los Angeles, New York City, and Washington, DC were the most expensive places to buy a home, not surprisingly, with St. Louis being the cheapest of any metropolitan area. Between 1978 and 1981, total housing costs had risen 60% on a national basis, with some areas doubling. Interest rates and prices were of course the biggest factors, but real estate taxes, hazard insurance, and utilities also made bunking with a neighbor an enticing possibility.[18]

Sharing a home with another family certainly made some sense but it did challenge one of the pillars of American life, something Margaret Daly astutely recognized. "Throughout American history, home ownership has been a symbol of both personal achievement and community stability," she posited in *Better Homes and Gardens* in 1982, adding that "but to many young people today, the dream of a one-family home on its own piece of land may seem like a fading fantasy."[19]

It could be seen how over the course of two generations, Americans and the federal government had formed a partnership of sorts, the common goal being for citizens to own rather than rent where one chose to live. The latter had offered attractive financial perks to the former in order to strengthen the democratic foundation of the country, a quid pro quo that had worked out well, unless one was a person of color. 44% of Americans owned their occupancy in 1940 while 65% did in 1980, this 50% gain in four decades likely making elected officials sleep better at night. "Owning a home provided families with roots and purpose," as Daly nicely explained why it had become a national priority, the deal also encouraging "a commitment to schools and churches, and a concern for community wellbeing."[20]

As the reality of owning faded in the early eighties, however, there was a flurry of attention devoted to the advantages of renting. "Renting doesn't mean abandoning the home-of-your-own dream," Thomas Tilling comforted readers of *Parents*, "it's putting you in a good position for when the climate is right." Tilling was right in that there were good and bad times to invest in real estate, a reflection of the natural highs and lows of an inherently fluid marketplace. For many, at this particular point in time, deferring ownership could be a wise choice, he pointed out. A petite apartment could be fine for smaller families, for example, with savings put away for a larger house and furnishings if or when more kids came along. Apartment living also allowed one to get to know neighbors well and offered great flexibility, the latter a good thing for those in the early stages of a career whose jobs might take them anywhere.[21]

While renting was not the first choice of most Americans, it was "an increasingly prevalent option these days," Amelia A. Newcomb of the *Christian Science Monitor* reported. Those looking at condominiums after realizing they were priced out of a house often found them to be small, expensive, in an unsafe neighborhood, or all the above. Renting could solve all these problems, making it a practical choice until interest rates and perhaps price tags fell somewhat. Enough Americans were making that conclusion for the rate of home ownership to flatten out and perhaps even start to decline, the first time that had happened for as long as anyone could remember.[22]

Were Americans giving up on the dream of home ownership? Not by a long shot, the Federal National Mortgage Association (FNMA) made clear after it completed a study on the matter in 1982. While affordability was indeed a great concern, making two paychecks almost a necessity, most renters had every intention of owning a property at some point in the future, according to the study's findings. A home should be not just a place to live but an investment, the respondents tended to say, and ownership really did allow for a deeper planting of roots in a community than could renting.[23]

Given the "hidden" (more accurately ignored) costs of home ownership, renting could be a blessing in disguise. While the financial benefits were typically emphasized, the truth was that a house could suck up money like a top-of-the-line Hoover vacuum. How could one know that a month after moving in, the plumbing would go haywire, those beautiful pines would suffer something called needle blight, and a letter from the city would arrive announcing a rise in property taxes? Add those expenses to the expected costs of maintenance, utilities, and insurance and one might begin to wonder if the American dream was as dreamy as imagined.[24]

Renters waiting for prices to go down were likely disappointed after perusing the real estate section of their local newspaper and finding that costs were continuing to go up. In May 1984, a milestone of sorts was reached when the Commerce Department reported that the average price of a new home was now in the six figures. In 1965, the price had been $20,000, and a decade later, it had increased to $42,600. Now, however, it was $101,000, a number that must have been seen as astronomical for those with moderate or low incomes. Fewer than three of ten families could afford to buy a home based on that figure and current mortgage rates, according to *Time*, whereas seven of ten could do so in 1950. Other analysts put the current percentage not at 30% but just 5%, which was likely more accurate.[25]

Fully aware that most of their customers couldn't qualify, banks and savings and loan associations were coming up with new forms of financing, such as adjustable-rate mortgages. Juggling the numbers could only do so much, however, as the full principal had to be paid at some point, no matter what. Developers, meanwhile, were building smaller and thus cheaper houses, trying to attract the lower end of the market.[26] Were tiny homes the solution to the nation's housing problem?

A Kind of Tradition

Probably not, given Americans' historical longing for land and to not be, to paraphrase a popular Cole Porter song, fenced in. In fact, despite all the imposing financial barriers, "the strength of the dream of owning a house remains undiminished," Matthew L. Wald of the *New York Times* reported in 1985. High interest rates and seemingly exorbitant construction costs notwithstanding, "the prospect of owning and living in a freestanding house on its own land is an enduring element in American aspirations," Wald continued. The classic American dream was certainly a resilient one, also impervious to the shift towards smaller, more fragmented families for whom condominiums, co-ops, or simply renting would likely make more financial sense. Wald's conclusion was based on results from a recent *New York Times*/CBS News Poll which showed that, much like previous generations, ownership of a house was a goal of most Americans.[27]

Nadine Brown of the *Michigan Chronicle*, Detroit's African American newspaper, didn't need any data to say much the same thing. A couple months after Wald presented the poll findings Brown wrote:

> There are many citizens of our community who have long yearned for home ownership and still live in the hope that it will happen one day. It seems to be a kind of tradition, and despite the fact that it's quite a chore to make ends meet, they hang on to the dream.[28]

In writing her piece, Brown was happy to report that there was reason for such hope. The city of Detroit along with two lending institutions had created a program that enabled prospective homeowners to obtain mortgages on "distressed" properties. Over the past four years, the New Owner Purchase and Repair Program (NOPAR) has led to the rehabilitation of 56 homes in the city worth $1.6 million, a great example of what could happen when public and private interests worked together to achieve a common goal.[29]

Thomas Tilling, who had espoused the benefits of renting in *Parents* in 1982, continued to offer a somewhat contrarian view. A home and a house were not the same thing, he pointed out three years later in the same magazine, warning readers not to get caught up in the strong emotions attached to the single-family house. The economy was rebounding nicely from the recession of the early 1980s, which had been triggered by tight monetary policies designed to control inflation. Fearing that it may be now or never, many had felt the need to buy a home during those years but, according to Tilling, "hysteria has diminished." There were legitimate financial arguments against buying a home, he maintained, challenging the prevailing sentiment that one wasn't quite fully American if one didn't own a piece of the country.[30]

With the economic turnaround of the mid-1980s, the American home appeared to be entering yet another era in its history. Builders were offering a significantly greater variety of houses to buyers, something *Better Homes and Gardens* took note of in 1986. "Contemporary architecture has broken the box," the magazine declared, claiming that there were "no more houses stamped from a pattern named 'Anywhere USA.'" Combining comfort with the latest technology was the common thread, although builders were prepared to personalize houses to fit the particular lifestyles of their occupants. Luxury bungalows (for retired couples), easy-to-care-for condos (for "hard-at-it city dwellers"), and the open-plan concept (growing families) were just a few options that buyers could now choose from. A major segment of the market was baby boomers, many of whom were moving up from the starter homes they may have bought in the 1970s.[31]

Also, home improvement had grown to a phenomenal $71 billion a year business by 1986, with no end in sight regarding how much money Americans would spend on renovating their dream house.[32] The booming home improvement industry was a sign of Americans' new obsession with fixing up or adding to their abode. (The television show *This Old House* debuted in 1979.) A return to traditional values was certainly playing a part in this ushering in of a new era of domesticity, even among previously countercultural baby boomers.

While there were innovations in houses that would put a smile on the face of the most discriminating of "yuppies"—multi-station kitchens, whirlpool tubs, skylights—regionalism remained alive and well. Much like depicted in a feature article in *Life* magazine in 1955, state-of-the-art builders were drawing on housing styles that were indigenous to a particular part of the country. New England Cape Cods, Midwestern farmhouses, Southern frame houses, Southwest missions, and Western ranches were all being constructed regardless of location and often with a modern twist. "Today's best housing borrows freely from the past, but looks forward, too," the magazine stated, adding that, "the American dream is alive and well—and changing."[33]

More evidence of that latter claim could certainly be found in Brooklyn as the Nehemiah Project gained traction. The project was the most ambitious of the community-based private housing initiatives that were appearing across the country targeted to low-income families. Under Reaganomics, the federal government had abandoned large-scale public housing, the thinking being that the tens of billions of dollars being spent on it was throwing good money after bad. The President believed a market-driven approach was a better path to take to address the housing crisis, although involvement from local communities was essential if success was to be achieved.[34]

That appeared to be the case with the Nehemiah Project, in which a coalition of powerful Brooklyn churches convinced Mayor Ed Koch to provide thirty blocks of vacant land on which to build. (The name of the project was inspired by the Old Testament character who was said to restore Jerusalem after the city was destroyed by the Babylonians). That, along with some creative financing (a below-market-rate first mortgage and interest-free second mortgage), was allowing families to buy a house at less cost than renting a public housing apartment, a win-win for all.[35]

A much-welcomed thing, of course, but there was an even greater problem woven into the housing crisis: homelessness. The precise numbers were unknown, but it was believed that in 1988 there were anywhere from 300,000 to three million Americans without homes. (The former was the federal government figure, the latter that of low-income housing advocates). Either way, it was too many, especially given the fact that about one in five homeless were children. Single mothers with children under five years of age were the most likely demographic within homelessness, many of whom had homes but were now living in shelters.[36]

The large and growing number of homeless Americans was viewed as a symbol of the sorry state of housing in the nation, this despite the whirlpools and skylights being installed in wealthier citizens' homes. The increasing economic polarization of the country, i.e., widening division between the haves and have-nots, could easily be detected in the landscape of housing. *Better and Homes and Gardens*, a magazine that usually devoted its pages to decorating how-tos and matters like protecting rose bushes from pesky aphids, was moved enough to devote a whole issue to the problem. Margaret Daly again took on the challenge, addressing everything from the plight of first-time home buyers to the disintegration of low-income housing. "It's time to renew our commitment to decent and affordable housing for all Americans," she wrote, recalling Congress's 1949 proclamation to strive for "a decent home and suitable living environment for every American family."[37]

Almost four decades later, Congress was at least studying the issue by forming a twenty-six-member, Senate-appointed National Housing Task

Force. It was, after all, impossible to completely ignore the problem given the growing number of homeless people on the streets in many cities. Behind each one there were many more right on the edge of homelessness, James Rouse, the chair of the committee (and big-time commercial developer), told Congress, just a lost job or medical emergency away from losing their home. Income was running behind rent, an equation that almost guaranteed more homelessness, and the costs to become homeowners remained too high for young adults. Home ownership had peaked in 1980 at 65.6% but had since slid to 63.8%, a disturbing trend.[38]

Solving the housing crisis was admittedly like turning a big ship around but worth the effort, most agreed. Reintroducing the kind of federal housing subsidies that had been scuttled by the Reagan Administration seemed to be the only real solution, and a new Housing Opportunity Program modeled after the Nehemiah Project would be of great help as well.[39] Meanwhile, the Reagans were moving into their new home in "old Bel Air," a decidedly tony part of Los Angeles. Their one-acre, $2.5 million estate ($31 million today) was right down the road from Elizabeth Taylor's and Zsa Zsa Gabor's digs, a sign that the couple understood the first rule of choosing a property—location, location, location. Best of all, the Reagan's didn't even have to buy the place, which included not just a three-car garage but two servants' rooms. It was acquired by an investment group who kindly leased it back to the couple, no doubt at a rate that would not be offered to the average Joe.[40]

Homeowning, Hollywood-Style

Quite fittingly, Los Angeles was a prime example of the two very different kinds of home ownership taking place in the country in the late 1980s. In Bel Air and other top-of-the-market neighborhoods like Beverly Hills and Brentwood, houses were selling in the millions of dollars, many of them with heated swimming pools, tennis courts, and giant hedges to keep the curious from taking a peek. On the other side of town, however, it was a major struggle for those with middle incomes and working-class families to buy a modest house, in part because of the lack of inventory. Black neighborhoods like Compton, Watts, Ladera Heights, and Baldwin Hills were still suffering from the white flight of the 1950s and 1960s, specifically a dearth of new construction. In Compton, for example, just 20% of the existing housing was built after 1960, as most developers simply had no interest in investing in the area.[41]

Happily, Congress had in 1987 passed legislation allowing tenants of public housing to buy their apartments or equivalent shares in a cooperative, an opportunity of which more folks were taking advantage. In Washington, DC, for example, residents of the Kenilworth projects began to purchase co-op shares in the buildings, although it was a victory that did not come easy. For seven years, Kimi Gray, a tenant, had fought to get her neighbors to organize and demand the right to own the apartment they occupied rather than continue renting. Kenilworth residents would have five years to buy shares, it was finally agreed, a story that was serving as a model for other public-housing communities. "This happens when people want change," Gray simply told *Time* in 1988.[42]

Even those with solid middle-class incomes were finding it difficult to become homeowners at the tail end of the eighties. Saving enough money to make the down payment was key, but for many, it was one step forward, two steps back. It was challenging to keep up with rising interest rates, making the money one had socked away not enough when they jumped a point or so. Realizing that compromises had to be made if it was going to happen, some renters were doing any or all of the following: lowering expectations, getting some assistance from family members, or assuming a risky kind of mortgage. "The house has no garage and no driveway, the bathroom's miniature, and the whole place is smaller than our apartment," said one new homeowner in Skokie, Illinois, after having done all three of those options to stop paying rent.[43]

Again, Los Angeles provided an entirely different picture of the real estate scene in the country. In 1999, television producer Aaron Spelling paid $10.25 million (in cash) to purchase what had been Bing Crosby's mansion in Holmby Hills. Spelling then proceeded to demolish it in order to build a $30 million "French manor," complete with a bowling alley. In Beverly Hills, meanwhile, a Japanese surgeon was taking apart Ronald Reagan's former bungalow to construct a "Moroccan palace." That house would have an art gallery, ten bathrooms, and two reflecting pools (not to mention five domes). "In the platinum ZIP codes of Holmby Hills, Bel Air and Beverly Hills, the noise of wretched excess is everywhere," *Time* noted.[44]

While "homeowning, Hollywood-style" represented the extreme end of the spectrum, "teardowns" were becoming standard operating procedure for the rich who want something bigger, better, and, most of all, newer. Hundreds of older homes in Los Angeles were meeting such an ignominious fate, meaning the number across the country had to be in the thousands. The taste of these new owners was highly questionable, but the rules of the marketplace were what they were. It was true that the cost of restoring or expanding a vintage house often exceeded that of putting up a brand-new one, but the homes being built were enormous by any measure. It was not unusual for 10,000 square-feet houses to replace 2,000 square-feet ones (the average size in the United States), making them stand out, quite literally, in what had been an older neighborhood.[45]

Beyond the great disparity in scale, these new behemoths (soon labeled "McMansions") often included amenities fitting with people who could be considered modern royalty. You name it—recording studios, tanning parlors, double kitchens (one for parties), and chandeliers (motorized, of course)—were part of interiors, while outside one might find polo grounds, putting greens, petting zoos, heliports, waterfalls, and, shades of Walt Disney, a miniature railroad surrounding the property. There had always been mansions, of course, but this over-the-top version did indeed seem excessive, particularly given the strain so many Americans were experiencing to try to get their diminutive slice of the pie.[46]

Indeed, some first-time buyers were pursuing a variety of creative strategies to get that slice. A fixer-upper was one way to go; true bargains could be had for those willing to do considerable work to what had once been a nice house. Bringing older dwellings up to code could be the first order of business as, after a century or so, walls and roofs tended to have their own sense of direction. Very attractive loans could be had for restoring a house in a historic district, however, although buyers had better be prepared to receive a hands-on education in the ABCs of construction. In such cases, hiring a professional contractor was usually a very wise decision, something realized after learning that the necessary repairs went much further than slapping on a new coat of paint.[47]

Purchasing a duplex was another option for those unable to afford a single-family house. There was actually a considerable number of multifamily housing communities around the country, many in ideal locations which would otherwise be unaffordable. Looking at such homes, one wouldn't know that there were in fact two attached dwellings, and duplexes typically included the proverbial two-car garage as well as a full-size laundry room and private courtyard entrance.[48]

Finally, there was the kit home. Building a house oneself from plans and materials obviously saved much money on construction costs, and sellers of kit homes usually were amenable to providing free consultation when asked. Traditional lenders were not keen on kit homes, however, making some creative financing usually necessary. That was the easy part, however, as assembly was a lot tougher than playing with Lego. First, there was excavation and then foundation work, followed by the putting up of the exterior. Then came doors, floors, and ceilings and, after that, insulation and wiring. Painting and staining came last, assuming one hadn't given up and called in a pro. As with real contractors, it was wise to build in a 50% overage in the time it would take to complete construction.[49]

The steps Americans were taking to have a home of their own reflected the power of the mythology of the American dream in real peoples' lives. The fact that home ownership had declined through the decade perhaps made the desire to buck the odds that much stronger, particularly among young adults. (In 1973, according to a study by the Joint Economic Committee of Congress, 23.4% of people under age twenty-five owned a home while in 1988 that number had dropped to 15.5%.) The average down payment for first-time home buyers had risen more than 50% through the 1980s, and average interest rates had climbed from 6% in the 1960s to over 10% by 1989.[50]

Many at the time seemed shocked to learn that home ownership in the United States had fallen backward, as such a thing went directly against our ethos of progress, but, given those financials, was it really any surprise? One last decade of the 20th century remained, however, offering the chance for Americans to reverse the tide of home ownership.

Notes

1 "Rent or Buy?," *Redbook*, September 1984, G-4.
2 "Rent or Buy?"
3 "Ayer Campaign to Push Idea of Home Ownership," *New York Times*, January 18, 1980, D11.
4 "The Housing Crisis," *Chicago Defender*, February 23, 1980, 8.
5 Brad Knickerbocker, "Home Ownership Impossible? One Plan Cracks Door Open," *Christian Science Monitor*, April 7, 1980, 4.
6 "Housing's Roof Caves In," *Time*, April 28, 1980.
7 Mary Winter, "Managerial Behavior of Young Families in Pursuit of Single-Family Home Ownership," *Journal of Consumer Affairs*, Summer 1980, 82.
8 Winter, "Managerial Behavior of Young Families in Pursuit of Single-Family Home Ownership."
9 Mary R. Jackman and Robert W. Jackman, "Racial Inequalities in Home Ownership," *Social Forces*, June 1980, 1221.
10 Lee Ivory, "Blacks Have Home Ownership Pride," *New Pittsburgh Courier*, July 5, 1980, 11.
11 William H. Morris, "The Disappearing American Dream," *Baltimore Afro-American*, March 21, 1981, 12.
12 Karen W. Arenson, "Housing: After 50 Years, the Heyday is Over," *New York Times*, March 29, 1981, F1. See Terry C. Blum and Paul William Kingston, "Home Ownership and Social Attachment," *Sociological Perspectives*, April 1984, 159.
13 Arenson, "Housing: After 50 Years, the Heyday is Over."
14 Nan Robertson, "Single Women as Homeowners," *New York Times*, April 23, 1981, A1.
15 Robertson, "Single Women as Homeowners."
16 Leah Fletcher, "Yes, You Can Buy a Home!," *Essence*, May 1982, 128.
17 Marshall Ingwerson, "Home Ownership: The Grass May Be Greener If It's Shared," *Christian Science Monitor*, August 11, 1981, B6. For more on changing patterns of household formation and the family, see Daniel A. Cox, "Emerging Trends and Enduring Patterns in American Family Life," *Survey Center on American Life*, February 9, 2022. https://www.americansurveycenter.org/research/emerging-trends-and-enduring-patterns-in-american-family-life/.
18 "Home Ownership Costs 'Devastating,'" *Weekend Chicago Defender*, August 22, 1981, 30.
19 Margaret Daly, "Housing Costs: Reshaping the American Dream," *Better Homes and Gardens*, June 1982, 33.
20 Daly, "Housing Costs: Reshaping the American Dream."
21 Thomas Tilling, "Reasons for Renting," *Parents*, September 1982, 57.
22 Amelia A. Newcomb, "Home Ownership Fades in Face of Uncertain Market," *Christian Science Monitor*, October 7, 1983, 27.
23 Amelia A. Newcomb, "Home Ownership Dream Still Alive in Americans' Hearts," *Christian Science Monitor*, October 1, 1982, 20.
24 Asa Hall, "Oh, Those Leaky Faucets: The Hidden Costs of Home Ownership," *Christian Science Monitor*, October 28, 1983, B4.
25 "Passing the $100,000 Milestone," *Time*, July 9, 1984.
26 "Passing the $100,000 Milestone."
27 Matthew L. Wald, "Americans Want to Own a Home, Despite Rising Cost," *New York Times*, February 28, 1985, C1.

28 Nadine Brown, "Home Ownership Made Easier," *Michigan Chronicle*, April 13, 1985, 8_B.
29 Brown, "Home Ownership Made Easier."
30 Thomas Tilling, "A Money-Saving Home Improvement Plan," *Parents*, May 1985, 92.
31 "Housing," *Better Homes and Gardens*, January 1986, 16.
32 "Housing."
33 "Housing."
34 "Building from the Bottom Up," *Time*, February 9, 1987.
35 "Building from the Bottom Up."
36 Margaret Daly, "Has America Lost Its Commitment to Housing?," *Better Homes and Gardens*, February 1988, 41.
37 Daly, "Has America Lost Its Commitment to Housing?"
38 "No Vacancy," *Time*, April 11, 1988.
39 "No Vacancy."
40 "Location, Location, Location," *Time*, April 11, 1988.
41 Curtis Bagley, "Real-Estate Tycoons," *Essence*, July 1988, 114.
42 "Bootstrap Homeowners," *Time*, November 7, 1988.
43 John Greenwald, "Gimme Shelter," *Time*, February 27, 1999.
44 "Million-Dollar 'Birthday Cakes,'" *Time*, May 1, 1989.
45 "Million-Dollar 'Birthday Cakes.'"
46 "Million-Dollar 'Birthday Cakes.'"
47 Susan Sheetz, "Smart Strategies for First-Time Buyers," *Better Homes and Gardens*, August 1989, 41.
48 Sheetz, "Smart Strategies for First-Time Buyers."
49 Sheetz, "Smart Strategies for First-Time Buyers."
50 "Home Ownership Found to Decline," *New York Times*, October 8, 1989, 31.

8 Opening Doors

"What's that I smell in the air? The American dream.
Sweet as a new millionaire, the American Dream.
Live like you haven't a care, the American dream.
All yours for 10 percent down, the American dream"

From "The American Dream" in the Broadway play *Miss Saigon* (1991)

In April 1999, theatergoers in New York City had the chance to see a new play called *Casa Propria* that had been written by Delores Prida. The Spanish-language play, whose title translated in English as "A House of Her Own," was a comedy populated by memorable characters from the playwright's life.[1]

Not an unusual thing, of course, but how the play came to life was certainly not typical. Prida had won a national contest sponsored by Fannie Mae for a play based on the subject of home ownership that was directed to Latino audiences. It cost $20 or $25 to see the show at the Gramercy Arts Theater in Manhattan, but there were a couple of free shows as well, the latter also sponsored by Fannie Mae, the national mortgage company. During the intermission of those shows (one in Brooklyn and the other in the Bronx), presentations on home ownership were made by community members, lenders, and Fannie Mae representatives, making the evening an interesting mix of fiction and non-fiction.[2]

The theatrical effort to inform audiences about the benefits of home ownership was symbolic of the landscape of real estate in the 1990s. After declining in the 1980s, the market rebounded in the final decade of the 20th century, especially in the mid-1990s when economic and social factors collided to form a powerful engine of buying. As the backdrop of *Casa Propria* suggested, much of the activity was centered around minority groups whose rates of ownership lagged behind those of whites. Doors opened for African Americans and Latinos this decade, something long overdue given the not-very-pretty history of the real estate business in the country.

DOI: 10.4324/9781003481485-9

A Safe Haven

Was home ownership all that it was said to be by its many champions? Larry Miller, the stand-up comedian, posed that question after going through the standard, often trying process of converting from a renter to an owner. Miller was perfectly content in his rental apartment that was near downtown Los Angeles, being able to walk to his neighborhood's restaurants, the Farmer's Market, and even the comedy clubs where he worked at night. Miller's neighbors in his apartment building were friendly and happy to get his mail while he was on the road, and the landlord was understanding if the rent happened to be a few days late because of his busy schedule. Miller also liked his old, beat-up furniture, not having to worry if a beer got spilled on it or if it got further scuffed.[3]

Realizing some career success, however, Miller was convinced by his "people" that it would be a good financial decision to buy a house. Very soon, assuming they were looking out for his best interests, Miller had bought a place in Los Feliz, a suburb about forty minutes away. Loans, title searches, and much more paperwork came next, which is when the real fun began—hiring and working with contractors and decorators to fix up the house. Actual costs were running five times the estimates, making Miller believe that the workers may have been gauging him because he was somewhat famous. Finally, his decorator chose Art Deco furniture, something Miller wasn't too pleased about. "I became the proud owner of six rooms full of the kind of ratty, wormed and threadbare pieces one can see too much of on *Masterpiece Theatre*," Miller half-joked, wondering if he should have stayed put in his rental.[4]

Still, despite Miller's humorous grumblings, home ownership naturally remained a much sought after goal among Americans. Perhaps the most remarkable thing about the desire for it was how it crossed all kinds of social divisions. Those who sold homes were fully aware of how many different kinds of people wanted the same thing, quite a rare thing in such a diverse society. "Young, old, and in-betweens—married, married with children, never-married, roommates, and extended families—all share a common interest," Robert G. Walter of Baird & Warner observed, that interest being "to own the place where they live." Because he was in the business, Walter had a keen read on why Americans would go to great lengths to own a home, understanding that the reasons went well beyond the financials. A home was perceived as "a safe haven from the pressures and cares of the world," he believed, an interesting take that was obscured by all the discussion about the economic benefits.[5]

Walter might have made a good psychologist if he hadn't gone into residential home sales. Some of his buyers saw a home as a symbol of success, others as a means of expressing who they were to the rest of the world. Interestingly, he had learned along the way that the usually dreaded mortgage had an emotional upside. For a married couple, a thirty-year commitment to pay back a loan was symbolic of the spouses' commitment to each other, as well as to the community where they had settled down. For men, a home tended to be a sign of achievement, Walter also explained, while for women it often conveyed togetherness.[6]

For others, however, owning a home was primarily about providing shelter. Since 1976, Habitat for Humanity had been building homes for low-income families, and by 1990 the international Christian organization based in Georgia had provided houses for many who otherwise may not have been able to have a roof over their heads. Scores of volunteers typically descended on a site, hammers and saws in hand, often in an area where there were significant numbers of run-down buildings and vacant lots. "Besides building homes for the families, we are also creating neighborhoods," said Diane Kirkpatrick, director of the organization, defining its mission as "a hand-up, not a hand-out." In place of money, homeowners had to invest 500 hours in the construction of their or another family's house, something Kirkpatrick called "sweat equity."[7]

Working up a sweat to earn a house was well worth the effort. "Take solace in the equity of a home," John Cunniff advised in the *Washington Post*, thinking "ownership is shelter from the latest storm." Housing prices were falling in the early nineties, making owners ponder if their investment was a wise one. History showed, however, that such dips were short-lived, and that values would recover and continue to rise, words of comfort during the current recession. "Homeowners are constantly paying down the mortgage, obtaining tax benefits and enjoying the kind of physical protection for one's head that no stock, bond or other security can provide," Cunniff explained, telling readers not to listen to the housing doomsayers.[8]

Nothing, it seemed, was able to knock the Great American House off its foundation. Other forms of housing were typically considered a compromise or temporary situation, the industry itself encouraging this kind of thinking through terms like "cooperative apartment" or "starter home." Americans had inherited their love of the freestanding house from Europe, of course, where land ownership conveyed status, security, and wealth. Whether it was a castle, manor house, villa, or just a cottage, the European country house was considered sacred, sometimes even deemed independent from the long arms of the church and state. The bucolic surroundings were a big part of this, naturally, the absence of the city's poverty, crime, overcrowding, and bad hygiene understandably making the house in the country seem like utopia. The suburban colonial, ranch, or Cape Cod was the Americanized version of this utopian domicile, the fact that one did not have to be wealthy or royalty to live in one making it no less desirable.[9]

Those not lucky enough to receive a hand-up from Habitat for Humanity had to explore other options if they were to become homeowners. The days of low-interest, government-insured loans for a first mortgage were long over; rather, it was high real property prices, economic uncertainty, and risk-averse banks that defined the housing climate (defaults were high). Brokers were calling it a buyer's market because interest rates had dropped, but coming up with what was more often than not a sizable down payment (10% was standard) was easier said than done. Many couples conceded that each spouse would have to work as long as they had their home if they were fortunate enough to buy one, a sacrifice that would likely impact how much time they could spend with their kids. Those who grew up in houses typically considered having one of their own as adults "normal"; this was another part of the deeply rooted psyche of home ownership.[10]

A 1992 Fannie Mae survey revealed how deeply home ownership was engrained in Americans' consciousness. Lorrie Griffey of the *Los Angeles Times* wrote after looking at the results of the survey:

> Most Americans say owning a home is so important that they gladly would work longer, travel farther, pass up career opportunities and take a second job just to get out of the ranks of renters, become an owner and start building equity.

Griffey concluded that "home ownership is still the American Dream." There was financial, psychological, and familial security embedded in owning a home, the national poll suggested, the intangible benefits seemingly as important as the tangible ones.[11]

Another survey, this one done by the National Association of Realtors® in 1993, also found that the more things changed in real estate, the more they remained the same. According to this poll, it was the investment aspect of home ownership that was the most compelling reason to buy (along with the dislike of paying rent), followed by the pride of having a place of one's own and the ability to make changes to one's liking. Not surprisingly, given the source of the survey, it was reported that agents played an important role in the buying decision, both as educators and as counselors.[12]

While the emotions attached to home ownership were certainly great, such surveys showed, it was the well-established economic benefits that made buying a rational decision. Those benefits were confirmed by the most recent "State of the Nation's Housing" report published by the Joint Center for Housing Studies. The 1992 report offered evidence that home ownership was a key element in realizing wealth, something that financial advisors had long pointed out. Home equity accounted for the bulk of the total wealth of owners regardless of their age, although it was younger homeowners who benefited most. (Young owners had fourteen times greater wealth than renters, an astounding statistic.) The division in median wealth between owners and renters was even starker based on race and ethnicity; African American homeowners had about ninety times the wealth of Black renters, and Hispanic owners almost 200 times the wealth of Hispanic renters. For whites, the spread was less but still significant (about twenty-five times).[13]

The great disparity in wealth between owners and renters, especially with regard to minorities, was partly behind Fannie Mae's "Opening Doors" campaign. The country's biggest provider of home mortgage funds had also done its own research, finding in its 1993 National Housing Survey that knowledge of the home-buying process was directly linked to the likelihood of ownership. It didn't take an expert to conclude that navigating the path to buying a home was complicated and, for some, intimidating. That fact had led Fannie Mae to test "Opening Doors" in Dallas/Fort Worth and Sacramento and, determining it to be a success, soon roll it out to Baltimore and Washington, DC. The campaign offered consumers, specifically families with low or moderate incomes, a guide to homebuying as well as contact information for dozens of mortgage lenders in their area.[14]

A Serious Problem

Such a guide was very much needed given the abstruse nature of real estate. The terms alone that a lender might reference—affordability ratios, mortgage structure, variable rate programs, consolidating nondeductible consumer debt—could make one's head spin, making it no wonder that many were reluctant to meet with a banker. The prospect of having house payments extending fifteen or, more likely, thirty years into the future was additional motivation to take the easier route of re-signing one's lease. Finally, looming costs such as college tuition for children, parental care, and retirement served as yet more rationale to conclude that home ownership was simply beyond one's capabilities if not comprehension.[15]

As Larry Miller had found, there were often unanticipated costs associated with buying a house, especially a new one. After the initial round—the down payment, closing costs, and moving expenses—there were a string of subsequent outlays over the course of the first year of ownership that accounted for one out of every seven dollars spent, according to the National Association of Home Builders. New furnishings and appliances (refrigerators, washers and dryers, televisions, and lawn mowers) as well as property alternations were typical expenditures after buying a new home, with the tab coming to more than 15% of the household's gross income. Landscaping as well as fixing or putting in decks, patios, fences, and driveways also didn't come cheap, and then there could be furniture, mattresses, linens, and knick-knacks to turn that house into a home.[16]

As the economy turned around again, however, more Americans were willing to take the plunge, extras included. Income growth combined with lower housing costs was the one-two punch that housing needed, according to Harvard's Joint Center for Housing Studies. "Not since the 1950s has single-family demand so dominated the housing market," H. James Brown, the director of the center, noted in reporting findings from "The State of the Nation's Housing 1994," which had been sponsored by the Ford Foundation. Even better, there were solid reasons to expect that the rise was not just a positive blip. Baby boomers might have been fighting the fact that they were aging every step of the way, but they were at the same time accumulating greater wealth, boding well for home ownership rates. Also, immigrants were moving up economically, this too a sign that the trend would be long term.[17]

Home ownership was also expanding in a more literal sense. The average square footage of a new single-family home had hit the magic number of 2,000 in 1989 and was continuing to grow, with two-story dwellings, garages, multiple bathrooms, central air-conditioning, and fireplaces now considered standard features. Media rooms and playrooms for the kids were also often popping up in new homes (even though families were smaller than in the postwar years), with more super-sized McMansions becoming a common sight in the suburbs.[18] By 1995, the typical American home was 40% bigger than it was in 1970, loaded of course with lots more electronic goodies.[19]

That same study reported that African Americans and Hispanics would experience the greatest increase in home ownership by the year 2000 (in part because their respective rates were currently so low). That, however, was just the good news, the bad news being that Blacks were still being denied mortgages at a much higher rate than both whites and Asian Americans. Fair lending laws had been more stringently enforced in the last few years, yet the loan denial rate was twice as high for African Americans than for those other groups.[20] A 1993 Fannie Mae survey had revealed that 52% of those polled said that discrimination in housing was "a serious problem," more evidence that racism in the industry had hardly gone away.[21]

Breaking down lingering racial barriers was just one of a hundred measures that President Clinton had in mind in June 1995 when he announced a plan to help more Americans buy homes. By the year 2000, eight million additional people would become first-time homeowners, he envisioned, assuming that his proposed partnership among dozens of public and private organizations moved forward. Cheaper construction costs and cheaper financing were the meat and potatoes of what was called the National Home Ownership Strategy, with HUD to play a key role in the ambitious endeavor.[22]

In fact, saving HUD from possible budget slashing was behind such major regulatory reform, as the agency had become a poster child of governmental incompetence due to the general failure of public housing. Housing Secretary Henry Cisneros stated in his support for Clinton's plan:

> I'm hopeful that in the year 2000 we can celebrate the long-term economic prosperity of the country at the turn of the century by touching people where it matters most, in the pocketbook, and watching a whole new generation of Americans be converted to homeowners.[23]

Not just HUD and FHA but all social service programs were indeed vulnerable to (Republican-led) Congressional cuts, making the President's far-reaching initiative a timely one. Cisneros made it clear that increasing minority home ownership was a major priority for the administration; without the FHA, he told a group of reporters, African Americans and Hispanics "could lose their best shot at grasping this part of the American dream." While about 70% of white households owned their homes, 43% of African Americans and 40% of Hispanics did, according to housing officials, who added that discrimination on the part of lending institutions played a part in this big differential.[24]

Should the federal government subsidize home ownership for lower- and moderate-income families and, if so, how? There was a long history of such, as since the 1930s national housing policies had frequently been crafted to encourage political stability and defuse "un-American" ideologies. Research had also shown there to be definite social benefits resulting from home ownership. Children of homeowners remained in school longer, were less likely to be arrested, and experienced fewer teenage pregnancies than children of renters, studies showed, evidence that there were a set of entirely practical reasons to increase home ownership in the country alongside all the psychological ones.[25]

If these were valid reasons to create greater home ownership, which they completely appeared to be, what approach should the government take if it was to help ease the financial burden? For the *Journal of Affordable Housing & Community Development Law*, Philip Halpern of the University of Buffalo Law School outlined the three major obstacles facing prospective home buyers: (1) too much debt to qualify for a mortgage; (2) not enough cash for the down payment (and closing costs); and (3) not enough income to make the monthly mortgage payments.[26]

Given those three hurdles, Halpern continued, there were four options the government could potentially take (outside of tweaking building codes, land-use requirements, and property taxes) to help those who wanted to buy a home but fell short on one or more of them: (1) lower a home's purchase price; (2) lower the mortgage interest rate; (3) subsidize the down payment; and (4) lower the required down payment. There were upsides and downsides to each, the larger question being whether Uncle Sam should be in the business of underwriting real estate for designated groups.[27]

Writing for that same publication a few months later, Duane E. Fleming provided a resounding yes. For the 1994 Congressional elections, the Republican Party had circulated something called "Contract with America" which carried the usual conservative agenda, allowing Fleming to suggest there instead be a government-endorsed "Contract for Home Ownership." "Home Ownership is the American Dream," he flatly stated, basing that supposition on studies showing that building equity was the key to building wealth. In its "The State of the Nation's Housing," the Harvard Joint Center for Housing Studies had reported that just 1.28 million households out of the 11.1 million renter households could afford to be homeowners, and it was this fact that Fleming felt needed addressing through some form of legislation like the recently proposed Home Ownership Plan (HOP).[28]

A Sense of Purpose

With those kinds of statistics, Cisneros had a good story to tell in promoting the President's National Home Ownership Strategy. Six months after its debut, he also had case histories illustrating how the program had been successful in turning renters into owners. One Latina single mother from California would soon be moving into her home after contributing to the construction of houses a la Habitat for Humanity, Cisneros let the media know, while in Ohio an African American woman and her two children had moved out of public housing and into their own home. That was made possible by a local lender being more flexible than he or she might have otherwise after determining that she was a good risk, and with the buyer cobbling together money from various sources.[29]

That was a small sample of what the administration's National Home Ownership Strategy was making possible, Cisneros was proud to say. The partnership among HUD, the housing industry, real estate agents, lenders, and nonprofits was helping reverse the decline that had taken place in the 1980s. "The American dream of home ownership had sprung a leak," he explained, but there was in place now a dam of sorts to stop the flow. The program was essentially targeting the four forms of subsidies that Halpern had identified, specifically reducing down payments, loosening loan requirements, simplifying the mortgage process, and lowering the cost of new construction. It didn't hurt that the economy was chugging along nicely, of course, and that both interest and mortgage rates were low.[30]

Economic factors may have played a larger role (inflation was also low), but that didn't stop the administration from flaunting the news that home ownership in the county had hit a fourteen-year high in 1995. The national ownership rate hit 65.1% in the final quarter of 1995 as 1.4 million more Americans joined the club that year. Not just Cisneros but Federal Reserve Chairman Alan Greenspan proclaimed the news that the rate was the highest since 1981, the result of a perfect economic storm of stable prices, consumer confidence, and a robust lending climate.[31]

That was good news, of course, but not mentioned was the fact that the increase in home ownership was taking place overwhelmingly in the nation's suburbs, according to a 1996 Harvard University study. Urban renters who could afford to buy houses were leaving cities in droves, attracted to better schools and services available in suburban communities. If the trend was long term, cities could become "a dumping ground for the least-advantaged people in our society," said William Apgar of the University's Joint Center for Housing Studies in reporting the findings. The housing industry was delighted with the migration, naturally, but more socially aware economists like Apgar could foresee a two-class society emerging if home sales and new construction continued to boom in the suburbs. Many urban neighborhoods were indeed deteriorating, reflecting the growing disparity in income between city folk and suburbanites.[32]

It wasn't made clear where their new homes were, but both African Americans and Latinos were taking out more mortgage loans in the 1990s. Between 1993 and 1995, home mortgage loans had risen by 48% for the former and 37% for the latter, and this was before the National Home Ownership Strategy had kicked in. In 1996, HUD launched a new initiative called Democratizing Data that was designed to help communities further increase home mortgage loans to minorities through the latest technology. The "World Wide Web," as it was commonly called then, could deliver useful information on mortgage lending, the government was learning, specifically data regarding applications, approvals, and denials that were sourced from thousands of financial institutions.[33]

Yet another HUD initiative was clearly intended to increase inner-city home ownership, however. Through its Target Lending Initiative, the Government National Mortgage Association (Ginnie Mae) would provide economic benefits to lenders to incentivize them to offer a total of $1 billion in secondary mortgage funds to residents of urban communities, Cisneros announced, all at no expense to the taxpayer. (Ginnie Mae was and remains a corporation owned by HUD that had been created to expand affordable housing through the secondary mortgage market.) Seventy-two communities across the country were targeted with this additional piece of Clinton's National Home Ownership Strategy, a clear sign that the President remained committed to his plan.[34]

Lenders responded to the government's incentives, although they were more likely to claim they were doing it for altruistic reasons. "With a sense of purpose and partnership, savings institutions are bringing home ownership within reach for many who've been shut out of the market or haven't been able to find their way in," William T. Marshall and Brennan King declared in *America's Community Banker* in 1996. In New York City, for example, the Dime Savings Bank created a Neighborhood Housing Services center to advise prospective low- and moderate-income home buyers and mortgage customers. In Pasadena, California, CenFed Bank did much the same and took part in a 23-member affordable housing advocacy council. And in Kansas City, Missouri, First Federal Bank FSB offered to share a Federal Home Loan Bank grant with other local institutions to provide down payment and closing cost assistance to affordable housing loan applicants.[35]

These kinds of public/private and national/local efforts were precisely what Clinton and Cisneros had envisioned to reach their goal of having eight million more homeowners by the year 2000. Renters, however, weren't happy with a recently signed piece of legislation which eliminated certain housing subsidies, allowing landlords to jack up rents (sometimes dramatically). The federal government spent $66 billion a year on mortgage interest and property tax deductions, the *New York Times* pointed out, which was about four times the amount spent on low-income housing. It was primarily upper-income families who benefited from these deductions, something Bernice P. Jackson made note of in the *Los Angeles Sentinel*. "As more landlords find it financially unfeasible to build or lease low-income housing and as the federal government gets out of the housing subsidy business, the question becomes where will millions of poor Americans live," she wrote.[36]

Needless to say, that question was not addressed by President Clinton when he announced in late October 1996 that home ownership had again climbed in the third quarter. Clinton was running for reelection, and a week before election day he made sure he delivered the numbers to the American public personally. (It was typically the job of Cisneros, who resigned from his post in January 1997 following a bit of a scandal and was replaced by Andrew Cuomo.) "My administration has worked hard to help more Americans own their own homes," his statement read, the bonus being that both African American and Latino home ownership was up.[37] If elected, Clinton would have to continue to convince Congress that his HUD and other housing-related programs were worth funding, more reason to report the progress being made.

The gains would continue through 1997, however, bringing the nation's rate of home ownership to 66%—the highest in history. Now it was singles who were being acknowledged as a significant new market of homeowners, a group that most lenders had traditionally ignored. Married or unmarried, there were good reasons to invest in property, something more banks were appreciating when pitching their mortgage products to consumers. Now, however, near the end of the 20th century, it was more understood that buying a house did not have to be a lifetime or even long-term proposition. People went through different stages as they aged, after all, making the dwelling in which one chose to live potentially a temporary one. Also, the country had become a more mobile society through the century, this too making home ownership a more fluid thing than it had once been.[38]

"Young unmarrieds," as single people were sometimes referred to in the trade, had until recently looked at ownership as something that would tie them down to a particular community. That appeared to be changing in the late 1990s, however, as it was easy to get caught up in the current real-estate rush fueled by high employment, modest inflation, and easier credit. Some singles had equated owning a house with marriage, but the idea of having a yard for a dog to run around in was enticing, as was the idea of not having to pay rent. (Single women were more likely to own a house than single men.) Condominiums and townhomes were proving to be as popular as the single-family house for this group of buyers, however, as those could be a better fit for the single lifestyle and offered the same tax-deductible mortgage.[39]

More immigrants—another group largely overlooked by lenders—were also taking meetings with bankers these days. As always, many newcomers to the United States were eager to climb the ladder of success and were willing to work hard to do it. Some were holding down two jobs to save enough for a down payment and have enough income to meet the payments; the opportunity to own property was viewed as a dream come true among those from countries where it was virtually impossible unless one was rich. Brokers were beginning to advertise in Spanish, knowing there was a large and growing market for potential buyers from Latin and South America.[40]

A Lot of New Picket Fences

Also as always, however, there was the chance that any homeowner would not be able to come up with the amount of money for the monthly payment. Losing a job, a medical emergency, divorce, or just overextension could lead to such an unfortunate situation, in which case the lending institution would have to take action. Despite the solid economy, "mortgage delinquencies" were not uncommon, often leading to foreclosure. (In a foreclosure proceeding, the lender gets a court judgment for nonpayment of the mortgage, with a court-appointed referee then auctioning off the property.) Too easy credit was cited as one reason for the increase in foreclosures, something that would surface on a much larger scale in about a decade. It also made sense that with record high rates of home ownership, more people would experience an event causing them to be short on cash.[41]

With foreclosures at their highest level in ten years, a new term—"home keepership"—entered the lexicon of real estate. Nonprofits, lenders, and local elected officials were holding discussions to find solutions to the growing problem. Getting help as early as possible was strongly advised, as financial difficulties tended to cascade until the hole was too deep to get out of. "Our interest is to help people attain the American dream, so we want to keep them in that house and do whatever we can to make sure that happens," said Lesley A. Wainwright, a senior vice president at Chase Manhattan Bank, thinking that there were no winners in a foreclosing (except perhaps the new buyer who was often getting a good deal). Working out a lower interest loan could be a solution, or a "time out" on payments could possibly be called until the owner was back on track.[42]

While foreclosures were the underbelly of the housing boom of the 1990s, the bigger story remained the historically high rate of home ownership, particularly among minorities. Not only had African Americans and Latinos realized their own respective historic highs, but the figures continued to rise. In 1999, the number of African Americans owning their own home was increasing nearly three times as fast as the number of whites, while the number of Latino homeowners was growing nearly five times as fast as that of whites. "That's a lot of new picket fences," Ronald Brownstein of the *Los Angeles Times* noted, thinking President Clinton hadn't received as much credit as he should have for creating policies that contributed to this progress. It could be argued that the social benefits of home ownership—the stabilization of neighborhoods and families, greater community involvement, and better student grades—were as great or even greater than the individual benefits, i.e., the accumulation of wealth.[43]

Given that the population of Latinos was rising rapidly, much attention was deservedly being given to home ownership among the group, particularly because it had lagged behind others. Mortgage brokers were known to charge Spanish-speaking people higher rates, just another example of the long history of bias in the nation's real estate community. Things were gradually improving, however, as bankers and agents recognized that Latinos represented a big business opportunity that would only get bigger in the years ahead. "This is a population that is very aspirational, that believes in the American dream," said Cisneros, who was, in 1999, president and chief operating officer of Univision Communications, the Spanish-language television network, thinking "continuous, systematic attention to the Latino consumer is a strategy that will pay off now."[44]

It received less attention than what was taking place in cities and among minority groups, but rural home ownership in the country was also at an all-time high. "Three out of four rural citizens have achieved the American dream," Agriculture Secretary Dan Glickman happily pronounced in 1999 during what not coincidentally was National Home Ownership Week. The 75.1% rate was actually higher than the national average of 66.7%, something made possible by a variety of government programs. Those included guaranteed rural housing loans (allowing eligible homeowners to obtain a mortgage without making a down payment), self-help housing (permitting groups of families to construct their own homes as a down payment on the purchase price), and direct ownership loans (enabling low-income families in towns of less than 30,000 population to purchase a house or a site on which to build a house).[45]

Doors to home ownership were also starting to open for members of Generation X (the 20 million or so Americans born between the mid-1960s and the late 1970s). Twenty- and thirtysomethings were more inclined to use the Internet when home shopping than older generations, however, often preferring to visit the websites of real estate agents and take virtual tours before seeing properties in the real world. (Many of them held technology-related jobs.) Gen Xers, who were fast losing their reputation as cynical slackers, were also going online to learn about the mortgage process, making them a different breed of prospective buyer. The generation was said to be now driving the starter-home market, with many baby boomers trading up to bigger, more expensive places.[46]

In his economics column for the *New York Times*, however, Louis Uchitelle made it clear that most Gen Xers were more tech-savvy than cash flush. His data on home ownership showed that it was older Americans who were driving the historically high rates, as it was they who had invested in property before the "affordability crunch." The postwar economic boom, combined with low-interest thirty-year mortgages, had stretched into the early 1970s, making that era an ideal time to buy a house. Things went south both economically and in housing after that, however, leading to a generation gap in home ownership that many analysts didn't recognize. More single-parent households and the trend toward later marriage compounded this age-based differential, leaving Xers and millennials with a lot of catching up to do in terms of becoming owners rather than renters.[47]

Regardless of one's age, champions of home ownership urged renters to do whatever they could to get in the game. The end of the 20th century was turning out to be a golden age of real estate, making it wise to take steps to leverage one's assets as much as one sensibly could. "Now is a terrific time to invest in a home," Carol Brann exclaimed in the *Washington Post* a couple months before the new millennium, working through hypothetical qualifying house payments and overall debt ratios. However the numbers tumbled, the main thing was to keep one's eyes on the prize. "Buying the home of your dreams may seem daunting, but not if you plan ahead," she assured readers, many of whom no doubt wondered if they really could make their dream a reality.[48] As always, however, the future was unpredictable, as events once again took the American home in a new direction.

Notes

1 "Play About Home Ownership, for Latinos," *New York Times*, April 25, 1999.
2 "Play About Home Ownership, for Latinos."
3 Larry Miller, "The Elusive Joys of Home Ownership," *Los Angeles Times*, February 4, 1990, K11.
4 Miller, "The Elusive Joys of Home Ownership."
5 "Home Ownership Still Top Goal," *Weekend Chicago Defender*, June 23, 1990, 43.
6 "Home Ownership Still Top Goal."
7 Tonya Harris, "Habitat for Humanity: Working to Provide Housing for Low-Income Families," *Louisville Defender*, August 2, 1990, B8.
8 John Cunniff, "Take Solace in Equity of Home," *Washington Post*, October 27, 1990, F14.
9 Roger K. Lewis, "Designing an Affordable Housing Future," *Washington Post*, November 23, 1991, E1.
10 Cheryl Devall, "Home Ownership is No Longer a Given," *Morning Edition* (NPR), December 30, 1991.
11 Lorrie Griffey, "Home Ownership Still the American Dream, Survey Finds," *Los Angeles Times*, August 16, 1992, VY_A20.
12 Alice McCain, "Reasons for Home Ownership Always Remain the Same," *Los Angeles Times*, July 4, 1993, VY_A14.
13 John Cunniff, "Country Needs Good Low-Cost Housing," *Pittsburgh Courier*, November 7, 1992, 2.
14 Ivy D. Jernigan, "Home Ownership a Reality? Fannie Mae Hopes So," *Baltimore Afro-American*, May 22, 1993, A6.
15 Thomas A. Haunty, "Money Pit," *ABA Journal*, October 1993, 108.
16 Nancy L. Ross, "Home Ownership Costs," *Washington Post*, January 12, 1995, 5.
17 "Home Ownership Up," *Weekend Chicago Defender*, July 2, 1994, 62.
18 James W. Hughes and Todd Zimmerman, "The Dream is Alive," *American Demographics*, August 1993, 32.
19 Alan Reynolds, "The Origins of Grumpiness," *National Review*, July 1, 1996, 52–53.

20 Nadirah Z. Sabir and Mark Lowery, "Home Ownership? Don't Bank on It," *Black Enterprise*, January 1995.
21 "More People in Survey Say Home Ownership is Possible for Young," *Wall Street Journal*, May 11, 1993, A12. Henry Buist, Isaac F. Megbolugbe, and Tina R. Trent, "Racial Home Ownership Patterns, the Mortgage Market, and Public Policy," *Journal of Housing Research*, 1994, 91.
22 Jon Greenberg, "HUD Releases Plan to Up Home Ownership," *Morning Edition* (NPR), June 5, 1995.
23 Greenberg, "HUD Releases Plan to Up Home Ownership."
24 Anthony W. McCarthy, "Cisneros Says Minority Home-Ownership Top Priority for HUD," *Baltimore Afro-American*, June 17, 1995, B8.
25 Philip Halpern, "Creating Fair and Efficient Subsidies for Home Ownership," *Journal of Affordable Housing & Community Development Law*, Spring 1995, 125. See also John I. Gilderbloom and John P. Markham, "The Impact of Home Ownership on Political Beliefs," *Social Forces*, June 1995, 1589.
26 Halpern, "Creating Fair and Efficient Subsidies for Home Ownership."
27 Halpern, "Creating Fair and Efficient Subsidies for Home Ownership."
28 Duane E. Fleming, "Wanted: A Contract for Home Ownership," *Journal of Affordable Housing & Community Development Law*, September 1995.
29 Henry G. Cisneros, "Home Ownership: Making the Dream into Reality for All Americans," *Michigan Chronicle*, December 13, 1995, 3_B.
30 Cisneros, "Home Ownership: Making the Dream into Reality for All Americans."
31 "Home Ownership Hit 14-Year High in 1995," *Wall Street Journal*, February 9, 1996, A16.
32 "Home Ownership Boom Skips Cities for Life in Suburbs," *Philadelphia Tribune*, July 2, 1996, 2B.
33 "Home Ownership Rates Increase for Blacks, Latinos," *Atlanta Daily World*, August 15, 1996, 2.
34 Kip Branch, "HUD Launches $1 Billion Initiative to Increase Inner-City Home Ownership," *Baltimore Afro-American*, August 31, 1996, A17.
35 William T. Marshall and Brennan King, "Building Partnerships top Boost Home Ownership," *America's Community Banker*, October 1996, 5.
36 Barbara Stewart, "New Rule Raises Rent and Fear for Low-Income Tenants," *New York Times*, June 30, 1996, NJ8; Bernice P. Jackson, "Home Ownership: The Lost American Dream," *Los Angeles Sentinel*, November 14, 1996, A7.
37 Randolph E. Schmid, "Home Ownership Climbs," *New Pittsburgh Courier*, November 16, 1996, 3.
38 Isabelle de Pommereau, "New Faces of America's Homeowners," *Christian Science Monitor*, November 14, 1997, 1. See Joseph Gyourko and Peter Linneman, "The Changing Influences of Education, Income, Family Structure, and Race on Home Ownership by Age Over Time," *Journal of Housing Research*, 1997, 1.
39 De Pommereau, "New Faces of America's Homeowners."
40 De Pommereau, "New Faces of America's Homeowners."
41 "After Home Ownership, 'Home Keepership' is Key," *New York Times*, November 16, 1997.
42 "After Home Ownership, 'Home Keepership' is Key."
43 Ronald Brownstein, "Minorities' Home Ownership Booms Under Clinton but Still Lags Whites'," *Los Angeles Times*, May 31, 1999.
44 Joshua Brockman, "Many Factors Seen Converging to Help Hispanics Buy Homes," *American Banker*, June 23, 1999.
45 "Rural U.S. Home Ownership a Record 75.1 Percent, USDA Reports," *Omaha World-Record*, June 15, 1999.

46 Hala Habal, "Gen X Travels Web, Not Main St., to Buy First Home," *American Banker*, June 22, 1999.
47 Louis Uchitelle, "In Home Ownership Data, a Hidden Generation Gap," *New York Times*, September 26, 1999.
48 Carol Brann, "The Route to Home Ownership: Now Is a Great Time to Buy a Home!," *Washington Post*, October 20, 1999, H12.

9 The Ownership Society

"Home ownership defines us as Americans."

Wendy A. Hoke, 2008

Six decades after the first Levittowners moved into the brand-new, soon-to-be massive community on Long Island, a fair number of current residents were struggling to keep their mid-20th century houses. Americans from coast to coast were in similar dire straits, but what was being called the subprime mortgage crisis was hitting Levittown especially hard in 2009. Home values in what many considered to be the quintessential American suburb had plummeted the last couple of years, so much so that what one owed on a house could be more than what it was worth. To make matters worse, the mortgage crisis had had a ripple through the nation's economy, triggering a recession, greater unemployment, and more bankruptcies. Home ownership was the very heart of Levittown, however, making its current state seem all the more heart breaking.[1]

How had the American dream turned into such a nightmare? Many had looked forward to the first decade of the new century and new millennium with great anticipation, thinking that more Americans, especially minorities, would be able to share the privilege of ownership. Indeed, President George H. Bush envisioned the nation becoming an "ownership society," in which citizens were not just more financially independent but more committed to the wellbeing of their communities. Something much different lay in store these years, however, as the underbelly of the American home was vividly exposed.

A Majority of Minorities

Until then, however, the lame-duck Clinton administration continued its efforts to increase home ownership among African Americans and Latinos. HUD Secretary Andrew Cuomo remained in charge of the initiative, urging the housing industry to help "a majority of minorities" realize that goal. Minorities still lagged behind whites in ownership, and Cuomo was pushing the FHA to issue more insured mortgages to African American and Latino

DOI: 10.4324/9781003481485-10

families. To make it work, however, other organizations—the National Association of Mortgage Brokers, the Mortgage Bankers Association of America, Fannie Mae, and Freddie Mac—would have to cooperate, and Cuomo asked that they enlist in the endeavor.[2]

It was a worthy goal, of course, but minorities were already shattering records in terms of home ownership. Two separate reports, one from Harvard's Joint Center for Housing Studies and the other from HUD, confirmed as much. "All racial and ethnic groups have shared in this home ownership boom," stated the latter's most recent State of the Cities report, with experts crediting the economic expansion of the 1990s for the good numbers. The total national figure had crept above 67% and was still rising, a positive thing for those who held that home ownership and social stability went hand in hand. That this was taking place while both home prices and rents increased and while welfare subsidies shrank was all the more impressive. Still, the gap that Cuomo had addressed was significant; about 73% of white households were owners in 2000 versus 47% for African Americans and 46% for Latinos.[3]

While that gap was gradually narrowing, the one between those who could afford to have any roof over their heads and those who couldn't was widening. Prosperity was welcomed, of course, but the rising rents were causing a greater number of families, even those with income from a job, to seek emergency shelter. Requests for beds at homeless shelters jumped 22% in 2000, as more renters could no longer afford their apartments. HUD estimated that more than five million Americans lived in "substandard or inadequate housing," an impetus for state and city officials to try to come up with alternative solutions to the problem.[4]

It was hard to overlook the irony, or perhaps tragedy, that so many Americans could not afford housing while home ownership had reached a historic high. Soon HUD (led now by Mel Martinez under the George W. Bush administration) raised the number of those who had "critical, unmet housing needs" to thirteen million, with an estimated 4.9 million families paying more than half of their income for shelter. The demand for low-cost rentals had doubled over the past decade, and for most income had not increased at the same rate. Those with low- or middle-income jobs in high-priced markets like New York or San Francisco were most likely of the employed to experience a housing problem. Some were taking second jobs, moving to a cheaper housing market, or commuting long distances to avoid becoming homeless.[5]

Foreclosures were yet another housing problem in 2001, particularly in low-income neighborhoods of inner cities. Just as there were many who couldn't pay their rent when it was hiked, losing a home due to not being able to make the monthly mortgage payments was occurring with more frequency. (The rate had doubled since 1997.) Looser lending standards and job instability were considered the primary causes, but predatory practices by certain lenders played a role. Unscrupulous parties were known to bury hidden costs and high fees in loan agreements, especially when dealing with buyers who were new to the game.[6]

Until solutions were found to such major such social problems, however, the tried-and-true rhetoric dedicated to the value of owning property made good copy. Picking up where President Clinton had left off, President Bush vigorously extolled the advantages of home ownership, seeing a combination of government programs and volunteerism as the means for more Americans to realize that worthy goal. Home ownership was "a key to upward mobility, an anchor for families, and a source of stability for communities," the President said in his weekly radio address in June 2001, suggesting that listeners "put hammer to nail and help people realize their dreams." Bush had just signed a $1.35 trillion tax cut (including $1.7 billion from HUD) and was relaxing on his Texas ranch at the time after his early morning jog while proposing that ordinary Americans building homes for the less advantaged could help solve the nation's housing problem.[7]

Bush actually had two governmental programs in mind that promised to increase home ownership among lower-income families, especially among minorities. The first was the American Dream Down Payment Fund which, as its name suggested, would make it easier for renters to make a down payment on a home. The $1 billion fund would be distributed to 650,000 low-income families for the following five years. The second initiative was the Renewing the Dream tax credit, which provided incentives for developers to build low-income housing. The goal was to create 100,000 new homes for low-income families, complementing the "pull" strategy of the down payment fund with more of a "push" one from the construction industry.[8]

While tax credits would certainly have been welcomed by builders, the construction business was doing just fine at the time despite a soft economy and post-dot-com stock market. Sales of new houses were strong and rising, fueled by low interest rates, governmental programs targeting minorities, and the growing population. Peripheral businesses—furniture, carpet, appliances—were also healthy, as consumers turned their houses into homes. Retailers like Bed Bath & Beyond, Lowe's, and Home Depot were benefiting from Americans' passion for all things home, although the usual concerns that the housing market could potentially suddenly collapse for some reason had not gone away.[9]

9/11 served as that potential reason. Immediately following the attacks, a war on terrorism was declared, drawing more of the nation's economic resources. The home ownership programs in place for low- and moderate-income families, including reduced closing costs and looser mortgage requirements, could be in jeopardy, experts worried. $1 billion a day was now going toward military efforts and domestic security, and funding for the FHA could be one bucket the administration might dip into. If first-time buyers were seriously impacted by budget cuts, there would be a domino effect through the housing market, as those wanting to trade up would have less chance in selling their homes.[10]

A few months after 9/11, however, there were no signs that the new world order would sink the American housing market. In fact, there were a number of positive developments. JP Morgan Chase had pledged $35 billion over five years to support mortgages with low or no down payments, and the AFL-CIO committed $750 million of its pension funds to be invested in low-cost housing. HUD, meanwhile, announced it would put an additional $235 million into programs designed to help first-time home buyers. The stated goal for all these initiatives was to narrow the wealth gap between whites and minorities and move more Americans into the middle class. Because African Americans were twice as likely to be denied a conventional loan by banks, however, there was a growing market for something called subprime lenders, i.e., those that charge higher initial fees and higher interest rates to reflect the greater risk.[11]

At the time, not much was being made of the transformation of the mortgage business. The traditional method was for local bankers to issue mortgages based on that market's conditions, with the loan then held by that bank. But now, for the sake of stability and efficiency, a full two-thirds of mortgages were farmed out to secondary markets on a national basis, taking locality out of the mix. The more mortgages issued, the greater the profit, an equation that was being expressed by the increasing number of houses that were being bought despite the ever-rising prices. The median price of an existing home in 2002 was $153,000 (a 6.7% increase from 2001), and for a new house, it was $176,700 (up 6.3%). More housing units were being sold and purchased than ever before in history, and the rising values of homes were functioning as a buffer against inflation.[12] With such positive data, was there any real reason to worry?

Clear Skies Ahead

Seemingly not, especially given the fact that the nation as a whole had benefited from the late 1990s economic boom, the clearest sign of that being home ownership. By the end of 2001, more people than ever (68% of adults) had realized the dream of owning a home, the highest percentage since the Census Bureau started keeping track.[13] Even with the economy blowing up in the early 2000s (much like it had in the early 1970s, 1980s, and 1990s), Americans were determined to keep their dream alive. Not just McMansions but luxuries of all kinds—many of them not costing an arm and a leg—were a ubiquitous part of American life, the outlandish consumerism of the times rivaling that of the late 1950s and late 1980s. A good chunk of the nation's ongoing shopping spree was being funded by easy home refinancing, with the dollars saved on the mortgage quickly spent at the mall. "The beginning of the 21st century is turning out to be yet another cavalcade of 'bling bling,'" observed John Schwartz of the *New York Times*, suggesting that Americans were reluctant to let the good times stop rolling.[14]

Meanwhile, the usual advice to build home equity wealth was doled out. "Fire your landlord," a 2004 article in *Essence* told readers, the conditions for qualified buyers (low interest rates, discounted closing costs, and minimal down payments) now very good to do just that. Of course, given the size of such an investment, there were sensible steps to take for one to buy a home and then be able to keep it. Cleaning up one's credit report was the first order of business, as mortgage issuers would be very interested in whether one had paid one's bills in the past. Shopping for the best mortgage was important, as just a fraction of a percent in interest rate added up to thousands of dollars over the course of a loan. And if approved, not buying more house than one could afford was a good idea, as there were a bunch of costs (property taxes, insurance, maintenance, and repairs) beyond the principal and interest.[15]

There were other reasons to fire your landlord if one could swing it. Home values were continuing to rise, for one thing, and the stock market had yet to recover from its phenomenal spike during the dot-com era. Americans could be said to be viewing real estate as "the new gold"—a source of stable wealth much like that of precious metals. If that weren't enough, history appeared to be on the side of property owners; there hadn't been a true housing bust on a national basis since the Great Depression. There were "clear skies ahead for home values," Stacy A. Teicher confidently stated in the *Christian Science Monitor* in 2004, seeing no dark clouds on the horizon.[16]

Despite all the good reasons to stop renting, many Americans were in fact reluctant to pursue home ownership. There were a reported sixty million renters, many of them assuming they couldn't afford to become owners and/ or intimidated by the financing process. The standardization and nationalization of the mortgage business had made that process much simpler than it had once been, however, a fact that lenders liked to point out.[17] Aware of the trepidation and misinformation that surrounded real estate, Freddie Mac was offering a free online tutorial called *Your Route to Home Ownership* for first-time home buyers that explained the process in understandable terms.[18]

As for many native-borns, owning one's own home continued to define the American dream for immigrants. About half of the nation's thirty million immigrants owned homes versus 70% of those born in the country, but the gap was closing as more of the former eventually became United States citizens. That a home was an investment and offered tax advantages was certainly important for immigrants, but other factors—a greater sense of security, belonging to an established community, and leaving a legacy for their children, in particular—were why the foreign-born considered home ownership their top priority. A cottage industry serving the immigrant housing market had not surprisingly sprung up, with feng shui consultants brought in to help design homes for Asian customers and real estate agents enrolling classes in cross-cultural marketing. Home Depot was putting more advertising dollars toward the Latino market, knowing that things like sponsoring the Mexican national soccer team and supporting the Hispanic Chamber of Commerce would help get Spanish-speaking customers into their stores.[19]

That real estate was the best path for anyone to realize financial security—and specifically a better place than the stock market for investors to have one's money—was confirmed by a 2004 report by the Joint Center for Housing Studies. The report, which had been commissioned by the NAR®, showed that home equity (the difference between the debt from a loan and the value of a home) accounted for 19% of total household wealth. That was greater than the percentage of wealth derived from stocks, evidence that owning a home offered not just more stability but a higher yield. In 2003, about half of the nation's households held stocks, significantly less than the 68% who owned homes, reason to believe that most Americans intuitively understood the financial advantages of the latter.[20]

To celebrate his second-term inauguration in 2005, President Bush returned to the theme of what he had called an "ownership society." "The more ownership there is in America, the more vitality there is in America, and the more people have a vital stake in the future of this country," the President had said in 2004 in promoting a number of policies based on that theme. More access and more choices in health care, tax relief to families and small businesses, and strengthening Social Security were all part of his vision of an ownership society. The heart of it was expanding home ownership, however, as it was that that formed the cornerstone of communities and provided long-term financial security. Through the American Dream Down Payment Initiative, affordable housing, the Self-Help Home Ownership Opportunities Program, and simplifying the homebuying process, Bush sought to leverage the progress made over his first term, particularly in urban neighborhoods.[21]

Alongside or in conjunction with these federal programs were a wide range of local ones designed to make housing more affordable for low- and middle-income families. The programs were scattered, however, leading The Home Ownership Alliance, a consortium of organizations affiliated with housing (bankers, builders, insurers, realtors, etc.), to identify which ones were proving to be effective. The Alliance compiled its findings in a report, "Affordable Homes: Best Practices for America," and made it available on its website to encourage information sharing. With the report, state and local housing officials could better determine which programs might work well in their own communities.[22]

The "best practices" culled from twenty metropolitan areas fell into five categories: (1) home-ownership tax credits (a success in Washington, DC); (2) housing cost assistance programs, in which funds were made available for down payments, closing costs, and mortgage payments (a popular thing in Seattle); (3) voucher assistance programs, whereby federal funds could be applied to mortgage payments (doing well in Pittsburgh and Philadelphia); (4) agency development initiatives, in which agencies increase local affordable housing via rezoning or annexing land (taking place in Minneapolis, Atlanta, and Riverside, California); and (5) developer incentives, where public agencies work with private developers to increase the supply of affordable housing (gaining traction in Chicago).[23]

Many younger adults—twenty- and thirtysomethings—could certainly have benefited from such programs. A myriad of factors—college student loans, low salaries, sporadic joblessness, career changes, the rising cost of healthcare, and the escalating price of a house, to name just a few—were making the prospect of buying a home untenable. "Young dream-seekers are strapped by debt," Marilyn Gardner noted in the *Christian Science Monitor* in 2006, with living paycheck to paycheck not a good formula to become a homeowner. Credit card debt was proving to be a particular problem among this group; news that one was "pre-approved" could be irresistible when there was no money in one's pocket.[24]

The Sky Will Not Fall

The financially challenged were perhaps happy to learn that houses may become more affordable because they were getting smaller. After more than three decades of continual upsizing, the average American house was finally topping out in square feet, the turnaround driven by younger buyers more interested in amenities than space. Higher costs for land and energy as well as rising interest rates were making those who could afford a tennis court-sized master bedroom to reconsider, with the growing number of empty nesters also contributing to the shrinking of the Great American House. In his *The New American Dream: Living Well in Small Homes*, James Gauer observed that "plywood palazzos" with their dreaded "loom factor" were now associated with greed and, in particular, the recent corporate scandals, not an image a new homeowner wanted to project to one's neighbors.[25]

The flourishing green movement too seemed to be part of the shift, with many now attuned to how big of a "footprint" each of us made on the environment. Bells and whistles like Sub-Zero refrigerators, exotic hardwood floors, high ceilings, and radiant heat now defined domestic luxury more than having the biggest house on the block, a sign of the times that quality was trumping quantity as a desirable attribute. The linguistic inspiration for McMansions, McDonald's, had recently discontinued its "supersized" French fries and soft drinks, in fact, another indication that the country was beginning to believe that bigger did not necessarily mean better.[26]

Owning even a small house, however, might have been more liability than an asset. Signs of the much-feared housing bubble popping appeared in 2005 with the news that the thirty-day past-due rate for subprime mortgages rose from 5.4% to 7.1% over the course of that year. That may not have sounded like much, but just a 1% increase in defaults triggered a cascade of financial problems not just through the mortgage market but the national economy. The lure to buy property by certain lenders was a powerful one; some didn't even ask for the prospect to show their income. The pendulum appeared to have swung the other way; banks and other financial institutions had for decades been criticized for being too cautious in making loans, but the appearance of the subprime mortgage market had incentivized them to be too eager.[27]

If the bad news was the jump in sub-prime past-dues, the worse news was the rise in foreclosures. The foreclosure rate for subprime loans was nine times that of primes in 2005, a clear sign of where the problem was. Neighborhoods with a predominantly minority and low-income population were suffering most, as it was those groups who shadier lenders tended to target with subprime loans. Rather than discriminating against African Americans and Hispanics, as in the past, less than ethical lenders were now exploiting them with low down payment, high-ratio, and interest-only mortgages. Such lenders knew full well that there would likely be trouble ahead for borrowers who may have had "impaired credit," but that wasn't their problem.[28]

Given such a climate in real estate, was it any wonder that potential first-time buyers were sitting on the sidelines? Just a couple of years earlier, there were bidding wars for more affordable homes, but now such properties likely had "For Sale" signs on their front lawn. Likewise, sales contracts had sped through the system during the peak (sometimes completed in a single day), but now they were moving at a snail's pace despite there being fewer deals made. Builders were lowering prices as inventory sat idle, and sellers were doing the same. If there was any good news, it was that buyers had more options to choose from and more time to shop for the best loan. Rash decisions were known to be made in a seller's market, something less likely to happen during a slowdown.[29]

Even some of those who were not facing default were having trouble making payments. Many buyers had taken out an adjustable-rate mortgage (ARM), attracted by their low initial interest rates. An ARM was especially desirable for those who had a checkered credit rating, wanted more house than they really could afford, or didn't plan to keep the property for very long. Over time, that rate changed based on certain criteria, however, and payments were going up as did the interest rate in 2006. ARMs accounted for a quarter of all mortgages at the time, making many homeowners less than pleased to learn what their payment would be when it adjusted (upward). Delinquency rates were predicted to rise, perhaps dramatically, making many wish that they had gone with a fixed-rate loan. Options for those in trouble were to refinance, negotiate the terms, sell the place, or rent it out.[30]

Should those unaffected by rising interest rates have sympathy for those who got themselves into a pickle through overextension or by taking out the wrong kind of mortgage? Perhaps and perhaps not, but all Americans had to worry about the implications. Having to write off more bad loans, banks would likely tighten credit standards, not just for housing but for all kinds of lending. That could trigger a slowdown in consumer spending and business investment, hurting the nation's whole economy. Wall Streeters, notoriously skittish, foresaw a possible looming credit crunch, and the market reacted accordingly in March 2007. Banks had already tightened standards for subprime mortgages, rather sensibly, but no one could say how this latest twist in the pursuit of the American dream would play out.[31]

Meanwhile, the media had taken to calling those who had got stuck with subprime mortgages "victims." Some of those facing a big "adjustment" were meeting with counselors who had expertise in such matters. It was true that a fair number of those with a subprime had never been informed of the possible downsides by their mortgage broker and were understandably taken aback when learning how much their payment would become. Some were hoping for some divine intervention, thinking God wanted them to be able to keep their house. Home rescue loans were being made by groups like the Neighborhood Assistance Corporation of America and, after some tussling with lenders, funds were used to refinance the mortgage at a thirty-year fixed, below-market rate.[32]

Not everyone agreed that those who had opted for a subprime were victims, even if their broker's main priority was to earn a commission. Stories abounded of people who had average salaries but somehow wrangled million-dollar houses, an exchange that defied common sense. Some of those people believed they owned the full value of the house, not realizing or wanting to believe their equity was just a small percentage of the value. While it was possible to beat the system in this manner, an unforeseen financial event could make it tumble like a house of cards. Dozens of the subprime lenders were themselves going belly up, turning the mess into a legitimate crisis. In a 2007 piece for the *Chicago Defender*, Harry C. Alford, the co-founder and President/CEO of the National Black Chamber of Commerce, made it clear that the ability to get a mortgage of any kind didn't really make one a homeowner. The uncomfortable truth was that one was a borrower who lived in a home owned mostly by the lender, but such a perspective took much of the magic out of the American dream.[33]

With delinquencies continuing to rise through 2006 and into 2007, however, such a reality check was certainly in order. The gravity of the situation was becoming ever clearer, making some worry that if more financial institutions failed, the nation's economy would collapse much like it did after the 1929 market crash. "Don't panic," assured Milton Ezrati, "the sky will not fall." Ezrati, an executive at Lord Abbett, a money management firm, pointed out that few delinquent mortgages reached foreclosure, as borrowers figured out some way to eventually pay what was due. Mortgage bankers themselves considered foreclosure the last thing they wanted to do, as they had no desire to be property owners. Plus, there was the fact that subprimes represented less than 10% of the dollar value of the total mortgage market, making it unlikely that there would be breadlines as in the Great Depression.[34]

Still, the Bush administration took active steps to ensure that the Chicken Littles would not prove to be correct. The Federal Reserve loaned billions of dollars to larger banks, referring to the money as "crisis prevention" rather than a bailout. That kind of money seemed enormous, but Treasury Secretary Henry Paulson explained that the kerfuffle represented less than 1% of the country's gross domestic product. Still, home prices had dropped significantly (5.1% in 2007), recalling what had taken place during the Depression and thus locating the mortgage crisis in historical terms. "A market reckoning is in order, one that teaches lessons as the receding tide lays bare all past mistakes and irrational exuberances," poetically wrote the editor of the *Christian Science Monitor*, calling for mortgages to henceforth be "built on the rock of honesty."[35]

What was perhaps most depressing about the subprime crisis was the possibility that some or even all of the progress made in home ownership over the past decade or two could be lost. Between 2003 and 2008, 2.8 million families bought their first homes, and ownership among people of color and Hispanics had reached new highs. Data showed that 2.2 million homeowners faced the possibility of foreclosure, however, so some kind of action had to be taken. Still, taxpayers didn't like the idea of their money being used to, as they saw it, rescue greedy bankers or folks who made foolish decisions. By early 2008, all kinds of other proposals were being considered to fix the problem, one of them being "bankruptcy relief" should things get worse rather than better.[36]

A Market Reckoning

Those kinds of big numbers didn't do justice to the reality of a family losing their home due to foreclosure. In April 2008, one in 519 American households received a foreclosure filing, up 65% over the past year. A drive down any block in suburban America would look normal, with the usual "For Sale" sign on the occasional front lawn, save for the fact that the house would likely be vacant. There was a sad story behind the scenes, however, the most frequent one being the balloon payment schedule that proved to be beyond what the homeowner could afford. The loss of a job, illness, or death might also have played a role in the sale, which meant, for the time being at least, the end of the American dream for that family.[37]

The loss of that dream, however, meant its gain for another family. In some neighborhoods, brokers were taking prospective buyers around in buses on "foreclosure tours," complete with a box lunch. In Solon and the aptly named Chagrin Falls, each a suburb of Cleveland, Ohio, ReMax Haven Realty was driving the bus, with an expert crew (home inspector, mortgage lender, and someone from a title company) also on board as guides. A seat on the bus costs $15, a good investment given the potential bargains that could be had for bank-owned houses in "short sale" (a transaction in which the lender, or lenders, agree to accept less than the mortgage amount owed by the current homeowner). Most of those who had been foreclosed had tried to sell their house but had failed to meet the deadline, leading to this depressing scenario. Some, angry about how it had played out, were known to take parts of the house with them, but it was little compensation for their loss.[38]

2008 was turning out to be a very bad year for the American home. "The mortgage foreclosure crisis is in full swing and not looking to ease soon," Rep. David Scott (D-GA) wrote for the *Philadelphia Tribune* in August of that year as both delinquency and default rates continued to rise. As predicted, the troubles of the subprime market had triggered higher conventional mortgage rates, impacting borrowers with perfectly good credit. Both the House of Representatives and the U.S. Senate had passed mortgage reform legislation; the American Housing Rescue and Foreclosure Prevention Act (H.R. 3221) was designed to ensure that there would not be another crisis like the one taking place and also allowed those at risk of defaulting to refinance with a government-guaranteed loan. Lawmakers feared that without such legislation, entire communities could be wiped out, taking out property-tax-funded schools in the process.[39]

Naturally, much fault-finding was taking place as the crisis worsened. Not just were home prices in free fall but the financial markets were suffering badly because of it. In short, many people were watching their net worth drop like a rock. In the bullseye of blame were the huge insurer AIG, investment banks, hedge-fund managers, rating agencies, and federal regulators. Going somewhat unscathed were Fannie Mae and Freddie Mac, however, despite their having owned or guaranteed about $5 trillion in home mortgages. Critics claimed they were responsible for the "exotic" (now rebranded as "toxic") financial products that had flooded credit markets, and the issue became a political football in the upcoming presidential election.[40] In the wake of the crisis, both Fannie Mae and Freddie Mac, which had previously been "government-sponsored enterprises," were nationalized as a means of greater control.[41]

While big corporations were bailed out by Congress (being considered "too big to fail"), thousands of homeowners found themselves "under water" or "upside down"—their properties were worth less than what they owed. How could such a thing have happened? "For decades, real estate was considered a sure thing," wrote Barbara Curtis two days before Christmas 2008, having believed that "owning a home meant shelter and savings all in one." After not saving for the proverbial rainy day, however, Curtis and her family had lost their home in the crisis. But much as in the 1946 film classic *It's a Wonderful Life*, friends, acquaintances, and even complete strangers helped them get back on their feet, making life imitate art.[42]

Such happy endings were far and few between, however. In their 2009 film *American Casino*, Andrew and Leslie Cockburn powerfully documented the financial and human costs of the subprime disaster. Beyond the millions of Americans who had lost their homes or were facing foreclosure, every citizen was paying an average $42,000 to bail out the banks responsible for the crisis, according to the filmmakers. Mortgage-backed securities were the cause of the problem, as Wall Street packaged subprime loans into financial products with names like collateralized debt obligations (CDOs) and credit default swaps (CDSs). Mortgages had been taken out by phone and signed in banks' parking lots, this alone a sign that something wasn't quite right. Minority communities were targeted for the subprimes, the film made clear; African American borrowers were 3.8 times more likely than whites to be given such loans, a fact that suggested that the actions taken represented a violation of civil rights.[43]

For the popular media, the mortgage crisis also made ideal grist for the mill. *GQ* (*Gentlemen's Quarterly*), for example, didn't usually cover such less-than-glamorous stories, but Joel Lovell, a writer for the trendy magazine, clearly had something to get off his chest. Lovell was a lifelong renter, and he felt strongly that Americans needed to get over their conviction that they wouldn't feel complete until they owned a money pit. The common wisdom—that renting was throwing your money away, one was not really an adult until he or she owned a home, buying a house was the best path to financial security—was hogwash, Lovell argued, the disaster area that was the current real estate market only more reason he was right and the rest of us were wrong. "Once you start crunching the numbers, it turns out the American dream is a total sham," he wrote, the home-as-nest-egg a big fat lie.[44]

Lovell had indeed crunched the numbers and, based on his own rent versus own calculations (in Brooklyn, it need be said, where the cost of an apartment was almost that of one in Manhattan), determined that should he buy a place it would take twenty-eight years to break even. Anything less than that, the down payment, thirty-year mortgage, property taxes, maintenance costs, homeowner's insurance, and other expenses made purchasing a home a bad deal, even if the property appreciated 5% per year. In pure investment terms, at least, home ownership was a losing proposition, he informed readers, unless one was prepared to stay put for almost three decades. The psychological and moralistic overtones associated with owning a home, and the flipside that renting was somehow suspect, were doing a real disservice to lots of Americans, Lovell concluded, hoping the popping of the real estate bubble would convince others similarly.[45]

Indeed, the cataclysmic housing crisis led some critics to suggest that the classic American dream itself was part of the problem. Richard Florida argued that it might be time for Americans to abandon their belief that home ownership symbolized achievement and/or success, agreeing with earlier critics who pointed out that the single-family home just did not make economic sense for many people. Besides being inflexible and expensive, a home of one's own did not make people happier, a recent study had found; the so-called "dream house" was often a major source of stress. Too many folks were "indentured servants to their homes," the University of Toronto professor wrote in 2009, proposing that the "house poor" and, especially, those at risk of foreclosure, rent rather than buy again.[46] Could Americans give up this central tenet of the good life even if it was a financial albatross around their necks?

Another academic, Joseph Gyourko, agreed that home ownership was not for everyone. Gyourko, who directed the Wharton School's Real Estate Center at the University of Pennsylvania, believed that too many Americans rushed into buying property when interest rates dropped, not a wise decision. After seeing that one's monthly mortgage payment would be about the same as rent, it was easy to fall into the trap of ownership, dismissing all the peripheral costs, i.e., property taxes, utilities, and repairs. Like Lovell, Gyourko challenged the generally accepted supposition that home ownership was a great long-term investment. He too did the math and determined that when adjusted for inflation, the average return on property since 1975 had been 1%, hardly a means to build wealth. (The return on Treasury bonds would have been higher.) It was nice to believe that building equity in a home offered a way to finance college for one's children and build a nest egg for retirement, but that was mostly wishful thinking.[47]

While not the golden goose many assumed it was, a home did offer many other benefits, Gyourko conceded. Owners had a sense of being in control, felt that they were part of a community, and were proud to have achieved something significant, he pointed out, and there was indeed evidence that they made better citizens and helped to stabilize neighborhoods.[48] Were such positives worth the risks that had just been so painfully demonstrated? Recent events would help answer that key question.

Notes

1 Randi F. Marshall, "Home Ownership Harder to Attain, Retain in Levittown," *Newsday*, February 19, 2009.
2 J. Zamgba Browne, "HUD Goal: Raise Minority Home Ownership," *New York Amsterdam News*, June 22, 2000, 15. See Stuart A. Gabriel, "Opening the Doors to Home Ownership: Challenges to Federal Policy," *Cityscape*, 2001, 31; Frederick J. Eggers, "Home Ownership: A Housing Success Story," *Cityscape*, 2001, 43.
3 Paul Van Slambrouk, "More Minorities Own the Roof Over Their Heads," *Christian Science Monitor*, June 27, 2000, 3. See Chenoa A. Flippen, "Racial and Ethnic Inequality in Home Ownership," *Sociological Quarterly*, Spring 2001, 121.
4 Alexandra Marks, "Prosperity Yields Two Views of US Housing," *Christian Science Monitor*, January 22, 2001, 3.
5 "Affording a Home," *Christian Science Monitor*, March 30, 2001, 10.
6 Noel C. Paul, "Home Ownership Can Be Short-Lived in Inner Cities," *Christian Science Monitor*, May 1, 2001, 2.
7 Lawrence L. Knutson, "Bush Promotes Home Ownership Programs," *Philadelphia Tribune*, June 12, 2001, 4_C.
8 "Home Ownership Reaches Record Levels," *Ogden Standard-Examiner* (Utah), July 30, 2001.
9 Guy Halverson, "Investors Build on Continued Housing Boom," *Christian Science Monitor*, September 10, 2001, 13.
10 Alan J. Heavens, "Minority Home Ownership Programs at Risk as Nation Fights Terrorism," *Philadelphia Inquirer*, December 2, 2001.
11 Alexandra Marks, "To Extend Housing Boom, A Push for Minority Buyers," *Christian Science Monitor*, January 28, 2002, 2; For more on the wealth gap based on race, see Kerwin Kofi Charles and Erik Hurst, "The Transition to Home Ownership and the Black-White Wealth Gap," *Review of Economics and Statistics*, May 2002, 281.
12 David R. Francis, "Up, Up, and…Then What?," *Christian Science Monitor*, May 6, 2002, 15.

13 Kathleen O'Brien, "Realizing the American Dream," *New York Times*, April 14, 2002, 9.
14 John Schwartz, "Supersize American Dream: Expensive? I'll Take it," *New York Times*, December 16, 2002, C8.
15 L.S., "Fire Your Landlord," *Essence*, March 2004, 108.
16 Stacy A. Teicher, "Clear Skies Ahead for Home Values," *Christian Science Monitor*, April 19, 2004, 13.
17 David Bradley, "Myths Prevent Home Ownership," *Philadelphia Tribune*, June 6, 2004, 6-B.
18 L.S., "The Road to Home Ownership," *Essence*, March 2004, 108.
19 Sue Kirchoff, "Immigrants Chase American Dream," *USA Today*, August 5, 2004, 1B. See Alvaro Cortes, Christopher E. Herbert, Erin Wilson, and Elizabeth Clay, "Factors Affecting Hispanic Home Ownership: A Review of the Literature," *Cityscape* 2007, 53; Amelie F. Constant, Rowan Roberts, and Klaus F. Zimmerman, "Ethnic Identity and Immigrant Home Ownership," *Urban Studies*, August 2009, 1879.
20 David Bradley, "Home Ownership Outearns Stocks," *Philadelphia Tribune*, December 19, 2004, 6-B.
21 https://georgewbush-whitehouse.archives.gov/news/releases/2004/08/20040809-9.html. See Sandra L. Barnes, "Positive Home Ownership Attitudes, Home Ownership Behavior, and Neighborhood Ties in Poor Urban Neighborhoods," *Cityscape*, 2004, 41.
22 "Best Practices for Housing Affordability," *Los Angeles Sentinel*, November 17, 2005, D1.
23 "Best Practices for Housing Affordability."
24 Marilyn Gardner, "Young Dream-Seekers Strapped by Debt," *Christian Science Monitor*, January 11, 2006, 13.
25 Fred A. Bernstein, "Are McMansions Going Out of Style?," *New York Times*, October 2, 2005, K1; James Gauer, *The New American Dream: Living Well in Small Homes* (New York: Monacelli, 2004).
26 "Are McMansions Going Out of Style?"; Gauer, *The New American Dream: Living Well in Small Homes*.
27 Sara Miller Llana, "Loans to Minorities Rise, But at a Price," *Christian Science Monitor*, March 24, 2006, 2.
28 "Loans to Minorities Rise, But at a Price." Anne B. Shlay, "Low-income Home Ownership: American Home or Delusion?," *Urban Studies*, March 2006, 511; Sabrina W. Tyuse and Julie Birkenmaier, "Promoting Home Ownership for the Poor: Proceed With Caution," *Race, Gender & Class*, 2006, 295; Donald R. Haurin, Christopher E. Herbert, and Stuart S. Rosenthal, "Home Ownership Gaps Among Low-Income and Minority Households," *Cityscape*, 2007, 5.
29 John Yantis, "The Waiting Game," *Mesa Tribune* (AZ), August 13, 2006.
30 Erik Spanberg, "Faced with Difficult Adjustments, Homeowners Weigh Their Options," *Christian Science Monitor*, September 25, 2006, 13.
31 Mark Trumbull, "Home-Loan Trouble Spurs Fears of 'Credit Crunch,'" *Christian Science Monitor*, March 15, 2007, 2.
32 Chris Arnold, "Home Ownership to Aid Subprime Victims," *All Things Considered (NPR)*, April 12, 2007.
33 Harry C. Alford, "What Is Home Ownership?," *Chicago Defender*, April 16, 2007, 7.
34 Milton Eztrati, "Subprime Home Loans: Don't Panic," *Christian Science Monitor*, April 26, 2007, 9.
35 "Ride Out the Mortgage Crisis," *Christian Science Monitor*, August 17, 2007, 8.

36 Jack Kemp, "A Smart Fix for the Subprime Mess," *Christian Science Monitor*, January 23, 2008, 9.
37 Wendy A. Hoke, "The Buyers on the Bus," *Christian Science Monitor*, May 27, 2008, 20.
38 Hoke, "The Buyers on the Bus."
39 Rep. David Scott (D-GA), "Legislation Is Needed to Protect Home Ownership," *Philadelphia Tribune*, August 1, 2008, 5-A.
40 Gail Russell Chaddock, "What About Fannie and Freddie?," *Christian Science Monitor*, October 9, 2008, 3.
41 Steven Horowitz, "Government Regulation, Not Free-Market Greed, Caused This Crisis," *Christian Science Monitor*, October 22, 2008, 9.
42 Barbara Curtis, "Living Through 'It's a Wonderful Life,'" *Christian Science Monitor*, December 23, 2008, 9.
43 "American Dream of Home Ownership Morphs into Nightmare," *Irish Times*, November 7, 2009.
44 Joel Lovell, "The American Dream, No Money Down," *GQ- Gentlemen's Quarterly*, February 2008, 78.
45 Lovell, "The American Dream, No Money Down."
46 Richard Florida, "Rent Out the American Dream?," *USA Today*, March 10, 2009, A11.
47 Neal Conan, "Rethinking American Dream of Home Ownership," *Talk of the Nation* (NPR), December 15, 2009.
48 Conan, "Rethinking American Dream of Home Ownership."

10 A House Divided

"The American dream of home ownership is not equally shared by all."
Zillow economist Stan Humphries, 2014

On May 31, 2023, President Joe Biden issued a proclamation declaring June of that year National Home Ownership Month. "I call upon the people of this Nation to safeguard the American Dream by ensuring that everyone has access to an affordable home in a community of their choice," Proclamation 10592 read, with the declaration soon entered in the Federal Register. Like previous heads of state, Biden understood the value Americans placed on the home, and expressed his deep commitment to enabling more citizens to share the benefits of ownership. "We recognize the power of owning a home when raising a family, planting roots in a community, building equity, and passing down generational wealth to continue the American Dream for generations to come," the proclamation stated, strong words that could be said to represent the heart and soul of what this nation was all about.[1]

Biden's proclamation followed what had in recent years been some sharp twists and turns on the rollercoaster ride of home ownership in America. The direction home ownership would take after the subprime mortgage crisis was unclear, as the value of buying property was increasingly questioned, both financially and emotionally. All agreed that too many people had become homeowners, and that the system had failed them and the nation as a whole. Minority groups had been especially hurt in the crisis, the latest example of how the real estate industry and government each created policies designed to make it difficult or impossible for people of color to own property. It was clear that a new kind of approach had to be taken to enable Americans to fulfill their dream of home ownership, an approach that perhaps needed to be reinvented from the ground up.

The Long Haul

The nation's housing market had of course been a particularly turbulent one in the first decade of the 21st century, so much so that even experts weren't sure about how Americans now felt about home ownership. In 2010, Fannie

DOI: 10.4324/9781003481485-11

Mae investigated the matter through a survey which delivered the good news that most of those asked believed that owning a home was "important" and preferable to renting. The foreclosure crisis was an unprecedented experience in the history of real estate in the country, and it was conceivable that the massive loss of homes and drop in values might have done serious, perhaps irreparable damage to consumers' confidence with regard to housing. Indeed, the number of people who viewed a home as "a safe investment" decreased from 83% in 2003 to 70% in 2010, according to the survey, an indication that Americans were going to be more cautious about buying property in the future.[2]

While the Fannie Mae survey was taken as evidence that Americans still had faith in home ownership, the crisis revealed that there were clear cracks in the system. For almost the past century, the benefits of owning one's home had been vigorously sold to the American people by both the government and private sectors, primarily as the best means to build wealth. Recent events painfully showed that for some folks it was a bad decision, however, suggesting that home ownership simply wasn't for everyone. As the percentage of homeowners approached 70%, a good number could not pay the mortgages that banks had urged them to take, pushing ownership down a few percentage points in 2010.[3]

With the numbers speaking for themselves, the generally accepted tenet that paying off a mortgage in order to gain equity (and essentially force a family to save more money than they likely would) was being reconsidered. "The case for trying to achieve a nation of homeowners needs to be rethought," stated economists Wenli Li and Fang Yang, authors of a study published by the Federal Reserve Bank of Philadelphia. Boosters of "universal" home ownership seemed to have overlooked the fact that unpredictable events took place in people's lives, wreaking havoc with the easy-to-understand notion that owning a thing—especially something as expensive as a house or apartment—made more financial sense than having to rent it. Not only were the financial underpinnings of home ownership being challenged in the post-subprime mortgage crisis period, but its alleged social benefits or "citizenship effects," striking a heavy blow to one of the pillars of the American dream.[4]

Richard Florida definitely questioned the assumption that home ownership was a worthy goal for all Americans. "Home ownership is overrated," the well-known author based at the University of Toronto stated in the *New York Times*, believing that Americans' view of possessing property as a "birthright and necessity" was misguided. While home ownership had contributed to national prosperity at different times in the 20th century, Florida conceded, what the country needed now was a more mobile workforce. "Owning a home may actually be a drawback given the economic flexibility required to power long-lasting recovery," he wrote, with his research showing that the nation would benefit if citizens could more easily "move on to new centers of opportunity."[5]

Against such a backdrop, it wasn't surprising that a new term—"sustainable home ownership"—entered the lexicon. "Sustainable" did not mean building houses with environmentally friendly materials but, as Al Heavens of the *Philadelphia Inquirer* described it, "buying a house and keeping it for the long haul." The originator of the phrase appeared to be Walter Molony of the National Association of REALTORS®, who used it in a paper titled "The Long-Term Value of Home Ownership in the U.S." Professionals like Molony understood that there was little point in someone buying a piece of property if it was from the get-go a risky proposition in which the ability to pay the monthly mortgage or annual taxes was questionable. Too many people had viewed a home as an investment rather than as shelter, Heavens added, drawn into ownership by Wall Streeters who viewed mortgages as just another financial asset rather than a life-changing obligation for the buyer.[6]

If there was any good news, it was that an ideal buyer's market had emerged out of the bursting of the housing bubble. Homes were more affordable as values dropped, there was considerable inventory, and interest rates were relatively low, an excellent mix for property shoppers despite the tighter lending standards. Experts had always advised prospective buyers about the true costs of owning a home, but in the wake of the crisis, these warnings were redoubled. Don't get more house than you need even if you qualified for that McMansion, real estate agents were now saying, and don't forget that there would be repairs to make, decorating expenses, and utility bills. (The general rule was that about a third of household income should be spent on PITI, or principal, interest, taxes, and insurance.) Some first-time buyers thought that utilities were included in the mortgage payment as it may have been for their rent, illustrating how and why so many new owners got into trouble when their income was interrupted for some reason.[7]

The worse news was that foreclosures had hardly eased up in some parts of the country, and that the gap between white and Black homeowners had widened during the crisis and the subsequent recession. That gap had gradually narrowed since the mid-1980s but now those gains had been erased, one reason being that African Americans tended to have more of their wealth invested in their homes. Blacks were also more likely to have been subject to the predatory lending practices that were a staple of subprime mortgages, and often paid higher interest rates than whites with similar credit histories.[8]

Younger adults, specifically "Gen Xers" (those born between 1965 and 1980), were also especially hurt by the crisis for a number of reasons. First and foremost, someone in their thirties tended to have less savings than an older person to use to pay a mortgage in case of job loss, increasing the chance of foreclosure. More than that, however, the value of one's home had typically dropped by a third, a significant loss for an individual still building his or her financial portfolio. Some Xers who had been burned by the experience were swearing off home ownership for good, thinking it was safer just to rent. Although banks and the government were usually blamed for having gotten them into the mess, baby boomers too were commonly seen as abettors in the process. Gen Xers had long accused boomers as being responsible for the former's limited opportunities, making it natural for them to believe that this latest kerfuffle was mostly the latter's fault as well.[9]

By 2012, however, there were signs that what was generally considered the worst downturn in the nation's housing market since the Great Depression was ending. Still, with rates of home ownership and property values having fallen, economists were saying that it would take years for the market to fully recover, assuming that it ever could. The fact that a home could be worth less than what one had paid for it was for some a revelation, and cause to rethink the entire proposition of ownership. Economists were also forecasting that home prices would continue to slide somewhat until stabilizing and, even then, would not significantly rise for years to come.[10] With such a bleak scenario, was it surprising that a segment of ex-homeowners had decided to pursue a different kind of American dream?

Not surprisingly, the media capitalized on this questioning of the nation's core mythology. A cover of *Time* magazine proposed, "Why Owning a Home May No Longer Make Economic Sense," an idea that in the past would likely have been considered absurd. CNN, meanwhile, suggested that "renting was the new owning," this too anathema in the creed of real estate. Renting, traditionally described as the means to make one's landlord wealthy rather than oneself by building equity, was now more apt to be praised for its flexibility by journalists looking for a story that challenged conventional thought.[11]

Did most Americans subscribe to such a message? In a word, no, at least according to one poll. A 2012 study by the Woodrow Wilson Center revealed that 84% of respondents believed that home ownership was "just as or more important as it was five years ago," suggesting that the subprime disaster, as bad as it had been, was more of an aberration than a permanent feature of the nation's housing landscape. Similarly, the poll showed that more than 90% of people subscribed to the notion that home ownership is part of the American dream, more evidence that not everyone was giving up on having their own little plot of land.[12]

A Renter with a Mortgage

That was good news, but the dream was more elusive than it had been for some time. The decline in home ownership and record rate of foreclosures and repossessions (more than five times the norm) had created a startling number of housing vacancies. Vacancies varied widely by region and metropolitan area, however. Detroit had been hit hard, as had overbuilt markets such as Phoenix and Las Vegas, but more upscale areas of California and the Northeast remained strong.[13]

While no doubt pleased that they had been able to ride through the crisis, homeowners were less than delighted to learn the current value of their dwelling. In 2000, the median asking sales price of a single-family house was around $90,000, a figure that had more than doubled by 2007. Five years later, however, the median ask was $135,000, which is what it had been in 2005. More troubling, the asking price could be significantly higher than what buyers were willing to pay, and more than a third of all sales agreements were being canceled due to appraisals being lower than the offers.[14]

Despite the new appreciation of renting, the law of supply and demand was making the economics of home ownership once again appear favorable. Rents were rising as ex-homeowners or nervous prospective ones opted for leases over sales contracts. With prices down and mortgage interest rates low, the financials of owning often were stronger than renting, something real estate agents were actively pointing out to clients. More astute buyers also recognized that the timing was right and were willing to take the plunge if only to be able to deduct the mortgage interest from their income. Again, however, the length of time one expected to be in the home mattered a great deal; if it was at least a decade, buying made sense, but if it was just a few years, renting was the way to go.[15]

For millennials, the generation born between 1981 and 1996, the idea of being in one place for at least a decade, not to mention taking on a load of debt, was a daunting proposition. It was commonly accepted that student loan debt played a major role in discouraging young adults from pursuing home ownership, although some disputed that claim.[16] Besides being mobile and liking to keep their options open, many millennials were holding off on marriage and having children, something that had also been demonstrated as a deterrent to investing in property. The numbers bore out this generation's values; home ownership rate for people under age 35 was 37% in 2013, down five percentage points from 2007.[17]

If millennials weren't following their parents' traditional path of settling down after college by getting jobs, starting families, and buying houses, where were they living? Pew Research found that 21.6 million of the 72 million millennials were residing in their parents' homes (something many boomers would not have considered doing during their rebellious youth.) Even renting their own place was beyond the reach of these eighteen- to thirty-one-year-olds; the usual plan was to try to get a good job, save some money, and eventually move out. Many envisioned buying a house and raising a family in the future, however, an affirmation of the classic American dream.[18]

According to some, millennials may have been better off postponing their dream of home ownership or abandoning it altogether. As committed renters had said in the past, new research was showing that spending (lots of) money on real estate did not lead to high levels of happiness. If that emotion was what one wanted more of in life, consumers would be better off spending their money on experiences such as traveling and dining out rather than material goods of any kind, according to the studies. "People are making so many trade-offs in order to have that home," explained Elizabeth Dunn of the University of British Columbia who included her findings in *Happy*

Money: The Science of Smarter Spending, with other research showing that homeowners weren't any happier than renters.[19]

A source of happiness or otherwise, home ownership in America was back on ascent by 2013. Home prices were rising fast as were both sales and new construction. Still, lenders were being extra cautious, not about to go back to the days when a worker at McDonald's making $8 an hour could get a loan for a $250,000 house. Housing accounted for one-fifth of the nation's total economy, making economists concerned that lenders' tight purse strings were slowing the recovery. Sounding more like a Republican, President Obama was proposing that the government play less of a role in housing, even suggesting that Fannie Mae and Freddie Mac be shut down for good.[20]

While it appeared that housing was back on track, a very old problem—discrimination against people of color in the mortgage process—resurfaced. According to a joint report titled "A House Divided: How Race Colors the Path to Home Ownership" issued by Zillow and the National Urban League, both African Americans and Hispanics were less likely than whites and Asians to apply for a mortgage to purchase a home and when they did, they were also much less likely to be approved. The 2014 report pooled a variety of data sources to reach the conclusion that divisions along the lines of race and class remained embedded in the real estate industry, discouraging news given all the efforts to make home ownership a more even playing field. The mortgage process took longer, and denials were higher for people of color, who were also much more likely to apply for an FHA versus a conventional loan because the down payment of the former was significantly lower.[21]

As Gregory Sharp and Matthew Hall pointed out in a 2014 essay in *Social Problems*, the racial divide in housing ran much deeper than discrimination in the mortgage process. Market exclusion certainly existed, as the "A House Divided" report showed, but it was market exploitation that presented the larger problem.[22] Ed Pinto, an economist for the (conservative) American Enterprise Institute, considered practices in the housing market to be a major factor in preventing people of color from building wealth. For decades, the mortgage industry had emphasized making loans affordable when they should have been offering loans that allowed buyers to gain more equity in their homes, Pinto argued. The standard 30-year fixed rate loan just wasn't a very good deal for most people, especially those with low- and moderate incomes, he believed, as the payment was heavily structured on paying interest for the first five or seven years. "You basically become a renter with a mortgage," Pinto said, thinking a fifteen-year mortgage would offer a much better way to pay down the principal and thus build wealth.[23]

Again, the question of whether the subprime mortgage crisis and the bursting of the housing bubble had triggered a fundamental shift in Americans' attitudes toward home ownership was asked. The trend toward renting, particularly among young adults, might have suggested there had been such a shift, but the findings from yet another study suggested that not much had actually changed. The Federal Reserve Board's "Report on the Economic

Well-Being of U.S. Households in 2014" found that most renters rented not because of some lifestyle choice but, quite simply, a lack of money. 50% of renters said that they just couldn't come up with the down payment to buy property, and another 31% said that they could not qualify for a mortgage. Interestingly, lower-income renters expressed a greater desire to be a homeowner than higher-income renters; it was the latter who were more likely to rent due to personal preference or not planning to stay in one place for long.[24]

In more expensive areas such as New York City, some renters wanting to be homeowners were partnering to come up with the required down payment. "Pooling resources with friends and siblings has become the quickest path to home ownership," Ronnie Koenig wrote in the *New York Times* after speaking with a few couples who had been priced out of the market by themselves. It was a more complicated proposition, of course, but there was no doubt that much more bang for the buck could be realized through a share. Splitting a house by level or wing with separate kitchens and bathrooms made the most sense, making the arrangement not unlike that in two-family houses which had been around for many years.[25]

That the dream of home ownership remained alive in America, however configured, was taken as good news, and understandably so. But what to make of the fact that the last time that the national rate of home ownership was 62.9%—the number in 2016—LBJ was president and the #1 song on the radio was the Beatles's "Help!"?[26] Americans weren't used to such statistics, of the belief that the country was always moving forward and progressing, especially with regard to something as sacred as the home. The national rate of home ownership had peaked in 2004 at 69.2%, making the number in 2016 just 6.3% lower.[27]

Media reports, however, made it sound as if most of the housing market had crashed, no doubt because of the way that large, powerful institutions had used mostly well-intentioned people as pawns in their financial game. It's clear that millions of people having lost their homes touched a collective nerve, a reflection of how deeply entrenched home ownership was in the national psyche. It was true that just seeing a foreclosed, vacant house on one's block was a heartbreaking experience, even if one didn't know the people who had lived in it. (Some blocks had many, making the neighborhood feel like a ghost town.) It was really the bank who had owned the house, or almost all of it, but that didn't take away from the feeling that seizing the property and displacing a family was wrong and, it might be said, un-American.[28]

A Valuable Institution

Charles Lane of the *Washington Post* had a much different take on the matter. "Contrary to entrenched conventional wisdom, the ongoing decline of the home ownership rate is actually good news," he wrote in 2016 after taking a deeper dive into the data. While the rate of home ownership had certainly fallen, current owners on average had the same amount of equity in their property as in 2004 (about 58%). The implication was that those who had weathered the storm could be credited with having made the housing market more secure and sustainable and were more personally equipped to ride out another crisis, should one come along. There was now more "ownership" in home ownership, in other words, as it was really equity rather than simply signing a sales agreement that brought stability to the economics of real estate. "The current situation approximates a happy ending to an unhappy story," Lane explained, that story being "the brutal real estate shake-out that impoverished and destabilized so many families across America."[29]

As Ed Pinto had argued, Lane believed that government policies supporting home ownership over the past couple of decades had taken a misguided approach. The Clinton and George H. Bush administrations had each effectively subsidized home ownership through federally guaranteed, low down payment mortgages as the means to allow those with low or moderate incomes to build wealth. Little or no equity had been created through such loans, however, making only a dramatic spike in home values the only real opportunity for owners to see their net worth rise. And should a market "correction" take place, those kinds of owners were likely to lose their homes, which is precisely what had happened. "We should de-emphasize house buying and explore alternatives that do not require people to bet on a single illiquid asset class," Lane proposed, thinking that "despite decades of rhetoric about the 'American Dream' from real estate lobbyists, politicians and well-meaning low-income-housing advocates, home ownership is not a surefire ticket into the middle class."[30]

Such thinking made much sense from an economics perspective, but it would have been difficult or even impossible to take the American dream away from those who had every intention of realizing it in their lives. Immigrants were catching up fast to native-born Americans in terms of home ownership; in 2015, half of the former owned homes compared to 66% of the latter, according to Trulia, a real estate research firm. The gap was narrowing as immigrants spent more years living in the United States, allowing them to extend their length of employment, improve their credit ratings, and save money for down payments. Also, immigrants were now required to have a certain level of economic resources to make their home here, giving them an edge in the ability to buy property.[31]

African Americans, meanwhile, continued to fall behind in realizing what Jonnelle Marte of the *Washington Post* labeled "the holy grail of home ownership." Many Blacks had financially recovered nicely from the Great Recession by then, making it all the more ironic that they weren't able to become homeowners. 43% of African Americans owned homes in 2017, according to the Joint Center for Housing Studies of Harvard University, a huge disparity versus the 72% rate for whites. (Like immigrants, Hispanics were now making gains.) Most disturbing, the gap had widened over the past three decades, making one question the value of the many efforts taken to take race out of the housing equation.[32]

Many African Americans, even those with solid jobs, were experiencing frustration in becoming a homeowner due to a variety of reasons. There were relatively few affordable homes as prices quickly rose after the crisis, for one thing, and there always seemed to be buyers who were willing to pay more for a property, perhaps to flip it. As often as not, desirable houses weren't approved for an FHA mortgage, and the down payment for a conventional loan was too much. Also, the higher lending standards were making it especially tough for people of color who could have lower credit scores resulting from the "toxic" loans they had taken during the boom. Higher fees were levied on such buyers, this too putting home ownership out of reach for middle-class African Americans.[33]

Even obtaining "the holy grail" hardly meant that one was on easy street, of course. One might have thought that Americans would have learned some valuable lessons in money management during the crisis but that didn't appear to be the case. Many new homeowners remained cash poor, ignoring the stream of advice regarding the need to allocate part of one's income to home costs outside of the mortgage payment and property taxes. Maintaining a home was the less glamorous side of ownership, as there was little joy to be found in fixing things that broke down. 72% of homeowners delayed making property repairs due to a lack of money, data from Discover Personal Loans showed, with even major projects often put on hold because of financial constraints. Others were making the necessary repairs if only to prevent water from pouring through what had been the roof or keep the temperature of the house above freezing after the furnace blew, but using credit cards to pay for the fixes.[34]

Sensibly prepared new buyers had put away six months of living expenses in an emergency fund to cover such unforeseen repairs. Fiscally prudent experts advised those shopping for a home to delay buying a place until such a fund had been built up, but most Americans ignored such practicalities. Exhausting the fund meant creating another as, veteran homeowners knew, there was always another needed repair waiting in the wings. Those caught in a money crunch often had to cut out certain luxuries like cable TV or gym memberships or else sell personal possessions in order to pay contractors, not an ideal situation. Others might take a second job to generate repair money, a case where one had to wonder whether the homeowner owned the home, or the home owned the homeowner.[35]

Problems in home ownership exceeded having to put off having that annoying leak fixed or buying a dishwasher that actually washed dishes. By 2018, it had been a full decade since the mortgage crisis, but a new kind of crisis was being said to have emerged. Buying a home had simply become impossible for many Americans, the result of too few new houses being built and costs that exceeded middle-class incomes. The problem was apparent not just in big cities but in small towns, suggesting that the economics of the real estate market were no longer viable for aspiring homeowners. Even existing homeowners with considerable equity were in a bind should they want to buy something bigger, as going from a two-bedroom house to a three-bedroom could cost twice as much money. As in the past, some buyers were heading out further into the countryside to find a house they could afford, and tech workers, especially on the West Coast, could seemingly outbid anyone with the kind of money they made.[36]

With the bedrock of the classic American dream showing some real cracks as a result of economic events in the first two decades of the 21st century, more policymakers and scholars were closely studying historical data in order to determine if home ownership was worth all the effort and resources many were devoting to it. Laurie S. Goodman of the Urban Institute and Christopher Mayer of Columbia University were two such experts doing so, publishing their important findings in the *Journal of Economic Perspectives*. After much tumbling of numbers and examining the subject from international, demographic, and financial perspectives, the pair concluded, quite simply, that "home ownership is a valuable institution." There were considerable variations depending on a host of factors, of course, but home ownership generally enabled families to build wealth and lead to considerable financial security. "While two decades of policies in the 1990s and early 2000s may have put too much faith in the benefits of home ownership," they wrote, "the pendulum seems to have swung too far the other way, and many now may have too little faith in home ownership as part of the American Dream."[37]

The Real Estate Landscape

It was understandable why and how many people of color had little faith in the home ownership part of the American dream. The Black Lives Matter movement that had gained greater momentum after the murder of George Floyd in Minneapolis in 2020 brought more attention to Black home ownership, as it served as a prime example of racially based economic inequities. Things had greatly improved with the passage of the Fair Housing Act of 1968, as prior to that, it was legal for real estate agents and homeowners to not show or sell homes to Blacks (or anyone else). Also, financial institutions could deny mortgages to people based on skin color or even the neighborhood where they intended to live. The anti-discrimination law helped to increase Black home ownership, which had peaked in 2000 at 47.3% (versus close to 73% for whites). Black ownership had dipped to 41.2% in 2018, while white ownership remained essentially the same as in 2000.[38]

In 2020, the rate of Black home ownership was the same as in 1968 due to many different factors (including the COVID-19 pandemic). One factor in particular was most disturbing, however. "Redlining is still alive and well in markets today," stated Alanna McCargo of the Urban Institute, finding that "segregated neighborhoods still exist, and ... there is still an appraisal bias."

According to a new report published by the Institute, "How Economic Crises and Sudden Disasters Increase Racial Disparities in Home Ownership," the median home value for a Black head of household was $155,000 versus $220,000 for a white head of household. The consequences of that disparity were that (1) it was significantly more difficult for people of color to build up home equity and thus wealth, and (2) there was more volatility in home values when the economy went south.[39]

In addition to those forms of discrimination, African American families annually paid 13% more in property taxes than white families given all other variables being equal. That's what economists Troup Howard of the University of Utah and Carlos Avenancio-León of Indiana University found in their 2020 study which drew upon much data analysis. Black-owned homes were regularly assessed at higher values, relative to their actual sale price, than white-owned homes, the researchers reported, something that African Americans had pointed out for decades, to no avail. The "Black tax," as the premium that African Americans paid was sometimes referred to, was common across the country, making it no isolated incident or error. Inequities in tax assessment were thus another contributing factor to lower home ownership rates among people of color, and another example of the systematic racism built into the nation's housing market.[40]

Recognizing the long, ugly, and persistent history of racism in their industry (and the damage they had done with subprime mortgages), some lenders were taking steps to try to enable more sustainable home ownership for minorities. Chase, for example, was offering Homebuyer Grants to those who purchased homes in low- to moderate-income communities. Buyers received a $2,500 grant to help with the down payment and a low-interest (3.25%) mortgage through a Fannie Mae loan, not a windfall but enough to make a difference in becoming a homeowner. The Chase program was one of many business initiatives designed to encourage racial justice as a response to the Black Lives Matter movement, with other banks soon joining in.[41] In 2022, Bank of America announced new zero down payment loans for first-time homebuyers in predominantly Black and Hispanic neighborhoods, and TD Bank was offering similar loans with grants of $5,000.[42]

Such programs were certainly helpful at the local level, but structural change had to take place if home ownership was to be truly equitable. As Keeanga-Yamahtta Taylor showed in her *Race for Profit*, the real estate business along with the government had consistently embedded racist attitudes in the housing market, resulting in a long list of discriminatory practices including redlining, restrictive covenants, and charging higher interest or fees on loans (based on the false assumption that African American buyers were greater credit risks). "Predatory inclusion" had been the latest such practice, and efforts were now being taken to extract racism from the way that homes were bought and sold in America.[43]

Racial justice in housing was also being pursued by the federal government. Like many previous presidents, Joe Biden wanted more Americans, particularly minorities, to become homeowners, and was creating policies to try to achieve that. Rather than make homebuying more affordable—something that proved to backfire when credit was made too easy—Biden was promoting higher rates of ownership as part of his ambitious American Jobs Plan. $213 billion was allocated in his 2021 budget to "preserve, retrofit or create" more than two million homes and commercial buildings, with incentives also provided to loosen up zoning codes. It was an interesting strategy, taking quite a different tack from the usual policies focused on financing. It was true that in virtually all areas of the country, there were many older (and sometimes vacant) homes that, with some work, could be entirely suitable for first-time buyers. In the plan, funds would be provided to those committing to improve existing homes and make them more energy-efficient, in the process also contributing to lessen neighborhood "blight."[44]

Even without the government subsidy, fixer-uppers have become a more popular choice for aspiring homeowners or those seeking a larger footprint. Such homes, often advertised as needing some tender loving care, were priced significantly lower than new ones of the same size (45% less, according to the home improvement site Porch). Correcting structural issues was expensive, however, as were new roofs and kitchen or bathroom upgrades. Still, because of the lower purchase price, it was easier to get a property in the area in which one wanted to live, the principal reason why folks were taking on the challenge. Repairs could be spread out over time, as long as the place was livable. Being handy was a big plus when considering a fixer-upper, as do-it-yourselfers not only saved money but didn't have to rely on contractors' well-established inclination to go beyond estimates of time and money.[45]

Whether their houses were fixer-uppers or brand new, Latinos have been hitting all-time highs in home ownership in recent years. While rates among African Americans lagged despite banks' attempts to make amends for their previous sins, Latinos were actively buying their first houses or trading up to larger ones. "The rise is altering the real estate landscape in many pockets of the country and making this demographic a growing force in the sharply rising housing market," Troy McMullen of the *Washington Post* observed in 2022, with Riverside/San Bernardino, California, Greater New York City, and Orlando the top markets for Latinos. COVID-19 appeared to play a role in the buying surge as apartment renters or owners of smaller dwellings sought more space after the pandemic lockdown. Whereas Latinos comprised roughly 18% of the population of the United States, they accounted for more than half of the country's home ownership growth in the decade prior to the pandemic, according to the Urban Institute. The Institute forecasted that 70% of the net new homeowner households in the nation would be Latino by 2040, while both Black and white rates would decrease over those years.[46]

More good news came in late 2022 when new federal data showed that the pandemic housing boom included all minority groups. Federal stimulus checks, rental subsidies, and student loan freezes put substantial money in the pockets of those who had had little, and the savings were being put to good use. Interest rates were very low following the pandemic, more reason why more Latinos, African Americans, and Asian Americans were scouring online real estate sites. Some who had no plans to buy but saw their rent going up and up cobbled together enough money for a down payment and, almost before they knew it, were holding housekeys. Policy experts were quick to caution that while the spike was a positive development, it didn't alter the historical lack of access to home ownership among minorities.[47] It was clear, however, that home ownership had taken another turn in its intriguing journey, with many more no doubt to come in the future past on its stormy past.

Notes

1 Administration of Joseph R. Biden, Jr., 2023, "Proclamation 10592—National Home Ownership Month, 2023," May 31, 2023.
2 Renae Merle, "Faith in Home Ownership Drops, Poll Shows," *Washington Post*, April 6, 2010.
3 David Wessel and Steve Inskeep, "Is the Home Ownership System Broken?," *Morning Edition* (NPR), June 22, 2010; See Alyssa Katz, *Our Lot: How Real Estate Came to Own Us* (New York: Bloomsbury, 2009).
4 Alan J. Heavens, "'American Dream' of Home Ownership Fizzles," *Philadelphia Inquirer*, September 13, 2010; See Rick Jacobus and David M. Abromowitz, "A Path to Home Ownership: Building a More Sustainable Strategy for Expanding Home Ownership," *Journal of Affordable Housing & Community Development Law*, Spring/Summer 2010, 313–344; Stephanie M. Stern, "Reassessing the Citizen Virtues of Home Ownership," *Columbia Law Review*, May 2011, 890; Brian J. McCabe, "Are Homeowners Better Citizens? Home Ownership and Community Participation in the United States," *Social Forces*, March 2013, 929.
5 Richard Florida, "Home Ownership is Overrated," *Wall Street Journal*, June 10, 2010, A17.
6 Al Heavens, "Your Place: 'Sustainable Home Ownership' is a Standard Buyers Should Consider," *Philadelphia Inquirer*, November 10, 2010.
7 Al Heavens, "Calculate the Real Cost of Home Ownership," *Philadelphia Inquirer*, April 8, 2011.
8 Robert Siegel, "Racial Gap in Home Ownership Widens in U.S. Slump," *All Things Considered* (NPR), August 24, 2011.
9 Audie Cornish, "Your Letters: Gen X Home Ownership Woes," *Weekend Edition Sunday* (NPR), November 20, 2011.
10 Julie Schmit, "Home Ownership, Prices Fall," *USA Today*, February 1, 2012.
11 Chris Armold, "After the Housing Bust, Rethinking Home Ownership," *All Things Considered* (NPR), June 4, 2012.
12 Armold, "After the Housing Bust, Rethinking Home Ownership."
13 Al Heavens, "Foreclosures Push Vacancy, Home Ownership in Opposite Directions," *Philadelphia Inquirer*, August 9, 2012.
14 Heavens, "Foreclosures Push Vacancy, Home Ownership in Opposite Directions."
15 Wendy Kaufman, "Renters No More: Newbies Lured to Home Ownership," *Morning Edition* (NPR), October 16, 2012.
16 For more on this debate, see Natalie Kitroeff, "Young and in Debt," *New York Times*, June 8, 2014, RE1; Lisa Prevost, "College Debt and Home Buying," *New York Times*, July 6, 2014, RE10; Lisa Prevost, "On the Home Ownership Path,"

New York Times, March 8, 2015, RE8; Jason N. Houle and Lawrence Berger, "Is Student Loan Debt Discouraging Home Ownership among Young Adults?," *Social Service Review*, December 2015, 589.

17 Tim Logan, "Is Home Ownership Fading?," *St. Louis Post-Dispatch*, November 23, 2013; See A. Mechele Dickerson, "Millennials, Affordable Housing, and the Future of Home Ownership," *Journal of Affordable Housing & Community Development Law*, 2016, 435–465.

18 Amy Banton, "American Dream Redefined," Home Ownership Poses Challenge for Younger Generations," *Aiken Standard* (SC), September 17, 2013.

19 Michelle Higgins, "Keys to Happiness. Or Not," *New York Times*, July 14, 2013, RE1.

20 Ari Shapiro, "Obama Focuses on Making Home Ownership More Accessible," *Morning Edition* (NPR), August 7, 2013.

21 Tim Grant, "Hispanics, Blacks Face Hurdles in Home Ownership," *Pittsburgh Post-Gazette*, January 2, 2014.

22 Gregory Sharp and Matthew Hall, "Emerging forms of Racial Inequality in Home Ownership Exit, 1968-2009," *Social Problems*, August 2014, 427–447.

23 Chris Arnold, "New15-Year Mortgage May Open Home Ownership Door for More Buyers," *All Things Considered*, October 3, 2014; See Christian A.L. Hilber and Tracy M. Turner," The Mortgage Interest Deduction and Its Impact on Home Ownership," *Review of Economics and Statistics*, October 2014, 618–637.

24 Richard Metcalf, "Home Ownership Dream Remains Alive in America," *Albuquerque Journal*, July 6, 2015.

25 Ronnie Koenig, "Together We Buy," *New York Times*, July 31, 2016, RE1.

26 Susan Salisbury and Jeff Ostrowski, "Best of Our Blogs: Home Ownership at 51-Year Low," *Palm Beach Post*, July 29, 2016; The Census Bureau began keeping track of the rate in 1965.

27 Charles Lane, "Why Less Home Ownership Is Good News," *Washington Post*, August 3, 2016.

28 Lane, "Why Less Home Ownership Is Good News."

29 Lane, "Why Less Home Ownership Is Good News."

30 Lane, "Why Less Home Ownership Is Good News."

31 Paul Davidson, "Immigrants Are Closing the Gap in Home Ownership," *USA Today*, October 13, 2016.

32 Jonnelle Marte, "The Holy Grail of Home Ownership," *Washington Post*, July 7, 2018.

33 Marte,"The Holy Grail of Home Ownership."

34 "Do You Have the Money to Keep Up with Home Ownership? Most Americans Don't," *Bloomington Pantagraph* (IL), July 15, 2018.

35 "Do You Have the Money to Keep Up with Home Ownership? Most Americans Don't."

36 Kirk Siegler and Lakshmi Singh, "We Asked: How is the Home Ownership Crisis Affecting You?," *All Things Considered* (NPR), August 11, 2018.

37 Laurie S. Goodman and Christopher Mayer, "Home Ownership and the American Dream," *Journal of Economic Perspectives*, Winter 2018, 31.

38 Michelle Singletary, "Black Home Ownership Key to Closing Wealth Gap, but Playing Field Still Uneven," *Washington Post*, June 12, 2020.

39 Singletary, "Black Home Ownership Key to Closing Wealth Gap, but Playing Field Still Uneven."

40 Andrew Van Dam, "Home Ownership's 'Black Tax,'" *Washington Post*, July 3, 2020.

41 Troy McMullen, "New Programs Widen the Path to Minority Home Ownership," *Washington Post*, October 30, 2020.
42 Ayesha Rascoe, "Zero-down Payment to Close the Racial Home Ownership Gap: What You Need to Know," *Weekend Edition Sunday*, September 11, 2022.
43 Alisa Chang, "The Racist Architecture of Home Ownership: How Housing Segregation Has Persisted," *All Things Considered* (NPR), May 4, 2021; *Race for Profit*.
44 Haisten Willis, "Biden's Plan Aims for a Big Boost in Home Ownership," *Washington Post*, June 10, 2021.
45 Terry Collins, "Fixer-Uppers Open Doors to Home Ownership," *USA Today*, September 20, 2022.
46 Troy McMullen, "Rising Latino Home Ownership Rates Alter the Housing Market," *Washington Post*, May 5, 2022.
47 Abha Bhattarai and Alyssa Fowers, "Pandemic Led to Spike in Minority Home Ownership," *Washington Post*, November 25, 2022.

Bibliography

Adams, James Truslow. *The Epic of America*. New York: Little, Brown, and Company, 1931.

Bigott, Joseph C. *From Cottage to Bungalow: Houses and the Working Class in Chicago, 1869–1929*. Chicago: University of Chicago Press, 2001.

Binford, Henry C. *The First Suburbs: Residential Communities on the Boston Periphery, 1815–1860*. Chicago: University of Chicago Press, 1985.

Burghardt, Stephen, ed. *Tenants and the Urban Housing Crisis*. Dexter, MI: The New Press, 1972.

Davies, Pearl Janet. *Real Estate in American History*. Washington, DC: Public Affairs Press, 1958.

Dean, John P. *Home Ownership: Is It Sound?* New York: Harper & Brothers, 1945.

The Editors of Harian Publications. *How to Retire on Real Estate Profits*. Greenlawn, NY: Harian Publications, 1959.

Federal National Mortgage Association, *The Fannie Mae Guide to Buying, Selling & Financing Your Home*. New York: Doubleday & Co., 1973.

Fennell, Lee Anne. *The Unbounded Home: Property Values beyond Property Lines*. New Haven, CT: Yale University Press, 2009.

Fishback, Price, Jonathan Rose, and Kenneth Snowden. *Well Worth Saving: How the New Deal Safeguarded Home Ownership*. Chicago: University of Chicago Press, 2013.

Garb, Margaret. *City of American Dreams: A History of Home Ownership and Housing Reform in Chicago, 1871–1919*. Chicago: University of Chicago Press, 2005.

Gauer, James. *The New American Dream: Living Well in Small Homes*. New York: Monacelli, 2004.

Hornstein, Jeffrey M. *A Nation of Realtors: A Cultural History of the Twentieth-Century American Middle Class*. Durham, NC: Duke University Press, 2005.

Katz, See Alyssa. *Our Lot: How Real Estate Came to Own Us*. New York: Bloomsbury, 2009.

Leigh, Wilhelmina A., and James B. Stewart, eds. *The Housing Status of Black Americans*. New Brunswick, NJ: Transaction, 1992.

Mayer, Martin. *The Builders*. New York: W.W. Norton & Co., 1978.

McCabe, Brian J. *No Place Like Home: Wealth, Community and the Politics of Home Ownership*. New York: Oxford University Press, 2016.

McCabe, Brian J., and Eve Rosen, eds. *The Sociology of Housing: How Homes Shape Our Lives*. University of Chicago Press, 2023.

Muller, Henry McCulley. *Urban Home Ownership: A Socio-Economic Analysis with Emphasis on Philadelphia*. Philadelphia: The Author, 1947.

Nickerson, William. *How I Turned $1,000 into a Million in Real Estate—in My Spare Time*. New York: Simon & Schuster, 1959.

Nickerson, William. *1965 Official Guide: New York World's Fair*. New York: Time Incorporated, 1965.
Nickerson, William. *Remembering the Future: The New York World's Fair from 1939 to 1964*. New York: Rizzoli, 1989.
Rothstein, Richard. *The Color of Law: A Forgotten History of How Our Government Segregated America*. New York: Norton, 2018.
Seligman, Amanda. *Block By Block: Neighborhoods and Public Policy on Chicago's West Side*. Chicago: University of Chicago Press, 2005.
Stacey, William. *Black Home Ownership: A Sociological Study of Metropolitan Jacksonville*. New York: Praeger Publishers, 1972.
Taylor, Keenanga-Yamahtta. *Race for Profit: How Banks and the Real Estate Industry Undermined Black Home Ownership*. Chapel Hill: University of North Carolina Press, 2019.
Winnink, Louis. *Rental Housing: Opportunities for Private Investment*. New York: McGraw-Hill, 1959.

Index

For Product Safety Concerns and Information please contact our EU
representative GPSR@taylorandfrancis.com
Taylor & Francis Verlag GmbH, Kaufingerstraße 24, 80331 München, Germany

www.ingramcontent.com/pod-product-compliance
Ingram Content Group UK Ltd.
Pitfield, Milton Keynes, MK11 3LW, UK
UKHW020002200926
475702UK00015B/2425
* 9 7 8 1 0 3 2 7 5 8 0 3 9 *